PROMOTING INCLUSIVE CLASSROOM DYNAMICS
IN HIGHER EDUCATION

PROMOTING INCLUSIVE CLASSROOM DYNAMICS IN HIGHER EDUCATION

A Research-Based Pedagogical Guide for Faculty

Kathryn C. Oleson

Foreword by Tia Brown McNair

STERLING, VIRGINIA

Published by Stylus Publishing, LLC
22883 Quicksilver Drive
Sterling, Virginia 20166-2019

Library of Congress Cataloging-in-Publication Data
Names: Oleson, Kathryn Carman, author.
Title: Promoting inclusive classroom dynamics in higher
    education : a research-based pedagogical guide for faculty /
    Kathryn C. Oleson ; Foreword by Tia Brown McNair.
Description: Sterling, Virginia : Stylus Publishing, [2020] |
    Includes bibliographical references and index.
Identifiers: LCCN 2020045637 | ISBN 9781620368992
    (paperback) | ISBN 9781620368985 (hardback) | ISBN
    9781620369005 (pdf) | ISBN 9781620369012 (ebook)
Subjects: LCSH: Inclusive education. | Education, Higher--
    Research. | College teaching. | Group identity. | Educational
    sociology.
Classification: LCC LC1200 .O44 2020 | DDC 371.9/046--dc23
LC record available at https://lccn.loc.gov/2020045637

13-digit ISBN: 978-1-62036-898-5 (cloth)
13-digit ISBN: 978-1-62036-899-2 (paperback)
13-digit ISBN: 978-1-62036-900-5 (library networkable e-edition)
13-digit ISBN: 978-1-62036-901-2 (consumer e-edition)

Printed in the United States of America

All first editions printed on acid-free paper
that meets the American National Standards Institute
Z39-48 Standard.

Bulk Purchases

Quantity discounts are available for use in workshops and for staff development.

Call 1-800-232-0223

First Edition, 2021

To Gordon, Sydney, and Jackson, with love.

CONTENTS

If there were ever a time to dare, to make a difference, to embark on something worth doing, it is now. Not for any grand cause, necessarily— but for something that tugs at your heart, something that's your aspiration, something that's your dream.

You owe it to yourself to make your days here count.

Have fun.

Dig deep.

Stretch.

Dream big. . . .

Believe in the incredible power of the human mind.

Of doing something that makes a difference.

Of working hard.

Of laughing and hoping.

Of lazy afternoons.

Of lasting friends.

Of all the things that will cross your path this year.

The start of something new brings the hope of something great.

Anything is possible.

There is only one you.

And you will pass this way only once.

Do it right.—Author Unknown

The COVID-19 pandemic brought many changes to our world, our communities, and our lives. For those of us in education, it exacerbated the growing inequities in our systems, structures, and practices, and reinforced the notion that what was once tolerated can no longer be ignored. The reality is that issues of access and privilege, if not addressed, will continue to perpetuate growing educational divides. This is the time to dare, the time to seek to make a difference and to identify the behaviors that need to be changed so progress can occur.

Promoting Inclusive Classroom Dynamics in Higher Education represents a pathway for change. Specifically, this book is a pathway for educators to make a difference during a time when inclusion and belonging are being rapidly replaced with a sense of loss of place for many students. In the midst of chaos, fear, and uncertainty, feelings of inclusion represent a lifeline for many students. In addition, as the definition of what constitutes a *classroom* becomes more expansive, we need more practical and reflective resources that challenge us to critically examine our own identities and beliefs in relationship to how those realities shape the design and implementation of the learning environments we seek to create. Deeper examinations of individual contexts and perceptions are taking on higher levels of significance and understanding how our individual ways of knowing influence our own decision-making are critical steps in the process of exploring what it means to be an effective educator.

Kathryn C. Oleson challenges readers to reflect on the function of who they are as people and as educators, and how that influences the way educational environments are designed and delivered. Similarly, Oleson encourages educators to engage in deep self-assessment and be open to learning new tools that can help manage difficult conversations among all learners, including students and educators.

The added value of the insights and practical strategies shared in this book come at a time when professional development opportunities for educators have, or will, decrease because of limited resources. There will be a growing need for resources that provide educational design guidance that can help faculty reflect critically on the practices that promote, and/or hinder, inclusivity and belonging for students in both in-person and remote learning environments.

Promoting Inclusive Classroom Dynamics in Higher Education provides a pathway for faculty to help students develop agency, achieve higher levels of learning and reflection, and have a sense of belonging.

Tia Brown McNair, EdD
Vice President for Diversity, Equity, and Student Success
Executive Director for the Truth, Racial Healing &
Transformation (TRHT) Campus Centers
Association of American Colleges & Universities

ACKNOWLEDGMENTS

There are so many people I want to thank for their support and assistance as I was writing this book.

I would like to acknowledge Nigel Nicholson, the dean of faculty who selected me to be the first director of Reed College's Center for Teaching and Learning (CTL). My supervisor Mary James, dean for institutional diversity, was a wonderful mentor and collaborator in creating inclusive pedagogy programming. At CTL I began to concretely think about applying my scholarly work to support faculty development. Based on this work, I decided to write the book that I would have liked to have as CTL director.

A hearty thank you for Reed College's support of my development as a teacher-scholar. In particular, I acknowledge the year-long sabbatical from 2016 to 2017 that provided sustained time to conduct research on student and faculty perceptions of the college classroom and to write my book proposal. The Blair Wellensiek and Karl Peters Faculty Research Fund and an American Philosophical Society Franklin Research Grant provided critical funding for this research. I am indebted to many students who conducted research with me as part of my inclusive classroom research group. These include a small group of students engaged in the initial research: Eileen Vinton (whose senior thesis was foundational to this research), Sidney Buttrill, and Robby Murphy. Building on this early research, many other psychology students became involved, including Alexa Harris, Tianfang Yang, Lauren Chacon, Cici Yin, Sydney Buffonge, Marshall DeFor, and Natalie Briggs.

I am grateful to Becky Packard, who provided an email introduction to John von Knorring. This introduction then led to a meeting with David Brightman, who encouraged me to send him a book proposal. He has been a supportive and thoughtful editor.

I would like to acknowledge the support of Alison Cook-Sather as I began my work in faculty development.

I am grateful to those who read drafts of my book proposal: Gordon Buffonge, Eileen Vinton, Sidney Buttrill, and Robby Murphy.

I appreciate the wonderful feedback from Gordon Buffonge, Sidney Buttrill, Robby Murphy, Alexa Harris, and Marshall DeFor on drafts of chapters.

Natalie Briggs, Lauren Chacon, and Cici Yin provided excellent work in organizing and formatting references. Sidney Buttrill created a compelling figure for faculty identity self-disclosure.

Thank you to the broader community of teacher-scholars who have engaged with me in wide-ranging conversations on the challenges and joys of teaching—particularly Carolyn Weisz for many mornings of "walking and talking" about inclusive teaching and Iliana Alcántar and Marc Schneiberg for talking about teaching at the dog park. I so appreciate the many colleagues who have presented with me on conference panels designed to promote teaching an increasingly diverse group of university students: Jonathan Cook, Michelle Nario-Redmond, Delia Saenz, Brooke Vick, and Carolyn Weisz. Thank you, Michelle, Brooke, and Carolyn, for letting me include your materials in this book. I also appreciate Susanne Morgan and Catherine Herne allowing me to include their faculty identity self-disclosure model, and Robert Sanchez providing permission to include an excerpt from his interview. I am thankful that Tia Brown McNair agreed to write the Foreword.

I am grateful to my many Reed colleagues who model teaching excellence. I am especially thankful for my psychology colleagues. The faculty members in my faculty teaching symposium on managing discomfort productively in the classroom were also helpful. A particular thank you to Jennifer Corpus and Kate Duffly for allowing me to adapt their materials for this book. Also I thank Margot Minardi, who I first heard use the term *cold moments*.

Finally, thank you to my family—Gordon, Sydney, and Jackson—for supporting me on all those weekends when I needed to work.

"Talking about rape and sexual assault, that makes people uncomfortable and it's possible triggering, but if it's not part of the conversation we can't make progress. . . . I know for a lot of people who are Caucasian, they're uncomfortable with talking about racial injustice because it's like, 'well I understand that there is racism, but I don't do it, and I'm uncomfortable that you're saying White people are doing this.' And it's just a lot of tension with that. But I think that's furthered by education. I think those feelings are lessened as they learn more." —Student (Oleson, 2017)

"We share in the classroom. It's going to change not only campus, it's going to change also our society. You're going to take it home. You're going to take it to your workplace. You're going to take it all over." —Student (Oleson, 2017)

With the growing diversity of the United States populace (Vespa et al., 2020) and of students heading to college in particular (Espinosa et al., 2019; Hussar & Bailey, 2014), there is a clear need for college instructors to have effective resources to teach this changing student population. As a faculty member, faculty developer, and dean, I am continually hunting for thoughtful, empirically grounded, and specific ways to empower *all* of my students so they thrive despite the barriers and obstacles they face. I am not alone in my search. Many faculty are uncertain about how to approach the difficult interactions that arise from complex classroom dynamics. They may feel unprepared to deal with the discomfort inherent in a diverse and inclusive learning environment. This discomfort may occur organically through interactions among students, instructors, and course content, as a class works through sensitive or difficult material. Faculty are also unsure how to effectively create discomfort that assists in tackling these challenging issues, particularly given the polarizing political times (Souza et al., 2018). Even those who report feeling prepared may not realize what they do not know (Samuels, 2014).

This pedagogical guide is designed to address these uncertainties and provide a versatile set of tools for approaching the college classroom. Each chapter focuses on palpable ideas and adaptive strategies to use right away when teaching.

This Book's General Approach

In this book, our object of focus is the college classroom, what hooks (1994) refers to as "the most radical space of possibility in the academy" (p. 12). I employ a social-psychological perspective that studies interaction among its various elements. I take into account the people in the classroom (instructors and students), the course content and methods of instruction, the dynamics between students and faculty, and the physical and psychological space. Often the college classroom—in discussion-based classes, or lab sections, or even in lectures—can be considered a small group (Billson, 1986), and thus I apply knowledge about group dynamics to understand it. One cannot fully understand the college classroom by examining its parts in isolation. For these teaching practices to be most effective, one needs to consider the potential synergy between the various class elements within their broader sociocultural or structural context (Adams et al., 2008; Oyserman & Lewis, 2017).

I use Kurt Lewin's (1946) psychological field theory as my foundation. Lewin proposed a simple formula that behavior is a function of a person and their environment. He noted that

> to understand or to predict behavior, the person and his environment have to be considered as *one* constellation of interdependent factors. We call the totality of these factors the life space (*LSp*) of that individual. . . . The life space, therefore, includes both the person and his psychological environment. (pp. 239–240)

In this book, I typically focus on the instructor's life space and then bring in the other features (e.g., students, course material, physical and psychological space, relationships between the individuals in the learning space) that compose it. As an example of this approach, consider for illustrative purposes the following classroom scenario of a White female college instructor, Alex. She is teaching a seminar on "Stereotyping and Prejudice" set in a small room where students sit around a table. The class consists of 11 White students, 2 Black students, and 2 Asian students. When discussing racial differences in test scores, a "hot moment" occurs. When one student contends that "maybe White students just work harder than Black students," another student responds angrily. Other students become quiet, seeming reticent to talk. This book probes each of the elements—the professor's identity, the course content, and so forth—individually and in tandem to provide strategies for the instructor to respond to interactions.

Although intended as a pedagogical guide for faculty, it is informed by students' points of view (Jennings, 2016). As much as possible, I ground the proposed strategies in empirical research in which both student and faculty perspectives are considered. The popular media often presents faculty and students' viewpoints—particularly on issues such as discomfort and safety on the college campus—as in opposition (Friedersdorf, 2015). My recent work demonstrates that there are misperceptions about faculty–student differences and suggests that there may be miscommunication when discussing classroom safety and discomfort (Vinton & Oleson, 2017). By considering the perceptions of both instructors and learners, we can develop a fuller understanding of the faculty member's "life space."

A Preview of the Chapters

To describe the learning environment of the classroom, the opening chapters provide a detailed exploration of the people—instructors and students—involved in creating an inclusive space, thinking through what each brings to it. In chapter 1 I consider professors' intersecting personal and social identities (e.g., racial backgrounds, gender identities, disability statuses) and their expectations for themselves and their students. I then examine implicit and explicit biases, their potential impact on the ways that faculty respond to students, and specific yet adaptable techniques to mitigate the influence of these biases. I explore approaches for faculty members to reflect on their own identities, emotions, and biases to become more self-aware and impartial in classroom interactions.

In chapter 2 I consider students' backgrounds, including class, race, disability, and gender, given the increasingly diverse group of students in college. I focus on what students bring to the classroom, exploring their basic psychological needs of autonomy, competence, and belonging; their approaches to learning; their intersecting personal and social identities that are linked to histories of privilege and exclusion; and their self-doubts and uncertainties. I concentrate particularly on obstacles or challenges to learning disproportionately navigated by marginalized students, presenting the influence of stereotypes on motivation, belonging, and performance, and considering ways to reduce the impact of stereotypes.

Next I provide the psychological and physical context in which students and faculty are interacting as well as the course materials and methods of instruction used. Chapter 3 draws on universally designed learning (Meyer et al., 2014) in combination with educational design rooted in social justice and multiculturalism (Evans et al., 2017) to describe ways to design academic spaces where students flourish academically and their basic psychological needs are met. In this chapter I focus on not only inclusive course design and content but also pedagogical approaches to make the classroom more inclusive across a range of academic disciplines. I present methods of instruction to make the classroom more engaging, meaningful, and welcoming, including effective ways to create collaborative small-group work and achieve desirable levels of difficulty, given the "*un*settlement" that thinking and learning involve (Dewey, 1920).

Chapters 4 and 5 focus on classroom dynamics, the heart of the book. My goal is to provide a comprehensive yet flexible model of *productive discomfort* that is essential for growth and learning, taking into account the role of intellectual safety and bravery. Chapter 4 primarily focuses on *preparation* for having difficult conversations in the classroom. I consider how instructors can not only create a shared understanding between themselves and their students about course content and values but also facilitate discussions about classroom norms and guidelines. Chapter 5 focuses on in-the-moment strategies to both *create* and *manage* discomfort about sensitive and controversial topics while supporting students of various social identities (e.g., gender, race, disability). It examines microaggressions, "cold moments" and "hot moments," and difficult dialogues. When concentrating on classroom dynamics, we bring in empirical research on these topics while also integrating practical approaches advocated by faculty developers, educators, and other higher education practitioners.

In chapter 6 I provide an overall integration of the ideas that have been presented throughout the book, considering how the various elements work together to influence classroom dynamics. Finally, I present more general college-wide programs to help faculty develop and improve their teaching, such as building faculty–student partnerships and creating learning communities in which faculty work together to create inclusive classrooms.

Some Suggestions for Getting the Most Out of the Book

Before going forward, I would encourage you to stop and reflect on what questions you're seeking answers for in this book. What are your challenges when you approach teaching? Take a moment to visualize your own teaching experiences. Reflect on a difficulty you've faced in the classroom. Consider the specific incident or interaction, your response, and the outcome. Was the outcome what you wanted? Where did you come up short? I urge you to ponder these challenges and successes as we go through this book. Use this guide as a resource to give you examples of different approaches and inspire you to make changes.

TABLE P.1
A Template for Reflection

What you are working on: _____

Description of relevant features or problems you're facing	What questions do you have?	What aspects work well?	What would you like to improve?

To provide a structure for your reflection, I offer a general template (see Table P.1). The website accompanying this book includes all the figures and tables in an easily downloadable format. Check out www.inclusiveclassroom dynamics.com for these resources.

At this point, set in motion your exploration of the various elements of the classroom space that this book addresses. What do you bring to the classroom? Prepare to examine your identities, expectations, and biases. What do your students bring? What are their needs, motivations, identities, doubts, preparation, and approaches to learning? Next consider what your teaching environments are like—both physically and psychologically. Are they accessible to all students? Do they convey that students of different backgrounds are welcome? Contemplate the course content. How do you design the course? What materials do you use? What are your methods of instruction? Next turn to reflect on the classroom dynamics among and between students and yourself. Finally, think about any broader campus issues that might influence your classroom.

This work is challenging, and this book covers a wide breadth of materials, so don't worry if you do not have reflections on a number of these factors or do not fully understand all of the terms and their definitions at this point. Assisting you in understanding each element is what this book is designed to do. It describes each of them in detail and provides you with possible strategies to approach each of them individually and in combination. To that end,

I would encourage you to pause and reflect on the themes of each chapter after you complete it.

Postscript

As this book is preparing to be typeset (May 2020), I am sheltering at home and teaching remotely as the country seeks to manage the COVID-19 pandemic. The challenges inherent in creating an inclusive university classroom have radically increased as I strive to teach students who have varied financial resources and access to reliable internet, are living in a range of time zones, feel stressed and/or without social support from family and friends, and show incredible resilience in the face of widespread hardships. Additionally, in this book, I envision the university classroom as a physical space (see especially Chapter 3)—a different environment than many of us are teaching in during this time. I encourage you, however, to take these ideas along with you as you teach—regardless of where the learning environment is. Now more than ever we need to work collectively to ensure that all students thrive

Finally, I want to add a note about the language I use in this book. I have sought to be inclusive, respectful, and clear as I present the diverse identities that students and instructors bring to the university classroom. However, the language considered respectful and clear is a moving target. I may have misstepped and inadvertently been offensive. Do let me know, so that I can correct the presentation in future work.

So, now, are you ready? Let's dive in and explore how to promote inclusive classroom dynamics.

I

INSTRUCTORS

"I think identity plays a huge role in the classroom. I don't think any of us can think outside. . . . We can think beyond our identities potentially, but we need to be aware we're doing so. . . . I don't think identity is a trap, but I do think . . . it's how we see the world, right? Our identities—and the groups we feel a part of, the groups we feel we belong to—are going to shape our perceptions."
—Faculty Member (Oleson, 2017)

"My identity shapes the classroom, all my students, all 30 students or 40 students or however many I have in the room, shape what's going on. And how do we best teach and reach students of all these varying identities? . . . It's about re-centering. . . . It's about bringing those marginalized identities into the center." —Faculty Member (Oleson, 2017)

This chapter focuses on *you*, the one teaching the course. What do you bring to the classroom in terms of your identities? What do you expect from yourself and your students? What are your biases and how do they impact interactions in the learning environment? This chapter provides the initial elements in this how-to guide for building an inclusive classroom. First, it gives a concrete set of questions to ask yourself about your identities, and if and when you should strategically disclose them. Second, it offers tangible strategies for both reflecting on your biases and mitigating their influence on your judgments of and interactions with students.

What follows are practical principles grounded in relevant research. However, their usefulness depends on your thoughtful application of these ideas to your own life. While reading the chapter, be open to both learning new ideas about identity and bias and reflecting on those aspects of your identities and biases you find most significant in terms of your classroom experiences as an instructor.

Faculty Members' Intersecting Personal and Social Identities

To begin, instructors bring *themselves*—their self-concepts—to the classroom. Their self-concepts include both their personal identities and their collective or social identities.

The Self

According to Baumeister (2010), one's self or self-concept has three key features:

1. Individuals have self-awareness and can look at themselves. For instance, I have knowledge about myself that includes ideas about my personal qualities (e.g., I am friendly; I like math) and my strengths and weaknesses (e.g., I often remember people's names yet sometimes forget how to pronounce certain names), among other things.
2. The self is social. It is created, maintained, and changed through interaction with other people. For instance, feedback from my students and my colleagues influences how I feel about my job and how competent I feel about my teaching.

TABLE 1.1

Worksheet: Applying Baumeister's Ideas About the Self-Concept to the Classroom

What are your important self-aspects/ personal qualities in the classroom?	While teaching, how are you influenced by your relationships, roles, and the environment?	In what ways do you exert control over and regulate yourself, your students, and the classroom environment?	What questions do you have? What aspects are working well? What would you like to improve?

3. One's self has the ability to act on the world, to self-regulate, and to make decisions. As a professor, I can exert a powerful role in the classroom, one that shapes my students' expectations, norms, and behaviors.

In Table 1.1, begin reflecting on yourself in the classroom, including both how you are *shaped by* and how you *shape* others.

Intersecting Personal and Social Identities

One's self is made up of more than personal identities. We also comprise social identities, "[those parts] of an individual's self-concept that [are] based upon the value and emotional significance of belonging to a social group" (Jones, 1997, p. 214). I identify as a social psychologist. I am a mother. I identify as White. To truly understand these social identities, one must also consider the ways that the social world intertwines them with each other, resulting in novel intersecting identities (e.g., I identify as a White woman or a cisgender White woman). Kimberle Crenshaw (1989) made clear the limits of considering identities in isolation when she introduced the term *intersectionality* in the realm of legal discrimination against Black women. More recently, Lisa Rosenthal (2016) stressed the importance of intersectionality in the field of psychology:

> Intersectionality highlights the importance of attending to multiple, intersecting identities and ascribed social positions (e.g., race, gender, sexual identity, class) along with associated power dynamics, as people are at the same time members of many different social groups and have unique experiences with privilege and disadvantage because of those intersections. Given its activist roots, focusing on systems of oppression and the need for structural change to promote social justice are central components of intersectionality. (p. 475)

Overall, instructors bring to the classroom their intersecting personal and social identities linked to histories of privilege and exclusion. When approaching teaching, your personal (e.g., "I see myself as smart or kind") and social identities (e.g., "I identify as a White woman") matter for students' perceptions, learning, achievement, and persistence (Carrell et al., 2010; Fairlie et al., 2014; Sorensen, 1989).

Rather than perceiving of and presenting one's self as a "disembodied *mind*—a possessor of knowledge and power" (Henderson, 1994, p. 436), a professor, Henderson (1994), suggests an "*embodied text*—produced by

TABLE 1.2
Worksheet: Personal and Social Identities in the Classroom

What are your identities? These could be single identities or intersecting multiple identities; briefly describe each.	In what ways is this identity important to you and/or to others?	What impact do you think it has on the way you see the world?	How does it influence your behavior in the classroom?	How does it impact how others respond to you?

certain personal and historical experiences" (p. 436). Building on this notion of embodied text, Mel Michelle Lewis (2011) considers how her intersecting identities impact her teaching of women's studies courses:

> I teach what I am, I am what I teach: an intersectionality . . . , an inter-disciplinarity, a complex epistemology, and pedagogical location. I live and perform my multiple social identities, both visible and invisible, and teach both through institutional knowledge and my own "embodied text" (Henderson, 1994: 436). As I teach through these embodiments, it has become apparent that the methods through which we teach women's studies must be intersectional and interdisciplinary, while recognizing the body as a site of learning and knowledge. (pp. 49–50)

You too have multiple identities that are significant in the university classroom. In Table 1.2, take time to reflect on identities that you consider important and/or that you think others consider important in the classroom, expanding on the initial work in Table 1.1.

Identities in the Classroom

Research, theory, and application to the higher education classroom often consider a focused set of important social identities. For example, Derald

Sue's (2015) work on "race talk" underscores the centrality of faculty members' racial or ethnic identities, whereas other explorations concentrate on gender (Miller & Chamberlin, 2000) or the intersection of gender with race (Chang, 2012; Pittman, 2010). I hope this book will be applicable across a variety of instructor identities, including race, gender, sexuality, relationship status, disability, social class, age, religion, political orientation, appearance, non-native English speaker, sexual assault survivor, cancer patient, to name some possibilities. This book provides a framework for approaching not only these identities but also unnamed ones that are or may become important for you while teaching.

I encourage you to explore your own identities and their potential for importance and relevance in the classroom. But identities are not weighted equally, nor necessarily consistently, at different times and in different classroom environments. There is a danger inherent in delineating such a broad collection of self-characteristics, as it may suggest that all are equivalent. I have some discomfort with my choice to include a long list of identities, because I realize that it could have unintended negative consequences. By including a range of diverse identities, individuals may underestimate the impact of some primary ones—such as race—that have an enormous societal impact (Crenshaw et al., 1995; Jones, 1997; Kendi, 2019; Oluo, 2019). For instance, recent research has suggested that when organizations define *diversity* with a broad range of categories—for example, including categories such as race or sex that are legally protected alongside categories such as personality—rather than concentrating on legally protected ones, individuals pay less attention to the organization's racial inequality (Akinola et al., 2017). The perceived impact of race is watered down by considering the other identities. To ensure that various social categories are not treated as interchangeable, current conversation has focused on anti-Blackness in particular and centered Black and Indigenous people when describing injustice experienced by people of color. The term *BIPOC* (Black, Indigenous, and People of Color) has recently become more commonly used. Keep this in mind. Also, while considering these wide-ranging identities, I particularly focus on the ways that these identities come to bear when discussing difficult, sensitive, or challenging topics in the classroom. The tools I am presenting are ones especially germane to managing these concerns.

Much of the literature on faculty identity involves qualitative research on faculty members' racial or ethnic identity, exploring the perspectives of both faculty of color (including Asian, Black, Latinx, and Native American) (Harlow, 2003) and White faculty members, especially within the classroom context when they are teaching about race (Sue et al., 2009). Other scholars have written about the potential impact of their male gender identity when teaching about sexual assault (Thakur, 2014), or as a gay male instructor teaching about homophobia (Gust, 2007). Additional narratives explore the intersection of gender and race (Pittman, 2010). I present these various accounts.

Faculty Members' Identities and Teaching Sensitive and Difficult Self-Relevant Material

This literature on faculty identities in the classroom helps us understand the challenges that instructors experience. Do they feel that they are doing a good job and that students perceive them as knowledgeable and effective? Do they feel that they have the strategies and skills necessary to thrive when teaching difficult topics? Use this research as a springboard to ask yourself these questions and to explore ways to approach challenges in your own teaching.

Faculty of Color Teaching About Race

Many of these rich qualitative studies highlight the experiences of professors of color. Faculty of color report having to manage the burden of their authority being questioned, with some research emphasizing that these instructors realize that race *does* matter, yet they have to act as if it doesn't (Harlow, 2003). Other research focuses on the impact of faculty members' race in the context of difficult racial conversations. For faculty of color,

> they all experienced discomfort at "being trapped" in the "expert syndrome." They are often expected to possess special expertise in handling racial topics and situations. When they were unable to do so, faculty of color were apprehensive that they would be perceived as less capable and competent. Last, most of the professors experienced powerful emotional reactions when they witnessed or were the targets of microaggressions. They described having their "buttons pushed" when they felt demeaned and/or watched other students of color become targets. Managing the feelings of anger and frustration, constantly providing proof of one's competency, and being expected to represent an entire racial group were described as emotionally draining and "exhausting." (Sue et al., 2011, p. 338)

Women faculty of color reported that their authority, teaching ability, and research knowledge were particularly questioned by White male students (Pittman, 2010).

White Faculty Teaching About Race

Recent qualitative research has also found that White faculty report challenges when confronted with difficult racial dialogues (Sue et al., 2009). Their anxiety levels are high. They experience a variety of fears, including concerns about (a) being *seen* as racist (Apfelbaum et al., 2008); (b) or even worse, acting in ways that made them realize that they *were* racist; (c) confronting White privilege; (d) not being seen as competent or legitimate to teach material about race; (e) and taking on accountability for reducing prejudice (Sue et al., 2009; Sue, 2013). These faculty accounts stress how individuals manage a challenging academic classroom where their authority and competence are questioned or where they are experiencing high anxiety. Faculty of color and White faculty both experienced obstacles when navigating difficult dialogues.

Gender Identity and Teaching About Sexual Assault

Other faculty members have written about their experiences discussing the sensitive topic of sexual assault with students. A pair of essays on teaching about rape in classics classrooms by Sanjaya Thakur, who identifies as male, and Sharon James, who identifies as female, provide a helpful understanding of how gender may come into play when discussing this topic. Thakur (2014) presents the challenges of teaching classics texts with descriptions of violence and rape, noting that he thinks many men avoid discussing these subjects. He suggests a list of reasons why these topics are actively avoided:

> (1) their desire not to offend, (2) they are afraid to somehow treat them "inappropriately," and they perceive that they do not possess adequate knowledge or training to discuss such topics, (3) their own comfort level with the material and subject, (4) their uncertainty of how even to begin a discussion about them, (5) they find them (or believe their colleagues and superiors might find them) unsuitable for discussion in an academic setting, (6) they hope other faculty or departments will cover them. (Thakur, 2014, p. 153)

Thakur also notes that many junior male faculty members express concerns about how handling these issues poorly could affect tenure and promotion; some report trepidation in approaching topics where female faculty are seen as having expertise. James (2014) too remarks that she has male friends who have stopped teaching Ovid's *Metamorphoses*, given its coverage of rape. She acknowledges that "teachers have good reason to be nervous about the topic, and perhaps even to avoid teaching it altogether" (James, 2014, p. 174). However, she and Thakur both stress that it is quite important to teach these topics in classics courses. James further notes that faculty must be prepared to talk about these topics during office hours and in more informal conversations, and that students are more likely to disclose sexual assault to female faculty members. Faculty members' gender identities can affect how they approach teaching (or not teaching) about rape and how students respond to the instructors' identities in terms of comfort with discussing the topic and disclosing personal experiences.

Stereotype Threat

These narratives and qualitative data complement empirical research on stereotype threat. While teaching, faculty from underrepresented groups may experience *stereotype threat*, the concern that their performance in the classroom could confirm a negative stereotype about their group's intelligence (Spencer et al., 2016). Instructors do not need to believe that the stereotype is true for these concerns to impact their teaching; they just need to know about the stereotype and be motivated to disconfirm it. While the majority of stereotype threat research has explored the performance of students rather than faculty, there is some research suggesting the junior women faculty in medicine are more vulnerable than junior men to stereotype threat (Fassiotto et al., 2016). Recent qualitative research (Block et al., 2019) explored the strategies that female scientists use to manage stereotype threat, including "fending off the threat," "confronting the threat," and "sustaining self in the presence of the threat" (p. 37).

Additionally, faculty members of color reflect on stereotype threat they experience in higher education; I provide two examples. Yolanda Flores Niemann (2012) considered the role of stereotypes in how she was treated during both her academic job interview and initial tenure process. When making a decision about what academic job to accept, she was asked by a senior male faculty member: "What are you, a scholar or a Mexican American?" (Niemann, 2012, p. 340). Doing research on ethnic studies meant that she was not a scholar. The threat to her academic identity was clear. Recently, Desdamona Rios (2018) explored the stereotype threat for faculty of color, presenting the threat that comes with being a woman, a Chicana, and a feminist: "less qualified, not legitimate, less knowledgeable, too political." This social identity threat led to feelings of anxiety, self-doubt, and lower performance in the classroom as she teaches about social justice. Strategies such as useful critical feedback from trusted colleagues and self-affirmation of her abilities were useful to reduce the impact of stereotype threat.

Before turning to a broader set of strategies used for identity management, I encourage you to return to Table 1.2. Are there additional intersecting identities that you would like to add? Do you have further insights regarding the potential impact of your identities on how you approach the classroom or how others respond to or perceive you in that learning environment?

Identity Management: Disclosure and Concealment of Identities in the Classroom

To feel comfortable and confident teaching difficult topics, faculty members make choices about how to manage their identities in the classroom. They must decide what aspects of their personal lives they discuss with their students. Do they talk about their relationships and families (e.g., their romantic partners, their children)? Do they share where they went to college and if they were the first one in the family to do so? Do they discuss how the class readings are personally relevant, based on aspects of their identity? These decisions involve juggling a number of competing motivations, such as supporting their students' learning, hoping to be genuine and transparent, creating connections with their students, and wanting to project knowledge and capability. Faculty might also decide some identities are irrelevant to the task at hand and could distract from learning (Herne & Morgan, 2013).

Social identity theory stresses that individuals are motivated to see themselves positively and that a person's identification with social groups is one beneficial path to accomplishing this positive self-view (Tajfel & Turner, 1986). Additionally, sharing certain aspects of one's self and one's social identities (e.g., "I've tried to teach my children that race, religion, or social class shouldn't affect their relationships with people," "There is nothing better than a good book to raise your spirit") could potentially enhance how students feel about their learning experience (Sorensen, 1989), particularly if students see the self-disclosure as positive and relevant to the course content (Cayanus et al., 2009). Professors must decide when, and if, and how much (Cayanus & Martin, 2008) to disclose or withhold discussing aspects of their personal characteristics and social identities. They may seek to discuss their identities in ways that reflect positively on themselves (Simpson, 2009), that protect their privacy, and that maintain their mental health and well-being (King, 2013).

Disclosure of Concealable Social Identities

Such self-disclosure is complicated because revealing important concealable social identities could prove stigmatizing (Chaudoir & Fisher, 2010). As an example, LGBTQ faculty members might consider whether to teach "out" in the classroom, given the potential for negative feedback. Although recent research (Boren & McPherson, 2018; Jennings, 2010) suggested that there may be few detrimental effects of coming out about one's sexual orientation in the college classroom, these researchers acknowledge that their findings do not necessarily generalize to the full range of classrooms. Russ et al. (2002) had previously found that students saw a gay male professor as less credible than a straight male one and reported learning less from him.

Scott William Gust (2007) wrote about his experiences as an out gay professor teaching *The Laramie Project,* which focuses on homophobia. Before entering the classroom, colleagues cautioned him to "look out for the football players and the frat boys. . . . (He) took the warning about 'football players and frat boys' seriously but still decided to make the choice to 'come out' in class" (p. 44). To his surprise, he found little pushback from the highly masculine male students. Instead he felt that male students whose masculinity had likely been questioned seemed more apt to respond negatively. Although Gust believes that he made the right personal decision to be an out gay teacher, he makes clear that each faculty member should choose what is best for themselves. "I do not, I repeat, believe that all queer teachers should disclose their sexual identities in class. I respect any choice that is carefully reasoned and does not deny the presence of sexual identity in all classrooms" (p. 51).

Faculty members also highlight the potential for self-disclosure to impact teaching and learning, the complexity of making decisions about disclosure, and the strategic nature of their choices. For instance, Rosamond King (2013) noted:

> Of course, no one strategy is appropriate for every teacher, class, or institution. Clearly, any instructor's approach to disclosing identity in the classroom needs to be one s/he is comfortable with—and, it should go without saying, which does not place the instructor in any kind of danger. (I suspect that age and professional rank, as well as race, gender, and sexual orientation are significant factors.) Nevertheless, any strategy that promotes education in its broadest sense, the opening of the mind, promotes the common good by serving as food for thought for us all. Any method of revealing aspects of one's personal identity that responds to the situation and context can be termed *strategic disclosure*, a term that refers to the individual's active determination of what information and how much information about themselves to share at any given moment. It allows the consideration of context, personal comfort, and protection. (p. 108, emphasis added)

King presented her own approach to students' personal questions, which involved telling students that she does not "answer such inquiries until the end of the term" (p. 102). And then, even at that point, she turns their probing questions into a "teaching moment" rather than just answering them. She likes her privacy, believes that professors should be free to keep their identities to themselves, and notes that "I have found that professors who cannot pass for heterosexual or White or born-in-the-USA Americans already have less privacy at work" (p. 102). However, she also presented examples of three colleagues' approaches that varied radically in terms of how directly they responded to student questions and how their responses engaged with their pedagogy.

Lad Tobin (2010) further presented faculty self-disclosure as a "strategic teaching tool" and offered some principles that he used when deciding whether to disclose personal information in his role as a composition teacher:

> In courses for first-year students, I often reveal personal characteristics designed to reassure my students that I am capable, confident, and consistent. In courses for teaching assistants and in writing about teaching, I often try to reveal the opposite. (p. 201)

His criteria suggested that his decisions are complicated ones that depend on the audience of his self-presentation and his goals for that interaction. He reflected that "there is value for teachers in developing protocols and criteria for making strategic decisions about potentially tricky self-disclosures" (p. 197). "In defending *strategic* rather than *all* uses of the personal, I am also acknowledging the role of differing applications and interpretations of pedagogical self-disclosure" (p. 200). While presenting his own set of guidelines, he encouraged faculty members to come up with their own.

Framework for Making Decisions About Self-Disclosure in the Classroom
In these faculty members' personal accounts, many factors relevant to self-disclosure are considered. However, each writer stresses that instructors need to come up with their own practices. In a presentation, Catherine Herne and Susanne Morgan (2013) suggested a series of questions that teachers could ask to determine whether to disclose particular identities, broadly framing these questions in terms of creating an inclusive and safe environment for students (see Figure 1.1).

In the first column they pose questions about the particular identity. Is it stigmatized? Is it one that is concealable/hidden, or is it visible to others? What is the impact of revealing or concealing the identity? In the second column they consider aspects of the particular classroom situation. Is the disclosure relevant to the academic discipline? To the students' learning environment? In the third column they present the broader university context, asking whether or not there is an inclusive climate and whether or not the person's job is secure. The second and third columns feed into the middle one with the final question, "Should I discuss it?"

Figure 1.1. Identity self-disclosure in the classroom.

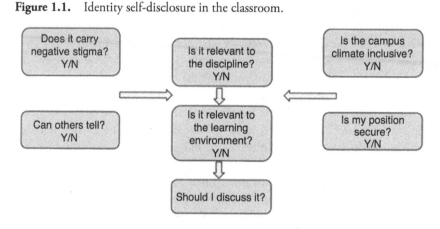

In terms of both the variables included and the framing of the variables as questions, Herne and Morgan's (2013) model is a compelling one. From my vantage point as a social psychologist, I have created an updated framework (see Figure 1.2). At the beginning of the process I include questions about the person's goals in disclosing the identity. In Herne and Morgan's model, a number of potential competing motivations are in play, yet the motivations are not made explicit in the visual. In their general model about disclosure processes, Chaudoir and Fisher (2010) have conceptualized decisions about disclosure as involving both approach and avoidance

Figure 1.2. Identity self-disclosure in an inclusive higher education classroom: Questions to consider.

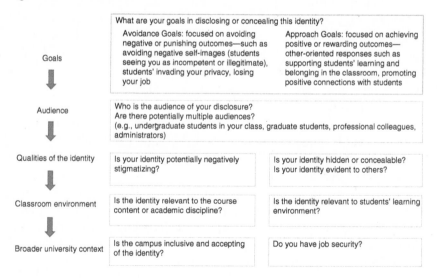

goals—goals focused on achieving positive or rewarding outcomes and goals focused on avoiding negative or punishing outcomes, respectively. Faculty might also have approach and avoidance motivations in the classroom when they decide whether to disclose (see Beck et al., 2019). For instance, in the classroom context, faculty members' avoidance goals could involve avoiding negative outcomes to the self, such as a negative self-image (e.g., students' seeing them as incompetent or illegitimate), students' invading their privacy, or losing their job. However, there are also approach goals, which could include responses oriented toward students, such as wanting to self-disclose in ways that support students' learning and belonging in the college classroom. Faculty members might also use self-disclosure to promote positive connections with students. They could disclose, for instance, that they were the first in their family to attend college as a way to connect, to serve as a role model, and to demonstrate that first-gen students belong there.

I also include questions about the audience of one's self-disclosure. As Tobin (2010) noted, his self-disclosure varies depending on who the audience is—first-year students, graduate students, colleagues. What is disclosed in the classroom does not always stay in the classroom, so questions about who is in not only the present audience but also the potentially broader audience could be important to ask.

Figure 1.2, building on Herne and Morgan's (2013) earlier flowchart, provides a series of five interrelated sets of questions to frame instructors' decisions about whether or not to disclose their identities in the classroom. It can also serve as a worksheet for you to fill in your specific goals, audiences, qualities, classroom environment, and broader university context.

Faculty Members' Biases and Prejudices

Thus far, I have focused on the expression of faculty members' personal and social identities in the classroom. In addition, faculty bring prejudices (evaluations of a group or an individual based on their group membership), stereotypes (beliefs about the characteristics of members of a social group), and expectations about their students' personal qualities and abilities (Kite & Whitley, 2016).

Explicit and Implicit Biases

Sometimes these attitudes are ones that someone consciously holds and freely reports on an explicit measure, for example, "Women are too easily offended" (Glick & Fiske, 1996) or "On the whole, Black people don't stress education and training" (Katz & Hass, 1988). In many contexts, though, expressing negative views about members of social groups is seen as unacceptable. Individuals keep these biases, or prejudices, to themselves (Crandall et al., 2002). They may not even realize that they have these negative attitudes (Dovidio & Gaertner, 2004). Often, these biases are subtle and hidden, what might be called *implicit* or *unconscious biases.* "Implicit attitudes and stereotypes . . . are evaluations and beliefs that are automatically activated by the mere presence (actual or symbolic) of the attitude object. They commonly function in an unconscious and unintentional fashion" (Dovidio et al., 2006, p. 94). Individuals may have learned negative stereotypes—including ones that they do not even realize they have—from images they see in the media (Ruscher, 2001) or from important figures in their lives, such as their parents (Miklikowska, 2016).

It may be difficult to acknowledge that we are influenced by automatic attitudes and stereotypes that are unintentional and largely out of our control. If these biases are in play, then we do not always treat our students fairly. It violates how we see ourselves or at least hope to see ourselves (O'Brien et al., 2010). However, understanding unconscious bias in general and in one's personal teaching is important to ensuring that the classroom is an egalitarian space where all students are treated in unbiased ways.

I consider a variety of potential biases, particularly focusing on racial bias because of its profound impact on students' academic lives (Weinstein et al., 2004). I highlight stereotypes and prejudices that are automatic or unconscious for I believe that it is important to raise awareness about these potential biases. However, even explicit prejudice can be seen as appropriate. For instance, Crandall et al. (2018) found that both Trump and Clinton supporters believed that it was more acceptable after Trump was elected (as compared to before) to express negative views about the social groups that Trump disparaged during his presidential campaign (e.g., Muslims, immigrants, disabled people). Therefore, I do not limit my focus to implicit stereotypes and prejudices; explicit ones are also implicated. Finally, I consider faculty members' biases. Chapter 5 considers biases in the classroom more broadly, including those of students (Boysen & Vogel, 2009).

Approach With a Growth Mindset

It is often difficult to talk about one's prejudices, particularly about race, without becoming defensive (Howell et al., 2015). To be aware of racial bias and its pervasiveness (Nosek et al., 2007) raises the concern that you might be racist, one of the worst possible ways to be characterized (Crandall et al., 2002). However, talking about these ideas and practicing being unbiased are essential for creating an inclusive classroom. I'd encourage you to approach these ideas with a growth mindset, in which you are seeking to develop your knowledge about how bias works in general and how it might be personally affecting your classroom teaching. According to Carol Dweck (2006),

> In this mindset, the hand you're dealt is just the starting point for development. This *growth mindset* is based on the belief that your basic qualities are things you can cultivate through your efforts. . . . The passion for stretching yourself and sticking to it, even (or especially) when it's not going well, is the hallmark of the growth mindset. (p. 7)

Your effort involves taking risks, making mistakes as you are developing your skills, but persisting to gain new knowledge. I encourage you to approach this challenging and rewarding task with cultural humility (Tervalon & Murray-Garcia, 1998). Although you may have learned negative cultural stereotypes and prejudices, it is important to realize that, with practice, you can reduce your racial biases and act in less prejudiced ways (Devine et al., 2012).

Reflective and Reflexive Processing Systems

To understand these subtle, often hidden biases, I consider how people process information about their social world. Psychologists, neuroscientists, and others suggest that humans have two different systems for processing information and drawing inferences about others—one that is more reflective and controlled and another that is more reflexive and automatic (Gilbert, 1989). Individuals can process information in a careful, regulated way, putting in lots of effort to understand the details accurately. But often they process the world in a more automatic way, coming to a fast conclusion with little effort or motivation needed; their perceptions are based on what quickly comes to mind. For instance, suppose I introduce myself to a new colleague at a conference, noting that I live in Portland. As an avid watcher of *Portlandia*, she automatically thinks I am a "yoga-doing, farmers-market-shopping, arugula-eating, library-card-holding, bike-riding, latte-sipping, liberal-blog-reading white person" (Steiger, 2011). Portland is linked to all of these ideas. More generally, individuals' social categories have associations that may be biased by their stereotypes, expectations, and previous experiences.

These biases could begin to play out as you step into the room on the first day of class, scanning the students sitting around the table. You begin to gain a sense of the various students. To do this, you likely categorize students based on their similarities; this categorization of individuals into social groups simplifies the world and gives you shortcuts for approaching the class (Macrae & Bodenhausen, 2000). You look around to see the backgrounds of students in the room—how many students of color are there? Students who identify as male? Students with visible disabilities? Older students? You are acknowledging students' personal and social identities. These identities could be quite important to the students, providing meaning and positive benefits. However, these social categories may also be associated with stereotypical qualities that become activated when you are thinking of students as members of social groups (Bargh, 1999). From this moment, your beliefs about these social groups—for example, stereotyping students with disabilities as dependent or incompetent (Nario-Redmond, 2010) or Asian students as strong in math (Cheryan & Bodenhausen, 2000)—may affect the ways that you respond to individual students (Klein & Snyder, 2003). In general, stereotypes and prejudices predict discriminatory behavior in the domains of education, employment, health care, and criminal justice (Cameron et al., 2012; Glaser et al., 2014). I provide some examples relevant to the college environment.

Biases in Higher Education

Katherine Milkman et al. (2015) found that biases against students based on gender and race have an impact before the student even comes to a professor's class. They sent an email to a sample of U.S. college professors, ostensibly from a student interested in pursuing a PhD. The professors did not realize that they were in an experiment (and that the student was hypothetical). The student wanted to have a brief in-person meeting in a week to talk about research opportunities. The student's name varied both in terms of gender (male, female) and race (White, Black, Hispanic, Indian, Chinese). They found "that when making decisions about the future, faculty in almost every academic discipline exhibit[ed] bias favoring White males at a key pathway to the Academy" (p. 1699). The potential student's name (signaling race and gender) impacted whether the professor ignored their email.

In other research, Jacoby-Senghor et al. (2016) asked White college students to prepare and teach a class lesson to another student. After learning the material, the other student, who was either Black or White, was tested on their knowledge. The videotaped teaching interactions were coded both for the teacher's level of anxiety and the quality of their lesson. Higher teacher implicit racial biases predicted lower test performance for Black (but not White) students. These more biased instructors also displayed more anxiety and created poorer quality lessons, which explained why the Black students performed worse. In a follow-up study, non-Black participants watched videotapes of the lessons given to Black students and were then tested for their knowledge. The teachers' implicit racial bias predicted lower performance for these students as well, making clear that the test performance was due to the lower pedagogical effectiveness of the teacher, not the student's race. This research underlines the potential for an instructor's biases to undermine the quality of their teaching, leading to student underperformance.

Finally, there is a growing body of research examining gender biases in recommendation letters written for academic positions. For instance, Madera et al. (2009) examined the linguistic content of actual letters of recommendations written for candidates for academic psychology positions. Female applicants were described with more communal terms (e.g., nurturing) than were male applicants; male candidates were described with more agentic terms (e.g., ambitious) than were female candidates. In a follow-up study, psychology professors read the letters of recommendation with all gender information removed. The professors rated how hirable the job applicants were, in addition to rating how communal and agentic they were. Higher communality ratings predicted lower hirability. These studies demonstrated that gender stereotypes of women's kindness in recommendation letters for academic jobs had the potential to negatively affect women's chances of being hired. Related research examining recommendation letters written for chemistry and biochemistry job applicants found that recommendations for male candidates contained more "standout" words (e.g., "excellent," "superb") than did those for female candidates (Schmader et al., 2007). Similarly, male applicants for postdocs in geoscience received recommendation letters that were stronger than female applicants' (Dutt et al., 2016).

These are a few examples of how stereotypes and prejudices might lead to discriminatory behavior in higher education. What should you do in response? In a recent *New York Times* video on implicit bias, Dolly Chugh suggests doing a self-audit to evaluate your biases (Reshamwala, 2016). For instance, you could count up the number of men and women (or individuals of various racial or ethnic backgrounds) in your social networks, or have a colleague sit in on your class and count how many students you call on from

TABLE 1.3
Worksheet on Biases

What is your bias? Describe briefly. Review past behaviors and consider future actions.	What are the possible sources of this bias?	What impact do you think that it has on the way you see the world?	How does it shape how you describe and evaluate students' abilities and qualities?	How does it influence your behavior in the classroom?	How does it impact students (e.g., their learning motivation, belonging)?

different backgrounds. Try to gather some data in your everyday life—whose emails you answer, who you call on in class, and so forth. Pause right now to consider your possible biases, even though this is difficult to do. Table 1.3 serves as a template to reflect on your biases.

Strategies for Mitigating the Influence of Biases

There are a number of approaches for mitigating the impact of one's stereotypes and prejudices on interactions with students. I begin by considering ways to control behaviors so that biases do not come out in judgments, evaluations, and behaviors. I focus primarily on Margo Monteith's (1993) self-regulation of prejudice model as a framework for helping mitigate the impact of biases. This model suggests strategies to help control behavior and not apply stereotypes and prejudices to individual students. Then I turn to methods for lessening the impact of implicit associations that come up automatically with our social categories.

The Self-Regulation of Prejudice Model: Controlling the Expression of Prejudice

In their recent review, Monteith et al. (2016) considered the conditions under which individuals may be able to reduce their expression of prejudice and act in egalitarian ways. As noted earlier, individuals' prejudices—even among those people who genuinely want to be non-prejudiced—may be activated when interacting with someone who belongs to a stereotyped group. Without individuals' having awareness or intention, stereotypes and biases can be activated automatically and lead to prejudiced behavior (Bargh, 1999), such as providing a Black student with a less effective teaching lesson. To overcome biases, individuals must be motivated to control their prejudice. For many faculty members, they are driven by their internal or personal standards to treat all students fairly. The motivation could also be influenced by external forces such as the norms and standards in their institution.

In the self-regulation of prejudice model, Monteith articulated how individuals motivated not to respond in prejudiced ways react when these automatically activated stereotypes lead to prejudiced behavior. They see themselves responding in ways that contradict their beliefs that they are not prejudiced. Awareness of this inconsistency and awareness that they acted in a biased way elicit negative affective responses, namely they feel guilty and disappointed about how they acted. This guilt motivates them to slow down and reflect on their behavior and consider ways to avoid being prejudiced in the future. With practice, individuals develop *"cues for control,* or the building of associations between stimuli that predict the occurrence of a discrepant response, the discrepant response itself, and negative self-directed affect resulting from awareness of one's discrepancy" (Monteith et al., 2016, p. 413). The prejudiced behavior becomes linked with negative affect and other features such as the person's social category. With practice, individuals can work to "break this bad habit of prejudice" (Devine, 1989).

Consider a concrete classroom example. Imagine that I am teaching about biomedical ethics. I get excited about the ideas and quickly toss out a couple examples of doctors' engagement and suggest in each that he plays an important role. I then turn to consider the nurse and her role in my example. At that point, I realize that I have linked gender with the roles of doctor and nurse. Discussing doctors activated the ideas that I associate with doctors, including that they are male. I look around and sense that my students—who are sitting in a class on ethics!—realize that I have not been egalitarian in my approach.

I may feel disappointed in myself for referring to nurses as women and doctors as men. I have reinforced gender stereotypes, as well as the gender binary. I would likely slow down in my presentation and try to be more thoughtful about my examples. I might bring in an additional example and reverse the pronouns. I might switch to using the pronoun "they" to refer to a single doctor or nurse in one example to demonstrate that medical professionals' gender identities are more inclusive than "he" and "she." I might bring the discussion back to a paper that we reading by an author who identified as female. I might tell the students that my examples were biased and explain that I will work to be more egalitarian in the future. Later when I put my class notes away, I might jot down to be careful next time and write out an example with a female doctor to use in class. In responding to my gendered presentation of medical staff, I am reflecting on the situation and starting to develop cues for control of my prejudice.

Importance of Awareness, Practice, and Planning

With practice, these cues can become present in upcoming situations to help individuals act in non-prejudiced ways (Monteith et al., 2002). Individuals become aware of their potential to be biased (Monteith et al., 2009). As part of this awareness, it is important to acknowledge race and other social categories. As Apfelbaum et al. (2009) have found, strategic color blindness ("avoidance of talking about race—or even acknowledging racial differences—in an effort to avoid the appearance of bias" [p. 918]), can elicit worse rather than better racial interactions. Treating race as unimportant when having a discussion about race does not make one seem less racist but instead may promote both negative social interactions and more implicit racial bias.

These cues for control cause individuals to seek to prevent themselves from acting in prejudiced ways and instead act *without* prejudice. They take the time to exert control and respond to the other person based on their individual qualities rather than their group membership. With practice over time, these new non-prejudiced responses can become more automatic, replacing the bad habit of prejudice (Devine et al., 2012). In addition, Mendoza et al. (2010) suggest that it can be possible to come up with clear concrete plans—for example, "if this happens, then do this"—to automatically control for biases in specific situations. These could be used in combination with cues for control. In response, Monteith et al. (2016) suggest this specific plan: "If I see a person of color, I will think before acting on stereotypes" (p. 423).

Controlling Prejudice in Ambiguous Situations

The self-regulation of prejudice model provides a compelling account of ways to develop cues for control and replace prejudiced responses with egalitarian ones. It depends on individuals realizing that their prejudiced behavior is discrepant from their desired egalitarian behavior. Often, situations are ambiguous, and someone does not realize that they have acted in a biased way. Importantly, stereotypes and prejudices are most likely to come into play in ambiguous situations (Dovidio & Gaertner, 2000; Kunda & Sherman-Williams, 1993). When a task is easy or clear-cut—for example, you are assigning a grade on an exam and the student scored 100% (or alternatively received 20% of the points)—one's biases likely have little effect on the evaluation. The perfect exam is given an A; the failing one receives an F. However, if you are evaluating a student's class presentation that includes some compelling points mixed in with some weak ones, your stereotypes may influence the overall evaluation (e.g., Darley & Gross, 1983). To give a Native American student a poor grade for a perfect exam is clearly discriminatory; however, a teacher could justify a poor grade for mixed performance based on factors unrelated to race or ethnicity. When the situation is ambiguous, it is more difficult to diagnose that one has acted in a prejudiced way; individuals may still see themselves as non-prejudiced (Dovidio et al., 2016). I would encourage you to especially consider your vulnerability to bias during ambiguous classroom situations. If your classroom experiences are like mine, many are ambiguous. Open yourself to the possibility that you might be biased, even if it is not clear.

Weakening One's Stereotypes and Prejudices

Another approach to reducing the impact of stereotypes is to change the initial stereotypes in a person's mind that could be activated. If the negative beliefs are reduced, then there is less that is activated. When I enter the classroom, I can try not to act on my stereotypes. However, it would be even better if I had weaker biases to begin with. Changing our stereotypes and prejudices is possible, but it is difficult to elicit long-term change (Forscher et al., 2017). Here are some promising ways to reduce one's biases.

Education about prejudice and diversity can play a role in changing prejudices. Rudman et al. (2001) found that students in a course on prejudice and conflict (as compared to students in control courses) showed larger reductions in implicit and explicit biases across the term. More recently, Hussey et al. (2010) found that students in a social psychology course with diversity content (compared to a social psychology course without it) showed more positive change in attitudes toward a variety of groups. A recent meta-analysis on education about diversity revealed that such education is not always effective, particularly in changing attitudes (Bezrukova et al., 2016). However, the analysis concluded that the knowledge gained about diversity issues in diversity training persists over time and longer training programs were more effective than shorter ones. A semester-long course may make a difference in one's knowledge, and in some cases, one's attitudes. But, as I consider in chapter 3, it often takes two or more classes to see benefits in intergroup relations (Bowman, 2010).

In addition, a 12-week intervention by Patricia Devine and her colleagues (2012) suggests a set of concrete strategies that individuals can use to "break the prejudice habit." In particular, they focused first on getting students motivated to reduce their implicit bias by raising awareness that they had implicit bias and increasing concern about their potential to act in discriminatory ways. They then taught the students specific strategies to implement in their everyday interactions to reduce their bias, stressing that students were receiving a toolkit to use. For these tools to be useful, however, they needed to practice and put effort into using them. Five strategies were presented: stereotype replacement (substituting non-stereotypic responses for stereotypic ones as described earlier), counter-stereotypic imaging (visualizing positive examples of members of stereotyped groups), individuating (coming up with personal rather than group qualities), perspective taking (taking the first-person perspective of a member of an out-group), and contact (having positive interactions with stigmatized group members).

Students in the intervention (as compared to a control group) showed reduced implicit biases for up to 8 weeks, increased awareness of their bias, and increased concern about discrimination. Further research using a similar intervention found increased concern about discrimination, too. This follow-up also found that two years later, the students who had participated in the intervention were more likely to write comments opposing a public forum that argued that stereotypes are useful and not harmful (Forscher et al., 2017). Making individuals aware of their prejudices, raising their concerns about discrimination, and giving them a toolkit to reduce their biases made a long-term difference.

Lessening the Activation of Social Categories

Yet another approach is to stop the categorization from happening. For some tasks, one is able to keep themselves blind to what social category someone belongs to, thereby preventing stereotypes from being activated at all. For instance, Goldin and Rouse (2000) examined the role of gender bias in selecting musicians for professional orchestras. When the auditions were "blind" (there was a screen so that no one could see the person who was auditioning), the number of women who were selected rose markedly. One could grade exams with students' names removed so that biases could not influence the evaluation. This approach is not recommended during classroom discussions relevant to student identities where ignoring or pretending to ignore students' social groups could have negative consequences.

Setting Clear Criteria

Finally, given that biases creep in when situations are ambiguous, it is important to set clear criteria when evaluating students, colleagues, job applicants, and others. When the criteria have not been set in advance, an evaluator may define criteria in such a way that they are biased in favor of one candidate over another. For instance, Uhlmann and Cohen (2005) found that when confronted with specific job files to assess, evaluators created criteria that favored men over women for the position of police chief but women over men for the position of women's studies professor. When they determined which criteria were important before seeing specific files, however, they did not show gender bias. When examining job candidates' files, decide in advance the criteria that you will use to evaluate them to reduce the impact of your biases.

In Table 1.4, I bring together these various strategies for mitigating the influences of biases and provide specific examples to use in the academic environment. I encourage you to refer to them in your attempts to reduce the influence of your biases.

Self-Reflection on One's Identities and Biases

To become more self-aware and impartial in classroom interactions, reflect on your own identities and biases and the relationships among them (see hooks, 1994). There is a template, Table 1.5, that you could use for your reflection. As Dena Samuels (2014) notes, we need to "consider what we don't know we don't know, so that we are prepared to teach to a variety of student identities" (p. 81). Taking time to reflect and get feedback from trusted colleagues and students can be invaluable for creating an inclusive classroom. This chapter considered faculty members' personal and social identities and strategically disclosing them (or not). Then it described faculty members' biases; their impact on judgments, evaluations, and interactions; and potential ways to mitigate their influence. As King (2013) stressed, you have the right to privacy and to feel safe in your position. You should also be perceived as capable to do your job. So monitor your identities as needed. That said, I would encourage you to be open to your potential for bias and to model for

TABLE 1.4
Strategies for Mitigating the Influence of Biases in the Classroom

Focus of Strategy	*Specific Suggestions*
Controlling and Regulating Biases	
Growth Mindset	Encourage individuals to frame their attempts at being unbiased in terms of growth and improvement. Personally model a growth mindset for your students.
Motivation	Reflect on your motivation and specific goals—e.g., to make your classroom more inclusive, to be unbiased in how you approach students of varying backgrounds, to promote social justice. Talk to colleagues about your motivation, and brainstorm together about ways to meet your goals.
Awareness of Bias	Do an audit of your behavior to see where you might be biased—e.g., whose emails do you open, who do you invite to be your research assistants, who do you eat lunch with, who do you follow on Twitter?
Practice	Treat controlling your bias like a bad habit that you need to practice to change. Set aside time to develop and practice, just as you would for other skills you are developing, such as learning to play a musical instrument or speak a foreign language.
Implementation Plans	Come up with specific plans—e.g., "If I see a person of color, I will think before acting on stereotypes."
Feedback	Ask a trusted colleague to provide feedback on your biases—e.g., ask someone to sit in your class and keep track of who you call on or encourage to speak.
Changing Biases	
Education	Attend workshops or classes to develop your understanding of biases. Read articles, books, and websites to educate yourself about bias.
Stereotype Replacement	Pause to notice when you are making stereotypic responses and replace them with non-stereotypic ones. Plan ahead in your teaching to ensure that you have non-stereotypic examples included.
Counterstereotypic Imaging	Learn about a range of individuals who are members of social groups so that you can easily pull to mind many counterstereotypic examples.

(Continues)

TABLE 1.4 (*Continued*)

Focus of Strategy	*Specific Suggestions*
Individuating	Ask students to introduce significant things about themselves during class. ("Tell the story of your name"— why were you given your first or middle name? Who were you named for? What does your name mean?) Have students complete a background questionnaire describing aspects of themselves that are important to them.
Perspective-Taking	Build in opportunities to learn about the first-person perspective of students in your class.
Contact	Create opportunities to interact with diverse sets of people—e.g., attending community organization meetings or churches, seeking activities beyond your work environment. Assign students to a variety of different class groupings, so that they interact with individuals of various backgrounds.
Lessening Activation of Stereotypes	Have students put their names at the end of the exams, so that you do not see them and cannot be influenced while grading.
Setting Clear Criteria	Come up with evaluation criteria before reading student papers or job candidate files.

TABLE 1.5
Self-Reflection on Your Identities and Biases

What you're working on: _____

Description of relevant features (problems you are facing)	What questions do you have?	What aspects are working well?	What would you like to improve?

your students that we all make mistakes and can learn from them. Modeling a growth mindset can be powerful to both you and your students.

Faculty of color have suggested that an effective strategy in racial dialogues is to acknowledge their prejudices and mistakes. They felt that it was important to be "human" and to show their students that they too make mistakes (Sue et al., 2011). White faculty engaged in racial dialogues similarly suggested that it was important to acknowledge and disclose their emotions, challenges, and fears (Sue et al., 2009). Personally, when I teach about difficult topics, I talk about the idea that we are all learners who make mistakes on the first day of class. In my role as director of the Center for Teaching and Learning, a key insight learned from interacting with faculty at all stages was the potential value of being more transparent about what we are doing in class and who we are. I think that I had implicitly or explicitly been taught that to be a professor—"to profess"—meant to be an expert who did not show weaknesses or gaps in knowledge. Today my understanding of teaching and learning fundamentally differs. I can be an expert about the topic of study and also be a learner who is developing, improving, and mastering knowledge rather than just demonstrating my knowledge (Elliot & McGregor, 2001).

2

STUDENTS

"During my first semester of my first year at Haverford, I constantly felt unsure of myself in the classroom. I believed that I was somehow less prepared than my peers to participate in class because I had not studied in an American high school and English was not my first language. This belief pushed me to undermine the value of my contributions, hindering my ability to participate confidently and sometimes even at all. . . . My identity, my beliefs, my worries, and my sense of uncertainty as I navigated the unfamiliar spaces of Haverford College all contributed to my sense of not belonging." (Cólon García, 2017, p. 1)

"Teaching well is a learning process that never stops and the student perspective is invaluable to that process." (Luker & Morris, 2016, p. 5)

Our attention turns to the students in your classes. You want to be able to support them and help them thrive and learn. It is therefore important to know what they bring to the classroom, including their psychological needs, their expectations, their personal and social identities, and their worries and concerns. Appreciating the richness of students' perspectives enhances your ability to create a classroom climate that promotes their well-being, motivation, and achievement. I begin by exploring students' basic psychological needs of autonomy, competence, and belonging (Ryan & Deci, 2000) and their varying expectations and approaches to learning and knowledge (Schrader, 2004). I situate these needs and expectations within a broader framework of their intersecting personal and social identities, which are linked to histories of privilege and exclusion (Case, 2013; Galliher et al., 2017). In addition, I bring to bear a constellation of worries and doubts that students may harbor: their self-doubts about their academic abilities (Oleson & Steckler, 2010), uncertainties about belonging in the college environment (Walton & Cohen, 2007), feelings of being an impostor (Clance & Imes, 1978), and threats to their social identities (Spencer et al., 2016). In particular, I focus on obstacles or challenges to learning disproportionately navigated by marginalized students and provide a set of tools to help all students thrive in the university classroom.

Basic Psychological Needs of Autonomy, Competence, and Belonging

When I enter the classroom on the first day of a new term and look out at my students, I am hopeful that they will be engaged and curious and ready to tackle the course. I strive to promote intrinsic motivation, "the inherent tendency to seek out novelty and challenges, to extend and exercise one's capabilities, to explore, and to learn" (Ryan & Deci, 2000, p. 70). But how should I foster this motivation?

Self-Determination Theory

Self-determination theory suggests that individuals' self-motivation and well-being is promoted when they feel that their fundamental psychological needs of competence, autonomy, and belonging are satisfied (Ryan & Deci, 2000). Learners thrive in academic environments fulfilling these needs (Niemiec & Ryan, 2009).

Competence is the belief that one is capable of achieving their desired outcomes. Individuals who feel competent perceive that they have the ability to effectively master their environment (White, 1959). In a classroom environment, if students feel unsure and lack the skills necessary to talk about difficult topics such as racism, they might feel incompetent during sensitive discussions. *Autonomy* involves feeling a sense of personal control and choice. Autonomous individuals see themselves as influencing their environment rather than being controlled by it (de Charms, 1968). A student who feels forced to discuss difficult topics does not feel autonomous. When individuals feel that they have a genuine connection and relationship with others, they feel a sense of *belonging* (Baumeister & Leary, 1995), or what Ryan and Deci (2000) refer to as relatedness. Students experience belonging when they feel as though they are part of a connected and welcoming classroom of learners. By supporting these basic psychological needs in the higher education classroom, instructors foster students' intellectual curiosity, promote their intrinsic motivation to learn for the challenge and enjoyment inherent in discovering new ideas and skills, and help them flourish and achieve.

Extensive research has documented the important role of autonomy, competence, and belonging on students' intrinsic motivation and well-being in classrooms from kindergarten through higher education (see Niemiec & Ryan, 2009; Ryan & Deci, 2017, chapter 14). Some researchers have examined self-determination theory with undergraduate and professional students, exploring the relationship between psychological needs and intrinsic motivation or well-being (Benware & Deci, 1984; Black & Deci, 2000; Levesque et al., 2004; Luyckx et al., 2009; Williams & Deci, 1996). Here I provide a few examples from higher education.

Satisfaction of Psychological Needs in Higher Education

Longitudinal studies with law and medical students demonstrate the value of seeing one's university as supporting autonomy. Sheldon and Krieger (2007) found that students who felt that their law school provided greater autonomy support reported enhanced satisfaction of all their psychological needs. Increased fulfillment of psychological needs predicted higher motivation, well-being, and achievement. Similarly, Williams and Deci (1996) found that when medical students saw their school as more autonomy-supportive, they reported feeling more autonomous and competent over time. As will be discussed in upcoming chapters, giving students autonomy over some aspects of the course can be valuable for classroom dynamics.

Trenshaw et al. (2016) recently explored autonomy, competence, and belonging/relatedness in a university-level engineering course. The class was restructured to focus support on students' autonomy by replacing required course work with a series of student-chosen team design projects. Instructors facilitated weekly team meetings to promote feelings of competence and belonging. A qualitative evaluation of the redesign revealed three main themes: "team projects promote relatedness"; "relatedness provides space for competence building"; and "without relatedness and competence, motivation declines" (Trenshaw et al, 2016, p. 1200). Belonging (or what they called, relatedness) was of primary importance in this college sample. In contrast, previous research with K–12 students has often focused on supporting autonomy (see Niemiec & Ryan, 2009). Trenshaw et al. (2016) argue that belonging may be more important in some college contexts (such as large undergraduate engineering courses). For younger children, belonging needs may already be met while their need for autonomy is unfulfilled. College students may already feel autonomous and are instead seeking belonging in their courses.

Other teaching interventions conducted with college students—while not explicitly framed in terms of the basic psychological needs of self-determination theory—are consistent with these findings. For instance, Mary-Ann Winkelmes et al. (2019) have begun encouraging instructors to be more transparent in their teaching. In particular they recommend that professors create assignments that clearly present three elements: the task they want students to do, the purpose in doing the task, and the criteria for how their performance will be evaluated (Berrett, 2015; Volk, 2015). Preliminary findings indicated that using transparent assignments enhances students' feelings of self-efficacy, belonging, and mastery of important skills (Winkelmes et al., 2016), suggesting higher competence and belonging. The impact of transparency was particularly strong for students who were first-generation college students, from underrepresented racial or ethnic groups, or from low-income backgrounds. For these students, transparency seemed to enhance autonomy by helping them develop an understanding of the tools needed to complete and assess their coursework.

Applying the Basic Psychological Needs Framework to Your Courses

I propose that you reflect on the courses that you are teaching and contemplate how students' autonomy, competence, and belonging are relevant, given the content and methods used in your courses. For my classes, I have high expectations for my students and seek to create discussion-based learning environments that demand great effort and commitment. I must be thoughtful in my pedagogical approach to design rigorous courses in which my students experience competence, autonomy, and belonging. This approach begins with the first information that students learn about the course.

On the Syllabus or First Day of Class

As you start the course, it is important to consider what material to provide at the beginning of the class and on your syllabus. This material should be presented in a tone that conveys respect and accessibility while providing information to support students in feeling autonomous, competent, and connected to others. The information could include: course content including topics covered and particular challenges in covering sensitive or difficult topics; expectations for student work, such as class preparation, participation, assignments, and exams; expectations and guidelines for conduct in class and during other course activities such as group work or office-hour visits; statements about disability and accommodations; plagiarism or honor policies; and other relevant campus resources (e.g., health center, financial assistance, food pantry, tutoring) and policies (e.g., how to report incidents of bias or sexual misconduct; mandatory reporting policies).

Seminar or Discussion-Based Courses

While this book focuses primarily on instructors setting up discussion-based courses where students are engaging with difficult topics, the basic psychological needs are relevant in a variety of classes. As an example, I present an excerpt in Figure 2.1 from a short piece on ways to support students' autonomy, competence, and belonging. My developmental psychology colleague Jennifer Corpus wrote this essay for our college magazine for a series in which professors described what makes a great class discussion. At Reed College, a discussion-based course is called a conference.

Before reading further in the chapter, I encourage you to use Table 2.1 to begin reflecting on your students and their psychological needs. First, describe places in your classes that you think students' needs might not be satisfied; second, articulate possible ways to support your students' needs in that area.

Figure 2.1.   Supporting psychological needs in discussion-based courses.

Autonomy is supported when students see value in what they're learning. How this is accomplished certainly varies by discipline, but in my field of developmental psychology we often consider how theory and research inform practice. For example, my students consider how socialization research guides the production of *Sesame Street*, how motivation research makes a case against high-stakes testing, and how developmental theories shed light on service-learning experiences. Of course, autonomy support is inherent to the conference method itself. When students take responsibility for their own learning through active discussion and debate, they become co-creators of knowledge. This sense of ownership is critical for fostering intrinsic motivation.

Competence flourishes when learning is structured, perhaps ironically even in a student-centered conference setting. This often means opening each conference with a few minutes of contextualizing commentary, followed by an "invisible" lesson plan of prompts and observations that guide students toward essential themes. Conference can also be structured through preparatory activities: In introductory psychology, for example, students complete written questions *before* conference that require them to extract design elements and interpret numerical data from each primary source reading. This type of scaffolding not only provides tools for understanding but also sends the important message that competence itself can grow.

Relatedness is supported when students feel security and connectedness in their learning environments. In my experience, this requires ongoing dialogue about active listening, openness to differences, and the learning that comes from articulating our ideas to others. It involves referring to students by name, and encouraging them to talk *to each other* and build on one another's contributions. It requires making space for all voices to enter the conversation. Research shows clearly that emotionally supportive classrooms promote well-being, intrinsic motivation, and achievement. We are drawn toward connection with others, and a great conference recognizes this aspect of our humanity.

Note. Excerpt from Corpus (2015).

TABLE 2.1

Worksheet: Supporting Students' Psychological Needs of Autonomy, Competence, and Belonging

Psychological Need	*Ways to Support Students*
Autonomy	
What you would like to improve; consider your students' challenges in terms of feeling that they can exert control and make meaningful choices.	Describe possible ways to support your students' autonomy.
Competence	
What you would like to improve; consider your students' challenges in terms of feeling able to deal with the challenges of your course.	Describe possible ways to support your students' competence.
Belonging	
What you would like to improve; consider your students' challenges in terms of experiencing connection with others in the class.	Describe possible ways to support your students' feelings of belonging.

Approaches to Learning: Epistemological Development

It is also important to take into account students' epistemological development, or approaches to learning (Schrader, 2004), when setting up the classroom climate. In particular, consider how students understand knowledge and the roles that they, other students, and the instructor play in their learning. Beginning with the classic work by William Perry (1970) with university students, researchers have explored the ways that students make sense of how they develop knowledge as they experience college. Based on his longitudinal research with primarily male college students at Harvard, Perry developed a framework of intellectual and ethical development that consisted of a series of nine different positions that students might take in terms of understanding knowledge. They are often grouped into four smaller categories (Hofer & Pintrich, 1997). These positions begin with "dualism" at one end, where students see knowledge as being absolute (true or false); they look to their professors to teach them this knowledge. In the middle positions, students develop a sense of "multiplicity"; they realize that there are multiple perspectives rather than one absolute one. Students tend to believe that everyone is entitled to their own opinions and these varying opinions are equally valid. At later positions, students see knowledge as being more "relativistic" in that it depends on the particular context and the supporting evidence. They begin to see themselves as agents in their own learning. At the highest positions, students have "commitment within relativism" to their own learning and identities as they come to terms with their understanding of the ambiguities in knowledge. They commit to ideas and values that are important to them.

Later researchers built on, refined, and expanded Perry's initial conceptual base to include the "ways of knowing" of a diverse sample of women (Belenky et al., 1986) and longitudinal research with both women and men (Baxter Magolda, 1992, 2001). To learn more, check out Hofer and Pintrich (1997) and West's (2004) summaries and comparison of Perry's (1970), Belenky et al.'s (1986), Baxter Magolda's (1992), and King and Kitchener's (1994) frameworks.

Schrader (2004) proposes that it is important to not only bear in mind the varying epistemological development of the students in a class but also think through the ways that students' frameworks fit (or did not fit) with the professor's epistemic approach. Additionally she stresses the significance of the context in which students and faculty are interacting, underscoring that it needs to be a caring and respectful environment. She puts forward a model of intellectual safety that includes both "the epistemic 'fit' between student and professor's epistemology, and the moral atmosphere or climate" (p. 91).

By understanding your own approach to teaching and learning and the varying epistemological positions of your students, you are better positioned to determine how to facilitate and support your students' learning while also challenging and pushing them beyond their current approach to learning. Schrader (2004) encourages

> "epistemic stretch" created by professors who are willing to make themselves aware of their own and their students' epistemological framework, take into account various aspects of the development of a moral climate in the classroom, and combine them together in designing educational experiences, contexts, and demands that both challenge and support students' epistemologies in an affectively and intellectually safe context. . . . Students may feel a slight discomfort in their current knowing system but they feel safe enough to let go of it and recreate a new way of thinking. (p. 88)

I return to these issues of intellectual safety and discomfort in chapter 4 when I consider classroom dynamics.

When I reflect on my own and my students' approaches to learning, I realize that I often count on my students to be responsible for their own learning. When discussing challenging controversial texts in class, I expect them to critically examine the evidence that supports or contradicts different perspectives to come to their own conclusion. Yet these expectations do not necessarily fit with my students' expectations and experiences. They often need help in developing these skills. Their previous educational experiences may not have promoted their being the creators of their own learning. For each of my classes, I need to take into account my students' backgrounds (e.g., they are mostly first-year students, they have not taken many psychology classes, many are international students who are learning cultural educational norms in addition to adjusting to college) and what they might mean for students' approaches to learning.

I then need to alter my approach to accommodate these varied approaches—for example, providing questions for students to ask themselves when they do the reading on a sensitive topic to help them develop critical skills. For some students these questions might be unnecessary, but for others they may be essential. For some topics, to ensure that students consider multiple perspectives, I use a "doubting and believing" exercise (see Elbow, 1973) that Alison Cook-Sather had shared in a faculty workshop I attended. Students are given a sheet a paper with a statement at the top ("Exposure to violence in media, including television, movies, music, and video games, represents a significant risk to the health of children and adolescents."). Underneath the statement are two columns; one is labeled "Believing" (What do you believe or embrace about this statement?) and the other is labeled "Doubting" (What do you doubt or question about this statement?). Students are asked to provide responses in both columns. I often follow up this writing task by having students write one of their responses from each column on the board. We use these responses to begin our class discussion. This activity provides a way for students to move beyond thinking of the right or wrong answer to reflecting on a variety of perspectives and the evidence for them.

At this point, I encourage you to reflect on your own and your students' epistemological frameworks and their potential impact on classroom dynamics, using Table 2.2 as a template.

Student Identity

To understand how to best support our students, we need to understand student learning within a broader framework of students' multiple intersecting personal and social identities (Galliher et al., 2017). As with faculty identities discussed in chapter 1, student identities are linked to histories of privilege and exclusion (Acevedo et al., 2015). I begin with Galliher et al.'s (2017)

TABLE 2.2
Worksheet: Epistemological Frameworks and Student-Faculty Fit

My Epistemological Framework(s)	My Students' Epistemological Frameworks
Potential Challenges, Given My Framework	Potential Challenges, Given My Students' Frameworks
Changes I Could Make to Improve Student Learning	Changes I Would Encourage My Students to Make

recently proposed developmental model for understanding the content of individuals' identities. Their model incorporates four levels of context:

> *culture*, capturing the historical, political, and structural factors in a society; *social roles*, pertaining to the relational contexts in which identities are developed and negotiated; *domains*, representing the various life spaces that individuals feel are central to who they are; and *everyday experiences*, capturing the day-to-day thoughts, feelings, and actions associated with individuals' identities. (p. 2013)

These interconnected levels of analysis are crucial in understanding the identities that students bring to their daily life in the university classroom. I now focus on these four different levels, taking these broad abstract ideas and making them concrete with everyday classroom examples.

Culture and Social Roles

At the most general level, an instructor needs to consider the cultural or historical background for undergraduate students' identities; in the United States, this context involves systems of power in which certain identities (e.g., White, male, heterosexual, wealthy) have higher social status and greater access to resources than other identities (Galliher et al., 2017). Members of these social categories are privileged, receiving "unearned benefits afforded to powerful social groups within systems of oppression" (Case et al., 2012, p. 3). If an individual's identity is the privileged or dominant one, they may not be regularly aware of their identity. Instead, they may see themselves as "normal" and be surprised by a question like "What is it like to be White?" (Sue, 2003; Tatum, 2017). However, those with nondominant or marginalized identities often do not have the luxury of being unaware. Instead they are navigating their social worlds, seeking to minimize the impact of prejudice and discrimination while creating positive social identities (Harlow, 2003; Jones, 1997). The task is even more complicated because many students are managing their academic lives with multiple marginalized identities (Patton & Simmons, 2008; Ro & Loya, 2015).

Independent and Interdependent Self-Construals
Individuals' culture also shapes how they construe themselves and their social roles, such that people view themselves as relatively more *independent* of others or *interdependent* with others (Markus & Kitayama, 1991). Markus and Conner (2013) describe individuals with independent selves as seeing themselves "as individual, unique, influencing others and their environments, free from constraints, and equal (yet great!)" (p. xii). They do not perceive themselves as restrained by social roles but instead as relatively autonomous actors who impact their world based on their own interests and choices (Markus & Kitayama, 2003). Those with interdependent selves, on the other hand, see themselves as "relational, similar to others, adjusting to their situations, rooted in traditions and obligations, and ranked in pecking orders" (Markus & Conner, 2013, p. xii.). Markus and Conner stress that individuals are both independent and interdependent (see also Brewer, 1991). However, they may experience cultural conflicts because cultural expectations and norms encourage either independence or interdependence.

In the book *Clash!*, Markus and Conner (2013) present eight cultural conflicts between independence and interdependence. Their book is primarily grounded in research examining East–West cultural difference across hemispheres (with the independent West and the interdependent East; see Markus & Kitayama, 1991). However, Markus and Conner also explore gender, race/ethnicity, class, religion, U.S. region, workplace, and global region. In the United States with its culture emphasizing autonomy and uniqueness, members of more powerful social groups—for example, Whites, men, those of higher socioeconomic status—often have more independent self-construals. Members of social groups that are marginalized often have more interdependent self-construals that are less in-step with the cultural norm of independence (Markus & Kitayama, 1994).

This cultural mismatch—being more interdependent in a culture that values independence—can have profound implications for university students who may be away from home for the first time. For instance, Nicole Stephens et al. (2012) have explored the transition to college and the ongoing college experiences of first-generation and working-class students (see also Jury et al., 2017). Universities commonly promote the norm of independence, presenting college as a time for individuals to be "on their own," making their own choices and living independently of their families. First-generation students may experience a mismatch with these norms, given that they report more interdependent selves (Stephens, Fryberg, Markus et al., 2012). Taking into account this mismatch, promoting independence (versus interdependence) in college can have negative effects on the academic performance of first-generation college students. For instance, after receiving a welcome letter to college framed in terms of independence (as opposed to one framed in terms of interdependence), first-gen students experienced higher stress and more negative emotions when presenting a speech (Stephens, Townsend et al., 2012) and performed worse on academic tasks (Stephens, Fryberg, Markus et al., 2012). For continuing-generation students (those who had at least one parent with a four-year college degree), their stress, emotions, and academic performance were unaffected by the manipulation of independent/interdependent norms. Additional longitudinal research revealed that students reporting higher interdependent selves had lower GPAs after two years of college (Stephens, Fryberg, Markus et al., 2012), suggesting long-term negative effects of this cultural mismatch.

Social Identity Contingencies
In addition, individuals routinely find that their social identities and social roles influence what is expected of them and how they are treated in specific situations (Steele, 2010). For instance, in a classroom, some college students expect that they will fit in and be treated with respect given their social identities. Other students may be concerned that they do not belong and will be treated as less worthy than others. Students are impacted by *social identity contingencies*, which Purdie-Vaughns et al. (2008) describe as

> the range of vulnerabilities and opportunities a person expects to face based on the settings' response to one or more of the person's social identities. When group members expect their social identity contingencies to be negative or to confirm that their group will be devalued, the setting can be characterized as threatening. When group members expect their social identity

contingencies to be positive or neutral, the setting can be characterized as identity-safe. Accordingly, social identity contingencies convey the degree of threat or safety with which one perceives the setting. (p. 616)

Purdie-Vaughns et al. (2008) found that cues in the setting, such as lower numbers of African Americans and colorblind messages focused on similarity, decreased African Americans' feelings of trust and comfort.

Disclosure of Concealable Social Identities

Given that students may fear that others' knowledge of their social identities will lead to negative outcomes, they might choose, if possible, to conceal some social identities (Chaudoir & Fischer, 2010). Many students' identities are not readily visible. For example, depending on the setting and its norms, students might not disclose that they are first-generation college students, have learning disabilities, are bisexual, are politically conservative, have survived family or relationship violence, are homeless, or have been diagnosed with anxiety. As this list makes clear, student self-disclosure during class can be challenging to approach as an instructor who wants to respect and acknowledge students' lived experiences but also provide a learning environment with appropriate boundaries (Borshuk, 2017). In later chapters, I will explicitly consider ways to set up classroom guidelines and approach classroom dynamics around sensitive and difficult topics.

At this juncture, it is important to note that faculty should facilitate students' disclosing—often in the privacy of the instructor's office—information about their identity that would support their learning. Many students have disabilities that need accommodations for them to have equal access to learning. If students have disabilities requiring accommodation but they do not disclose this information to their university or instructors, then faculty are not able to provide learning-supportive accommodation. I encourage you to approach disability accommodation in a straightforward and supportive way so that students feel that they can trust you to use this information to improve their learning and not be biased against them. Recent research examining self-disclosure for students with disabilities revealed some positive outcomes of disclosure. For instance, disclosing a disability status for social motivated reasons (e.g., to help others get to know you) predicted academic persistence and well-being (Troxell Whitman & Oleson, 2016a, 2016b). Having more positive views about the effects of one's disability predicted more disclosure to college peers (Hilarides & Oleson, 2008). As an instructor, you should create an environment in which students feel empowered to disclose their disability status to you by providing information about accommodations on the syllabus and making clear that you want to work with students to ensure that they thrive in class.

Domains and Everyday Experiences

I turn briefly to explore the third and fourth levels of Galliher et al.'s (2017) developmental framework of identity content, bringing in students' central life domains and their everyday thoughts, feelings, and behaviors. For college students, important life domains include occupation, values, politics, religion, family, romance, friends, and gender roles (McLean et al., 2016). Although faculty members often interact with students within a specific classroom setting, students' multiple identities are not separate from one other; students' lives in these various intersecting domains impact the learning environment. For instance, a student's conservative political beliefs and her friendships with other students in the course may impact how she responds during a classroom discussion about racial or gender bias. The opening quote to this chapter presents the complicated ways that students are navigating their identities each day in the classroom, with the second quote making clear that "the student perspective is invaluable" (Luker & Morris, 2016, p. 5).

Take a moment to reflect on your students' perspectives—particularly the multiple intersecting identities that they bring to your classroom and the potential ways that these identities influence their interactions with you and other students. Use Table 2.3 as a template for your reflection.

TABLE 2.3
Students' Identities in the Classroom: Culture, Social Roles, Domains, Everyday Experiences

What identities do your students bring to your classroom? These identities could be single ones or intersecting multiple identities; include brief descriptions. Consider culture, social roles, domains, and everyday experiences.	How do these identities influence your students' behavior in the classroom?

Students' Worries, Doubts, and Uncertainties

We next turn to explore the host of worries, doubts, and uncertainties that students bring to the classroom. They may have general doubts about their abilities and whether they will be able to successfully complete the work demanded in academic contexts (Oleson et al., 2000). They may be uncertain that they belong at the university, in this major, or in this course (Mendoza-Denton et al., 2002; Walton & Cohen, 2007). They may feel like an impostor (Sakulku & Alexander, 2011) who somehow got lucky to be accepted at the college. Additionally, the challenging academic environment may create fears that they will not perform well and that this negative performance will reflect poorly on their social groups (Thoman et al., 2013). These feelings of threat and uncertainty may be further exacerbated by the belief that how smart they are is set and not open to improvement (Dweck, 2006). Believing that their intelligence cannot be changed may cause students to see academic problems as evidence that they are not smart and lead to less persistence when they hit academic challenges (Yeager & Dweck, 2012). Next I consider each of these various doubts, uncertainties, and threats and how they impact students' academic lives.

Self-Doubts About Academic Abilities

Students may have uncertainties or self-doubts about their ability to perform well in challenging academic contexts (Braslow et al., 2012). Oleson and Steckler (2010) describe this uncertainty "as doubt about one's self-worth and self-efficacy based on questioning one's competence; this uncertainty is a fundamental one. . . . Individuals ask themselves, 'Do I have what it takes to be successful? Am I able to avoid failure?'" (p. 380). Given that competence, as discussed earlier, is a basic psychological need (Ryan & Deci, 2000), students will likely be motivated to cope with their feelings of doubt about their competence by developing strategies to manage it.

For instance, self-handicapping is one strategy that students use to manage their self-doubt (Arkin & Oleson, 1998). When fearful that they might fail, students may create or claim an obstacle to performing well. For instance, they may procrastinate, drink too much, or not study before an important performance, thereby creating an explanation for performing poorly. Failure is not due to their lack of ability; instead it can be blamed on lack of effort or putting off the task. Ironically the student's desire to protect the idea that they are smart and capable potentially leads to their sabotaging their performance. They may fail, but they can still believe that they have the ability to succeed. Some students, however, are not willing to fail. Success is quite important to them. In this case, when doubtful about their ability, they may put in extra effort to ensure that they will not fail. But by putting in this extra effort, they are not able to diagnose their true ability. Their self-doubt persists, and they may feel that they should continue to put in extra effort in the future to be successful (see Oleson & Steckler, 2010). These strategies may help students handle their doubts about their abilities at the moment but may lead to maintenance of their self-doubt. Your students may have nagging and persistent concerns about their competence that influence classroom dynamics.

Belongingness Uncertainty

An additional source of uncertainty for some of your students is whether they belong at college or in their major. This concern may be exacerbated if they are a member of a social group that is underrepresented—such as women in engineering programs or African Americans at predominantly White colleges—because they may question not only if they belong but if their whole social group belongs (Cohen & Garcia, 2008; Mendoza-Denton et al., 2002). Like competence, belonging is a fundamental psychological need (Baumeister & Leary, 1995; Ryan & Deci, 2000). As Walton and Cohen (2007) argue,

> One of the most important questions that people ask themselves in deciding to enter, continue, or abandon a pursuit is, "Do I belong?" Among socially stigmatized individuals, this question may be visited and revisited. Stigmatization can create a global uncertainty about the quality of one's social bonds in academic and professional domains—a state of *belonging uncertainty*. As a consequence, events that threaten one's social connectedness, although seen as minor by other individuals, can have large effects on the motivation of those contending with a threatened social identity. (p. 94)

For example, in a series of studies Walton and Cohen (2007) found that, for African American students, feeling that they might not have many friends in their major or experiencing everyday difficulties resulted in feeling lower belonging, whereas White students' belonging was relatively unaffected.

College students' feelings of belonging have profound implications for their academic lives (Strayhorn, 2012) and well-being (Gummadam et al., 2015). A sense of belonging—at the college level, in their majors, and even in specific classes—is related to academic persistence and achievement. For example, Hausmann et al. (2007) found that, for both Black and White first-year college students, a sense of belonging at their university predicted their intentions to continue in college. Good et al. (2012) established analogous findings within the field of mathematics, with both men and women's sense of belonging in math predicting their desire to take future math courses. Additionally, Good et al. found that for women (but not men) the perception that students in their math class saw both intelligence as fixed and women as less capable at math predicted lower belonging in math. Belonging also matters for specific classroom dynamics (Zumbrunn et al., 2014). A supportive classroom environment predicts greater belonging. Students who reported higher belonging saw their instructors as more enthusiastic and as caring more about students' learning. Belonging predicted elevated feelings of self-efficacy, which in turn predicted both higher engagement and achievement. Overall, for all students, a sense of belonging is important for encouraging them to thrive academically, with some research revealing that marginalized and underrepresented students' sense of belonging is often disrupted by environmental cues.

Impostor Phenomenon

Students may also feel as though they are impostors who do not deserve their accomplishments. They may worry that others will discover that they are not as capable as they seem (Clance & Imes, 1978). Individuals feeling like impostors do not see their successes as a result of their intellectual abilities but instead attribute successes to external factors, such as luck, error, or being in the right place at the right time (Clance, 1985; Topping & Kimmel, 1985). Impostors may also experience a host of negative affective and psychological outcomes, including self-doubt or low confidence about their abilities (Kumar & Jagacinski, 2006; Oleson et al., 2000), anxiety (Kumar & Jagacinski, 2006; Topping & Kimmel, 1985), and psychological distress and depression (McGregor et al., 2008; Peteet et al., 2015).

Initially, Clance and Imes (1978) documented evidence for the impostor phenomenon in a sample of highly successful undergraduate, graduate, and professional women (see also Clance, 1985). However, subsequent research makes clear that perceived fraudulence also affects men (Cokley et al., 2015; Topping & Kimmel, 1985), African Americans (Bernard & Neblett, 2018), and individuals in a range of careers (Sakulku & Alexander, 2011). Both students (Bernard et al., 2018; Kumar & Jagacinski, 2006; Thompson et al., 1998) and professors, especially untenured ones, report feeling like impostors (Hutchins, 2015; Topping & Kimmel, 1985).

Students may have experiences with other people questioning their intellectual capabilities, possibly causing them to feel that they are frauds.

Recent research, for instance, has begun to explore racial discrimination, psychological distress, and feelings of being an impostor with African American college students (Bernard & Neblett, 2018). For instance, Bernard et al. (2018) conducted a longitudinal investigation in which they examined racial discrimination and the impostor phenomenon with African American college students at a predominately White institution. They found that students' earlier reports of racial discrimination predicted higher levels of feeling like an impostor over time. Other work suggests that these impostor feelings have profound implications for African American students' psychological functioning. For instance, Cokley et al. (2017) recently concluded that "the current findings suggest that among African American students, impostor feelings are a stronger factor in mental health than perceived discrimination and possibly minority status stress" (p. 149). Additional research highlights that gender should be taken into account in addition to race when considering impostor feelings, racial discrimination, and mental health, because the experiences of Black men and women might differ (Bernard et al., 2017).

Stereotype Threat

Students' social identities, such as race, gender, and socioeconomic status, may also cause them to experience stereotype threat (Steele, 2010). As it was described in an amicus brief to the U.S. Supreme Court,

> Stereotype threat is the pressure that people feel when they fear that their performance could confirm a negative stereotype about their group. This pressure manifests itself in anxiety and distraction that interferes with intellectual functioning. If one belongs to a gender, ethnicity, or race that is viewed as intellectually inferior, a challenging academic task can trigger this particular form of anxiety, which prevents a student from performing as well as he or she is capable. The student need not believe that the stereotype is accurate to be affected. The student only needs to be aware that the stereotype exists and to care about performing well. This can occur regardless of the actual level of prejudice in a classroom or test-taking situation. (Brief of Experimental Psychologists, 2012, p. 3)

Most research on stereotype threat has focused on its impact on academic performance (Spencer et al., 2016).

However, these fears about confirming negative intellectual stereotypes about one's group—for example, that women are bad at math (Spencer et al., 1999) or that African Americans perform poorly academically (Steele & Aronson,

1995)—have influences going beyond academic performance on specific tasks. Such fears also impact students' learning and motivation more broadly (Thoman et al., 2013) and can disrupt intergroup classroom dynamics (Goff et al., 2008). For instance, in their motivational experiences model of stereotype threat, Thoman et al. (2013) argue that the cues that activate stereotype threat—for example, identifying as a woman in a male-dominated field (Inzlicht & Ben-Zeev, 2000), or having to indicate one's gender (Danaher & Crandall, 2008) or race (Steele & Aronson, 1995) before completing an academic task—also affect one's orientation toward achievement, sense of belonging, and intrinsic motivation. Specifically, when feeling stereotype threat, individuals worry more about avoiding failure and experience a lowered sense of belonging and intrinsic motivation. One's intrinsic motivation and belonging can then impact how much one wants to continue taking courses in the field of study and how much one identifies as a part of the field.

Additionally, stereotype threat can impact the intergroup dynamics between White and Black students in a classroom setting. In this setting, White students may believe that they are stereotyped as being racially prejudiced (Vorauer et al., 2000; Vorauer et al., 1998). They may then fear that they will act in biased ways that confirm this negative stereotype. Goff et al. (2008) set up a series of studies to examine how White male students approach difficult interracial conversations with Black male students. In particular they were interested in how close or far away their participants would sit from their partners (who were either two Black men or two White men). They found that participants sat farther away from Black partners. Interestingly, how far away participants sat was not predicted by their implicit or explicit prejudice. But when expecting to talk about racial profiling, a racially sensitive topic, participants who thought more about the stereotype of Whites being prejudiced sat farther away. Being concerned about being prejudiced resulted in behavior—sitting farther away from Black students—that could be interpreted as being more prejudiced. Just as the threat of one's group being seen as less intellectually competent interferes with one's academic performance, the threat of being prejudiced results in stymied social interaction.

I urge you to stop to consider your students' uncertainties, self-doubts, and concerns and how classroom discussion and engagement can be affected by them. For instance, in my classes I sometimes have students who talk too much. There are many possible explanations for their behavior. One possibility is that they are putting this extra effort into participation to make sure that everyone (including themselves) thinks that they are smart. Alternatively, a student who never speaks in class may have concerns that their insights are not as profound as other students' or that they do not belong in the course.

TABLE 2.4
Worksheet: Students' Self-Doubts, Uncertainties, and Feelings of Threat

What self-doubts, uncertainties, and threats do your students bring to class? Think about concerns about academic ability and belonging. Reflect on potential stereotype threats. Describe them in the space provided.	How do these identities influence your students' behavior in the classroom?

They may feel unsure about how college works and how to participate in class. They may feel as though they are an impostor or that their saying foolish things might reflect poorly on their social group.

It is important to try to understand the particular fears that might be impacting your students' interactions with their peers and with you in order to develop ways to mitigate them in class (Aguilar et al., 2014). Use Table 2.4 to describe potential concerns, doubts, threats that your students are experiencing. Further reflect on the impact you think these doubts are having in class.

Strategies to Mitigate Students' Self-Doubt, Belongingness Uncertainty, Impostor Feelings, and Stereotype Threat

Given the large potential for students' various self-doubts, uncertainties about belonging, impostor feelings, and stereotype threat to negatively impact their academic experiences, many researchers have considered ways to mitigate their adverse effects in higher education (see Cohen et al., 2012; Jury et al., 2017; Schmader & Hall, 2014; Walton et al., 2012; Wise Interventions, n.d.). Much of this work has the goal of reducing inequities based on individuals' social identities (e.g., race, socioeconomic status, gender). Note that these approaches involve *all* students. Targeting "at-risk" students serves to reinforce stereotypes associated with groups (Aguilar et al., 2014).

I end this chapter by considering four broad approaches for reducing the impact of these uncertainties and threats on students' academic lives in the classroom: promoting belonging; encouraging students to use their identities and values as resources against threat; creating a growth-oriented inclusive curriculum; and educating students about strategies for managing their anxieties. See Table 2.5 for specific examples to use in your academic classroom.

Promoting Belonging
As a foundation, it is essential to create a welcoming classroom environment where students feel as though they belong (Zumbrunn et al., 2014). Given that many students experience concerns about whether they do belong at the university, in a particular major, or in a specific course, teachers can help students frame this uncertainty as something that is typical of students at their college but is temporary. For instance, in a series of belonging interventions (Walton & Cohen, 2007, 2011), Black and White undergraduates learned about a racially mixed group of previous undergraduates at their college who were initially worried about belonging but eventually felt these concerns lessen. Over time, Black student participants' feelings of belonging increased, as did their academic performance. The narratives of previous students provided a more productive way for participants to frame concerns about belonging—it is normal to worry and over time you will feel better—that relieved their concerns. Finally, as will be discussed in chapter 3, it is important to remove any cues in the environment that signal that some students do not belong. Instead provide cues that you value diversity. For instance, a syllabus with perspectives from individuals from a range of backgrounds signals that the topic is an inclusive one. During class discussion or in lectures, including photos of authors of articles— assuming that it is a diverse group—can promote a sense to students that they are a welcome part of the academic field.

Encouraging Students to Use Their Identities and Values as Resources Against Threat
It is critical to acknowledge that students have a host of important identities and personal values. For instance, Ambady et al. (2004) found that having students consider their individual qualities and traits before a challenging math test eliminated stereotype threat. Similarly, asking students to write about their important personal values reduces stereotype threat and promotes academic performance and persistence (Harackiewicz et al., 2014; Miyake et al., 2010).

Stephens et al. (2014) further propose that learning about how one's identity matters—both positively and negatively—can help students adjust to college.

TABLE 2.5
Mitigating Students' Worries and Concerns

Focus of Strategy	Specific Suggestions
Promote Belonging	
Create a welcoming classroom environment[1]	Have students partner on the first day of class and then introduce each other. These introductions provide a way for students to share their gender pronouns for their partners to use in the introduction. Learn to pronounce all of your students' names correctly. Colleges can purchase apps in which students record their names. Instructors then listen to these recordings outside of class to practice their pronunciation.
Frame concerns about belonging as common and temporary[2]	Talk about how students often feel as though they don't belong when they first come to college, and for many students these concerns decrease over time.
Remove cues signaling that some students do not belong and instead signal that you value diversity[3]	Include non-stereotypic art, such as nature posters. Include a variety of images, including positive images of members of marginalized groups.
Encourage Students to Use Their Identities and Values as a Resource Against Threat	
Acknowledge that students have a host of important identities and personal qualities[4]	When doing partner introductions, ask students to share three self-characteristics: a relatively unique quality (e.g., I have 10 siblings), a quality that is similar to many others in class (e.g., psychology major), and quality that they are unsure how many other students share (e.g., I rode my bike to school). Faculty members introduce themselves with the same three qualities.
Foster the idea that students' identities matter and can be sources of strength[5]	Provide information from previous students about how their social identities have impacted their academic lives in positive and negative ways.
Ask students to affirm important values to buffer them against threats[6]	Early on in the term, ask students to select two or three personal values from a list. Then ask them to write a few sentences reflecting on why these values are important to them.
Create a Growth-Oriented Inclusive Curriculum	
Frame assessment as learning-oriented[7]	Consider using more frequent, low-stakes testing. Frame assignments as learning opportunities. If you use similar assignments across the semester, provide extensive concrete feedback that helps students improve on the next one.
Promote a growth mindset toward learning[8]	Help students embrace every learning resource available to them, including office hours, tutors, and working with peers. Model a growth mindset in your own learning: acknowledge your mistakes and use them to improve.

(Continues)

TABLE 2.5 *(Continued)*

Focus of Strategy	Specific Suggestions
Ensure that students see individuals like themselves in the course material and the classroom[9]	Include course content with diverse representation. Integrate it throughout the term so that it is clear that these perspectives are central to the course. When creating small groups, try to avoid having only one member of a social group included. A more equal distribution of social identities is preferable.
To reduce students' concerns about critical feedback being biased, emphasize high standards and students' ability to meet them[10]	When providing critical feedback, note your high standards, your belief that the student can meet the high standards, and concrete steps for the student to improve. Foster students' attributing their negative feedback to their instructors' high standards and desire for students to reach their potential.
Teach Strategies for Managing Threat and Anxiety	
Educate students about stereotype threat to provide external attributions for threat[11]	Encourage students to keep in mind that, if they are feeling anxious while taking a test, this anxiety could be the result of negative stereotypes and have nothing to do with their actual ability to do well on the test.
Equip students to reappraise arousal as a challenge rather than a threat[12]	Help students "turn the knots in their stomachs into bows" by construing their affect as helpful for performance. Frame difficult tasks as challenges rather than threats. Nurture students' idea that (a) feeling aroused signals that the task is important and challenging and (b) that they can use the arousal to do better.

[1]Zumbrunn et al. (2014); [2]Walton & Cohen (2007, 2011); [3]Cheryan et al. (2009), Fryberg et al. (2008), Latu et al. (2013), Purdie-Vaughns et al. (2008); [4]Ambady et al. (2004), Rydell et al. (2009); [5]Stephens et al. (2014), Stephens et al. (2015); [6]Harackiewicz et al. (2014), Martens et al. (2006), Miyake et al. (2010); [7]Smeding et al. (2013), Steele & Aronson (1995); [8]Aronson et al. (2002), Yeager & Dweck (2012); [9]Dasgupta et al. (2015), Grover et al. (2017), Inzlicht & Ben-Zeev (2000), Shaffer et al. (2013), Purdie-Vaughns et al. (2008); [10]Cohen et al. (1999), Yeager et al. (2014); [11]Johns et al. (2005); [12]Alter et al. (2010), Jamieson et al. (2010).

In their research, first-year students (both first- and continuing-generation students) listened to a panel of upper-level students discussing their college adjustment. In the difference-education condition, these students' adjustment narratives stressed that their socioeconomic status impacted their college experiences. This condition was compared to one where these narratives did not discuss the impact of socioeconomics. First-gen students who heard how socioeconomic status matters achieved higher GPAs and reported more frequent help-seeking (emailing professors with questions, meeting with professors outside of class, going to the writing center). Additional results showed positive long-term effects for both continuing- and first-gen students in the difference-education condition: as second-year students they seemed more comfortable talking about their backgrounds (including family, friends from home, academic preparation) when giving a speech than did those in the control condition (Stephens et al., 2015). Also, for first-gen students in the difference-education condition, when completing academic tasks in the lab, their physiological responses suggested they were better able to handle academic stress than those in the control panel.

This difference-education approach is an intriguing one because it reveals positive effects of emphasizing differences, consistent with research on intergroup dialogue (Gurin et al., 2013). Stephens et al. (2014) suggest that discussing the potential impact of one's background can have a positive impact if students learn about these differences "in a supportive, constructive, and identity-safe manner" (p. 950). As I consider in chapter 3, the environment is critical in creating positive intergroup outcomes (Hurtado, 2005).

The value of this method, according to Stephens et al. (2015), is that it "can help students to make sense of the source of their particular experiences in college and, at the same time, equip them with the tools they need to manage and overcome the challenges their different backgrounds might present" (p. 950). This intervention acknowledges that different backgrounds might make a difference but helps students see that their background can be beneficial. This approach is in contrast to Walton and Cohen's (2007, 2011) research discussed earlier that seeks to reduce threat by emphasizing that one's concerns about belonging are common and temporary experiences of students of various backgrounds. I think that both approaches can be useful. Reducing threat by helping students see that their peers, regardless of their background, are uncertain about whether they belong can be beneficial. At the same time, it can be important to acknowledge students' differences and the strength that can come from them.

Creating a Growth-Oriented Inclusive Curriculum

I'd encourage you to consider your pedagogical approaches. It is essential to focus on students' learning and mastery of material. For instance, Smeding et al. (2013) found that when a university course presented testing as designed to help students improve and master course content rather than as a way to compare students, the achievement gap between low- and high-socioeconomic-status students was reduced. Similarly, Steele and Aronson (1995) found reductions in Black–White achievement gaps when a difficult test was framed as a problem-solving task rather than as diagnostic of one's ability. Also, as I stress throughout this book, it is important to promote the idea that one's intelligence improves with practice. Aronson et al. (2002) found that teaching students that one's intelligence can grow and improve predicted higher grades, particularly for African American students.

Additionally, instructors should strive to ensure that students see others who share their social identities in the course material and in the classroom. If an individual is a solo representative of their social group, stereotype threat and lowered performance can occur (Grover et al., 2017; Inzlicht & Ben-Zeev, 2000). Although instructors often cannot influence the numbers of students of different backgrounds in their courses, they are able to impact the diversity of the representation of the course content. As will be stressed in chapter 3, material that speaks to students' lived experience promotes academic achievement (Gay, 2018). The way that this information is presented may make a difference. For instance, Shaffer et al. (2012) examined men and women's performance on a challenging math test after learning about women's representation in science, technology, engineering, and medicine (STEM) fields. In all conditions, women in STEM were presented as performing at a high level. Participants either learned that the number of women in STEM fields was increasing so that there were nearly equal numbers of men and women (balanced condition), or they learned the same information about increases in numbers except that it was stressed that women were still underrepresented (unbalanced condition). Participants in the control group did not learn about women in STEM. When representation was presented as balanced, women performed better than when it was presented as unbalanced or they did not learn about women's representation. Men were not affected by the information about balance. Seeing their group as successful and well-represented buffered women against stereotype threat.

Finally, when thinking through your teaching approach, I urge you to carefully consider how you provide critical feedback to students. A key issue is that students might be concerned that your feedback reflects bias against them because of negative stereotypes about their group. For instance, Cohen et al. (1999) found that Black students responded more negatively than White students to critical feedback from White evaluators. They saw the feedback as biased and were not motivated to make use of it. But when this feedback emphasized that the evaluator had high standards and believed that the student could meet the standards, then both Black and White students responded with high motivation to improve. To improve, it is essential that students learn from critical feedback. You can buffer the sting of negative feedback by being clear that it is designed to help a promising student reach your high standards.

Educating Students About Strategies for Managing Their Anxieties
A final method for reducing the impact of concerns and threat is to help students learn strategies to handle the arousal and anxiety they feel in challenging

academic situations. For instance, Johns et al. (2005) found that inform-ing women about stereotype threat can be helpful in minimizing its impact. Women were less affected by stereotype threat when they learned that

> it's important to keep in mind that if you are feeling anxious while taking this test, this anxiety could be the result of these negative stereotypes that are widely known in society and have nothing to do with your actual ability to do well on the test. (p. 176)

These women had an explanation for their anxiety that was not about them or their lack of ability. A related approach is for students to construe their arousal as helpful for performance. Jamieson et al. (2010) taught one group of students to reappraise the arousal they experienced under difficult testing situations as being able to help them. These students performed better on the GRE than the second group of participants who were not taught reappraisal techniques. They argue that reappraisal helps students "turn the knots in the stomach into bows."

In Table 2.5, I have summarized these strategies for mitigating students' worries, concerns, and feelings of threat as a handy reference. Lessening these concerns can help ensure that all students in your classroom thrive.

In this chapter, I have focused on what your students bring to the uni-versity classroom, including their psychological needs, their expectations, their personal and social identities, and their worries and concerns. I encour-age you to pause at this point to reflect on the students in your particular courses before turning to consider the class context and content.

3

CONTEXT AND CONTENT

"What are the biggest challenges and rewards of working to diversify the canon? For me, the biggest challenge and reward amount to the same thing. Like most of us, I have a relatively standard background in the history of western and analytic philosophy. So being committed to diversifying the canon means that I am always having to learn something new and, in some ways, starting over. This can be disorienting and it's always a challenge, since it requires having to look at the old anew and trying hard not to look at the new a-old. But I have come to see the discomfort of this form of travel as part of the growing process. For me, the never knowing what philosophy really is, is the beginning of philosophy." —Robert Sanchez (interviewed by Maxwell, 2018, emphasis in original)

In this chapter, I bring in the various features that make up your learning space, such as the *context* of the classroom, including the physical and psychological elements; the *content* that faculty and students are engaging with in the classroom; and the *methods of instruction*. As a foundation, I return to Kurt Lewin's (1946) psychological field theory. As presented in the preface, Lewin proposed a simple formula that an individual's behavior is a function of the person (in our case, a faculty member or a student) and their psychological environment.

I begin by exploring ways to design academic spaces where students flourish academically and their basic psychological needs are met. This chapter draws on the empirically and conceptually grounded ideas of universally designed learning (Meyer et al., 2014) in combination with educational design rooted in social justice and multiculturalism (Couillard & Higbee, 2018; Evans et al., 2017). A Universal Design for Learning (UDL) approach considers the varying needs of diverse college students and attempts to devise curricula and instructional components effective for all students (Nario-Redmond, 2016).

I then turn to focus on course design and content, presenting the benefits of adding more inclusive content into courses across a range of academic disciplines (Branche et al., 2007). I encourage faculty members to reflect on their own courses to consider ways to make their materials, pedagogical approaches, and methods of instruction meaningful and welcoming to a range of students. These methods include effective ways to create collaborative small-group work, achieve desirable levels of difficulty, and promote high-impact practices. By seeking to make all aspects of the course's context and content inclusive, we are equipping students to be able to have respectful conversations about challenging topics.

Designing Inclusive Learning Spaces for All Students to Thrive

We first delve into the various physical features of students' classroom spaces to ensure that they facilitate students' ability to thrive academically. These include basic structural elements (e.g., air quality, lighting, temperature) where a university course takes place and more symbolic cues present in the environment (e.g., everyday objects that indicate who belongs, such as artwork). As Cheryan et al. (2014) make clear, both the structural physical features and the symbolic aspects are important in shaping students' academic experience.

Structural Physical Space

Thoughtful design of the physical space can facilitate an instructor's goals and help create effective classroom dynamics as students interact with each other, the professor, and the course materials (Strange & Banning, 2015). The physical space can also support students' needs for autonomy, competence, and belonging (Sjöblom et al., 2016). For instance, students' competence is hindered when working within a cramped or poorly lit chemistry lab space. At the most basic level, classrooms with satisfactory air quality, appropriate lighting, optimal temperature of 68 to 74 degrees, and limited external noise promote student achievement (Cheryan et al., 2014; see also Lei, 2010).

Symbolic Space

Faculty members should also consider the symbolic cues present in their classroom and strive to create spaces where students feel that they belong and are valued and safe (Purdie-Vaughns et al., 2008; Schmader & Sedikides, 2018). Does the university classroom convey that all students are welcome there? Does it promote academic thriving for students of a range of backgrounds? If not, which students are left out? A variety of elements in the learning space— including furniture, technology, artwork, and other classroom objects—can signal what is going to happen in the space and who belongs in it (see Burgess & Kaya, 2007; Cheryan et al., 2009; Sanders, 2013; Steele, 2010). I would encourage you and your faculty peers to take a significant role in the planning and creation of student learning spaces (see Lippincott, 2009). I realize that, given the costs, some redesign is impractical. But even small (and often less expensive) design details (e.g., artwork, types of desks or tables, lighting) can impact students' learning experience (Cheryan et al., 2014; Henshaw & Reubens, 2013; Parsons, 2017).

Furniture, Classroom Layout, and Technology

For instance, Finkelstein et al. (2016) were recently involved at McGill University in a redesign of a number of classroom spaces, including a tiered lecture hall, a basic flexible classroom space, and an active-learning classroom (see Finkelstein et al., 2016, for before and after photos of the redesign). Each of the renovated classroom spaces included some basic structural improvements—such as better lighting, acoustics that limited distracting noise, and upgraded ventilation—that are critical for learning. Importantly, the designers also focused on classroom layout, furniture, and technology that supported their learning goals based on the National Survey of Student Engagement themes, engagement indicators, and high-impact practices (National Survey of Student Engagement [NSSE], 2015). Specifically, they concentrated on creating classrooms that supported *academic challenge* (deep engagement with course content), *learning with peers* (interaction with student peers of varying backgrounds), *experiences with faculty* (constructive interaction with instructors), *campus environment* (inclusive learning spaces across campus), and *high-impact practices* (such as service-learning, learning communities, research with faculty, internships of field experience, study abroad, and culminating senior experiences) (NSSE, 2015).

Here I focus on McGill's flexible and active-learning classrooms to give readers sense of some classroom updates that might be useful for learning goals. For the flexible layout, the redesign team provided tables with large surfaces to make it easier for students to engage with the course content. In the active-learning environment, they also included comfortable furniture and technology to support academic challenge in which students are engaging with materials in multiple ways. To encourage learning with peers, their classrooms contained furniture set up for face-to-face interaction. In the flexible classroom, this involved "lightweight, sturdy wheeled tables and chairs" that allowed students to collaborate easily with their peers or write on whiteboards that were on multiple walls, while the active-learning classroom was outfitted with "round tables for collaboration; shared digital and physical workspaces (screen-sharing and writable walls)" (Finkelstein et al., 2016, p. 30). To enhance student–faculty interactions, instructors were accessible to all students, had shared screens with students, and were able to control classroom technology while moving around the classroom. In their flexible classroom, the movable furniture and close access to the professor promoted interaction with faculty. In the active-learning classroom, the teacher's podium was placed in the center of the room, from which the instructor could move around. An acoustics system with different sound zones supported both small-group student–student interactions and whole-class faculty–student interaction. Finally, these classrooms fit into the broader campus environment and could be used flexibly for various high-impact practices.

Finkelstein et al.'s (2016) redesign seems quite promising and is informed by research; however, it is also important to assess the impact of any classroom renovation (Rands & Gansemer-Topf, 2017). For instance, at Iowa State University, Rands and Gansemer-Topf (2017) conducted a qualitative evaluation to understand the impact of changing a traditional classroom (fixed seating, no classroom technology) to an active-learning classroom (flexible seating, technology). Both faculty and students reported that the active-learning classroom promoted closer student–student and student–faculty connections. They also felt that the supplemental audiovisuals (portable whiteboards, extra computer monitors) encouraged students to engage with the material at a higher level. They reported that the space promoted holistic learning and allowed faculty to use a wider array of teaching approaches.

Artwork and Objects

The objects and artwork in classrooms or other learning spaces can also impact students' academic experiences. For example, the decorations can provide cues about what groups of people belong in the space. In a series of studies, Cheryan et al. (2009) explored how male and female undergraduates responded to computer science learning spaces that varied in terms of the stereotypicality of the objects in them. In one environment, the objects were ones associated with stereotypes of computer science majors (e.g., *Star Trek* poster, comics, pop cans, technical magazines) while the other environment contained similar but non-stereotypic objects (e.g., nature poster, art, water bottles, general-interest magazines). They found that stereotypic objects conveyed a masculine image for computer science that caused women (but not men) to feel as though they did not belong in the field. Women also reported being less interested in pursuing computer science when in the stereotypic environment compared to the non-stereotypic one. Men's interest was not diminished. Based on these findings, the computer science and engineering department at the University of Washington redesigned their computer lab space to be welcoming to all students. As Cheryan et al. (2014) note, "changes such as repainting the walls and hanging nature posters were relatively inexpensive and took less than 2 weeks to implement" (p. 8). The updates have been well-received by students and faculty.

Additional research supports the idea that objects can suggest that some students do not belong. In one set of studies (Schmitt et al., 2010), college students completed a questionnaire in a cubicle that included a small Christmas tree or no Christmas tree. If the Christmas tree fit with their identity (e.g., they celebrated Christmas, they were Christians), the students experienced positive outcomes such as feeling included. If the Christmas tree did not fit with their identity (e.g., they did not celebrate Christmas; they were Sikh or Buddhist), they reported negative affect and lower inclusion at the college. Interestingly, both Christians and non-Christians thought that the impact of the Christmas tree would be positive. Another investigation (Latu et al., 2013) conducted in a virtual-reality classroom found that when seeing a photo of a male leader (Bill Clinton) or no photo in the audience, women's performance on a persuasive speech was worse than men's performance. Seeing a photo of a female leader (Hillary Clinton, Angela Merkel), however, improved women's performance to be as persuasive as men's. Men's performance was unaffected by the photos. Simple objects like Christmas trees, Star Trek posters, or images of male leaders not only signal who does and does not fit in a particular space, but they also impact students' performance.

The implications are clear. Universities can hang nature posters in computer science spaces. Colleges can refrain from putting up Christmas trees and include images highlighting the achievements of less powerful groups. However, one needs to consider the best ways to alter spaces so that they create a sense of inclusion for all students. Cheryan et al. (2014) provide two cautions. First, the objects or artworks need to be respectful and not stereotypical. For example, seeing stereotypical Native American images (e.g., Pocahontas, sports mascots) predicts both lower well-being and describing one's self in less achievement-oriented ways among Native American students compared to seeing no images or positive images of Native Americans (Fryberg et al., 2008). Second, one's students come from a variety of backgrounds, including more advantaged or privileged ones. Efforts to create an inclusive environment can lead to defensiveness and feelings of threat and exclusion from men or White individuals (Dover et al., 2016; Wilkin et al., 2017). Making clear that one's inclusiveness is *all-inclusive* and contains European Americans helps ensure that White students do not feel excluded (Plaut et al., 2011).

TABLE 3.1
Worksheet: Symbolic Space

For each of the elements, taking into account your students and their identities and needs, describe updates to make them more inclusive.

Describe the students in your class and dimensions on which they might not feel included.	Furniture	Classroom Layout	Technology	Artwork and Objects

Using Table 3.1, stop to reflect on what you could do to make your classroom more inclusive. Take into account your students and their identities. Then consider the furniture, classroom layout, technology, artwork, and objects. What cues do you think students see in the space? What are ways you could improve it?

Universal Design

Principles of universal design are also important to the creation of inclusive classrooms. In architecture, universal design is an approach to making buildings accessible to individuals with disabilities. But rather than making specialty designs to accommodate disabilities, it involves designing buildings and structures that can be used by everyone "to the greatest extent possible" (Mace et al., 1991, p. 160). For instance, when designing a learning space, one could place it on the first floor with easy access for all students, regardless of whether they use wheelchairs, are on crutches because of sports injuries, or are carrying heavy backpacks. The accessibility of the space helps all students, including those with disabilities. As Goff and Higbee (2008) note,

> Universal Design promotes the consideration of the needs of all potential users in the planning and development of a space, product, or program—an approach that is equally applicable to architecture or education. It also supports the notion that when providing an architectural feature—or educational service, for that matter—to enhance accessibility and inclusion for one population, we are often benefiting all occupants or participants. (p. 1)

Goff and Higbee (2008) make clear that universal design is relevant to educational service, which I turn to next.

Inclusive Course Design, Content, and Methods of Instruction

I examine the role of universal design in higher education classrooms, explore the benefits of including a diversity of perspectives in one's course content, and focus on additional inclusive teaching methods. In each case, one sees the value of infusing inclusivity into both one's pedagogical approaches and course content on students' academic lives.

Universal Design for Learning

Basic principles of universal design have been applied to higher education to help provide equitable access and support to the increasingly diverse population of university students (Roberts et al., 2011; Tobin & Behling, 2018). There have been a number of different approaches for applying universal design to university learning, including Universal Design for Instruction (UDI; Scott et al., 2003), Universal Instructional Design (UID; Silver et al., 1998), and UDL (Meyer et al., 2014). I focus primarily on UDL, which is grounded in the conceptual framework and research of the Center for Applied Special Technology (CAST, 2018).

Employing research from neuroscience and education, CAST applied the principles of universal design to education by creating guidelines to capture three key aspects of learning: why (students' engagement and motivation), what (students' perception and understanding of information being taught), and how (students' expression and demonstration of their knowledge) (CAST, 2018). For each aspect, CAST established strategies to meet the needs of a broad range of students: (a) *engagement* (why): offer multiple ways for students to engage meaningfully with the material; (b) *representation* (what): present the course content using a variety of methods; and (c) *action and expression* (how): include various methods for students to express what they know and demonstrate their learning (Meyer et al., 2014).

These strategies are consistent with satisfying students' basic psychological needs of autonomy and competence (Ryan & Deci, 2017) discussed in chapter 2, as they stress student choice and independence and give students many ways to demonstrate mastery and competence. While not emphasized in the UDL guidelines, meeting students' needs for belonging is also important, particularly for marginalized and underrepresented students (Good et al., 2012; Walton & Cohen, 2007). It can be challenging to ensure that everyone is supported, given competing needs (Nakamura, 2019). For instance, one student may request to bring their emotional support dog to class but another student is allergic. In addition, Nakamura (2019) stresses that one needs to be careful when describing universal design techniques to one's students because students who feel as though they do not fit within universal design may feel even more alienated. Relatedly, when applying universally designed learning to the educational context, it is important to consider issues of privilege and identity in the classroom by focusing on students' possible intersecting social identities that may experience systemic inequality, such as being students of color, students with minoritized sexual or gender identities, from low socioeconomic backgrounds, students with disabilities, and/or older students (e.g., Couillard & Higbee, 2018; Evans et al., 2017; Hackman, 2008).

As an example of ways to incorporate each principle of universally designed learning into the college classroom, I provide Michelle Nario-Redmond's (2016, 2018) recent course design that incorporates engagement, representation, and action/expression in Table 3.2. Nario-Redmond (2016) recommends taking three steps when starting to use UDL: reflect on what you are already doing, consider ways to apply universal design, and evaluate any changes. Throughout this process, she stresses that the instructor consider what is "essential" about an assignment, establishing how the assignment fits with their key course goals and desired outcomes. I also recommend Higbee and Goff's (2008) book as a useful resource. It provides many illustrations of individuals incorporating universal design into their university classrooms, particularly applying UID. Higbee et al. (2008), for instance, provide a compelling set of examples for first-year courses.

Consistent with many frameworks of course design (e.g., Understanding by Design, Wiggins & McTighe, 2006; Integrated Course Design, Fink 2013), an instructor should determine their learning goals or objectives before coming up with the specific course materials and assignments; you are considering what is essential for students to learn. For instance, Wiggins and McTighe (2006) suggest using backward design: define what you want

TABLE 3.2

Example of Implementing UDL for Redesign of Freshman Writing Course

Implementing UDL Redesign of "Freak, Gimp, Crazy, Crip" Course	
Learning Objectives: • Experience different ways of learning and being in the world. • Evaluate the impact of different environments, supports, and barriers to learning. • Distinguish among stigma, discrimination, and the fit between differences in people and the contexts that impact participation. • Develop personal insights on the challenges and values associated with physical and mental difference, and the importance of variation to the human experience.	

(Continues)

TABLE 3.2 (*Continued*)

Implementing UDL Redesign of "Freak, Gimp, Crazy, Crip" Course

Assignments/Activities	**Examples of Specific Assignments**
Alternate Formats/Accessibility Apps Demonstration	*Demonstrating Education Apps*
• Essay 1: Personal essay on experiences with stigma	• Create a short but engaging demonstration of an app:
• Essay II: Comparative essay evaluating alternative learning formats experienced	• The purpose of the app/feature
• Essay III: Source paper on solutions to learning barriers/accommodating diversity	• The steps for how to use it
• Learning preferences reflection journals, daily readings, quizzes, discussions, clips on ableism and social change.	• Evaluation of the app/feature
• Campus Accessibility Tour and Evaluation	• Use easy to follow steps with audio, graphics
Examples of Specific Assignments	*Comparative Essay on Alternative Learning Formats*
Solutions Paper: Accommodating Diverse Learners	PURPOSE: Compare pros and cons of using two methods for accomplishing same task. Examples: Read text versus listen to a text. Dictate versus type. Study in library versus dorm. Use app-based versus paper calendar. Take notes with 1-pencil versus by hand.
• Focus on a problem affecting college student achievement and inclusion: What's the population? What are challenges faced? How are they accommodated or not? What strategies work to improve participation or performance? What do insiders say?	• Step 1. Choose your two methods for comparison: _____ vs _____
• The paper can take a number of forms: a persuasive essay with recommendations; a proposal for a new policy; an educational-awareness paper; a self-advocacy statement or plan for the college.	• Step 2. Identify five criteria to evaluate each method
• Incorporate at least three scholarly sources (e.g., on UDL, accommodations, advocacy, assistive technologies, educational campaigns).	• Motivation/interest in material
• Students can build on previous work.	• Effort/challenge
	• Performance/mastery of task or skill
	• Step 3. Conduct self-experiment of each method for 30 minutes–1 hour over 2–3 days.
	• Step 4. Complete comparison evaluation template + 1 scholarly source.
	• Step 5. Take a stand on which method was more effective in fitting your capabilities.

Source. Nario-Redmond, 2018.

to achieve in the course (i.e., learning goals); then, decide how you know whether or not these goals had been met; and finally, design the content and methods of instruction to reach those goals. Using UDL principles, you would offer many flexible means to motivate students to achieve the course goals, demonstrate their knowledge, and learn the information. As discussed in chapter 2, you should be transparent with your students, making clear the task they are being asked to do, its purpose, and how it will be evaluated (Winkelmes et al., 2019).

As an example of using backward design in my social psychology course, one of my goals is for students to be able to apply the research that they are learning to a new real-world context. Currently students read a number of articles about social influence, conformity, attitude change, and persuasion. We have class discussions about these topics. They then each create an advertisement utilizing various principles learned in class. It could be a print ad, radio ad, television ad, or a face-to-face persuasive attempt. Finally, they write a two-page paper, explaining the techniques that they used and citing the relevant research literature.

In Table 3.3, consider your classes. If it is a new class you are developing, I encourage you to start with your learning goals and then consider assignments, readings, and assessments. If you are updating a course, it probably makes the most sense to begin with a current assignment that fits with your goals and think through how you could update it. Ask yourself the following: What are my learning goals? How would I know that a goal has been met? What content and methods do I use to reach the learning goal?

TABLE 3.3
Worksheet: Backward Design

Learning Goals	How would you know that this goal had been met?	Content to reach your learning goal	Methods to reach your learning goal

Next, ponder ways to update your proposed assignment to include UDL. For instance, when reflecting on my social psychology assignment, I can see that in many ways it is consistent with a UDL approach. In terms of *engagement*, I offer students multiple ways to engage meaningfully with the material. They have great choice in terms of their "product" and their style of presentation. In recent years, students have tried to persuade the class to not smoke, practice safer sex, buy baby carrots, vote for a political candidate, or use a new app, among other things. Students can choose something they care about deeply, such as a political issue, or something that is fun, like baby carrots. Their ads have been print ads, short video clips, PowerPoint presentations, and in-person skits. In the ads, they also have multiple ways to *express* what they have learned. They could, for example, apply the persuasive principle of authority or another of Cialidini's principles of influence (Cialdini & Sagarin, 2005).

Generally, I ask all students to write a paper and complete the assignment individually. I could provide multiple ways for them to demonstrate their learning, such as working with a partner or presenting the principles they have used rather than writing a paper. In my class, they write many individual papers, and my learning goal of applying the material would be accomplished even if they did the project with a partner or did an oral presentation. This last year—after having written this chapter—I gave students the option of creating their ad individually or with a partner; a number of students opted to work with a partner. I would continue including these choices in the future. Finally, I could develop different means of *representation* of the course content on social influence and persuasion. In addition to the readings and discussion, I could include a video about advertising with the captions on (to represent that information both verbally and in text), or I could ask someone whose career is in advertising to join us for one day of our discussion. I urge you to use Table 3.4 to consider ways that you could update a current assignment to include multiple methods of engagement, representation, and action/expression.

Inclusive Course Content

In addition to ensuring that the pedagogy of your courses is inclusive by using multiple flexible ways of presenting information, you also need to reflect on whether the *information itself* is inclusive (e.g., presents multiple perspectives, includes authors from varying backgrounds, promotes positive interactions across students of different groups) (Hackman, 2008; Higbee et al., 2010; Littleford & Nolan, 2013). Think through the type of material you are teaching and how the question of inclusivity fits with your

TABLE 3.4

Worksheet: UDL—Updating a Current Assignment

Describe a current assignment and the learning goals it is designed to achieve. Then, in each of the boxes to the right, describe potential ways to update it to include multiple methods of engagement, representation, and action/expression.

Current Assignment and Learning Goals	Engagement	Representation	Action/Expression

course content. Consider the students in your class and how their backgrounds could interact with the course content. For instance, you could be teaching sensitive content in the humanities (e.g., classics courses covering death, disability, sexual violence, homosexuality, or slavery, Rabinowitz & McHardy, 2014), the social sciences (e.g., social science classes considering torture, racism, intimate partner violence, Lowe & Jones, 2010), classes focusing on race and diversity (Perry et al., 2009; Quaye, 2012), courses exploring privilege (Case, 2013), and research methods and natural science courses (Weisz, 2016). You might be teaching a course fulfilling a university-wide general diversity requirement or a course in your academic discipline. The content and methods of your course may vary in terms of how inclusive they are of the range of students' backgrounds (see Nelson Laird, 2011, for a consideration of the dimensions on which diversity inclusivity can vary). The goal here is not to be non-biased or non-racist but to be anti-racist, where you actively challenge racial inequity (Kendi, 2019).

Benefits of Inclusive Content

There are many potential benefits to using inclusive course content. First, in terms of student learning and engagement, course material that speaks to students' lived experiences is more personally relevant, memorable to students, improves well-being, and promotes academic engagement and achievement (Gay, 2018; Ladson-Billings, 1995; Stephens et al., 2015). Seeing oneself in the curriculum matters for thriving in college for students from a range of backgrounds.

Next, the presentation of presenting diverse representation can enhance the content and make course material more accurate, representative, and comprehensive (Gay, 2018; Trimble et al., 2004). As Trimble et al. (2004) argue about the field of psychology,

> It is especially important that introductory psychology course materials be current, accurate, fair, and inclusive. . . . The inclusion of diverse viewpoints and diversity issues is one such improvement that is of utmost scientific and social importance. . . . Incorporating diversity issues into textbooks is not a matter of political correctness. It is a matter of scientific and professional responsibility. . . . By exploring psychological processes across diverse populations and contexts, we gain deeper insights into how these processes operate. (p. iv)

They stress that it is important to "infuse" diversity throughout each of the topics within a textbook. Integrating the presentation of multiple perspectives throughout the semester makes clear that these perspectives are central to the course (Banks, 2016; Saunders & Kardia, 1997).

Finally, course materials in which students learn about different social groups (e.g., different racial or ethnic groups) can positively impact intergroup attitudes and behaviors and reduce prejudice (Banks, 2016; Bowman, 2010; Gurin et al., 2004; Hurtado, 2005; Lopez, 2004; Neville et al., 2014; van Laar et al., 2008). Many researchers have found that White students experienced long-term positive effects from learning diversity-related course content (Lopez, 2004; Neville et al., 2014, van Laar et al., 2008). Across the first year of college, Lopez (2004) observed that White students taking more curricular experiences related to understanding other ethnic groups reported increased awareness of inequality and support for policies confronting inequality. van Laar et al. (2008) found that across a 5-year period White students taking ethnic studies courses tended to develop more friendships with members of other racial/ethnic groups relative to their number of White friends. Similarly, Neville et al. (2014) discovered that across a 4-year period White students who took more diversity-related courses reported a greater drop in colorblind racial ideology ("set of beliefs that deny, minimize, and distort the existence of racism in its many forms [e.g., individual, interpersonal, cultural, and institutional] and the role of race in people's lives," Neville et al., 2014, p. 180). For White students, engaging with course material dealing with race or ethnicity predicted long-lasting positive inter-group attitudes and behaviors.

Complexities and Challenges of Inclusive Course Content

However, the effects of more inclusive course content, particularly material that considers race or ethnicity, may be complicated and not always positive (Denson & Bowman, 2017; Hurtado, 2005; Patton, 2016). For instance, African American or Latinx students may respond differently than their White peers to taking diversity-related courses (Gurin et al., 2004; Lopez, 2004; van Laar et al., 2008). While van Laar et al. (2008) found positive movement (e.g., friendships) toward those of other groups among White participants, they found movement toward their own group among Black and Latinx students. These positive in-group attitudes for Black and Latinx students were accompanied by increased tolerance for the out-group. These differing effects were similar to results seen earlier by Gurin et al. (2004) and Lopez (2004) in which White students showed stronger positive out-group effects than other ethnic groups. Overall, van Laar et al. (2008) suggest that the differential findings for the White, Black, and Latinx students could be helpful to create change on campus, because students of all backgrounds showed increased tolerance. Both the White students (who are in the major-ity) showing more openness to students of other racial backgrounds and the Black and Latinx students (who have less status) showing more in-group movement might spur on collective action to make changes to inequities that exist on campus.

Student Resistance. Alternatively, students of a variety of backgrounds may experience resistance when taking diversity-related courses (Aleman & Gaytan, 2017; Atwood, 1994; Ukpokodu, 2002). For instance, Case and Cole (2013) recently proposed, based on faculty narratives about teaching about privilege, that students demonstrate three types of resistance: world-view protection, target group resistance, and narrative resistance. With *worldview protection*, students are resistant to learning information that threatens fundamental beliefs they have about the world, such as the belief that anyone through hard work can achieve success. *Target group resistance* reflects stu-dents' resistance based on less privileged social identities. Members of mar-ginalized groups may feel that they need to protect themselves when the class discussion covers a topic in which they could be tokenized or stereotyped. For instance, when considering the Israeli-Palestinian conflict, a student who is Jewish may opt not to engage with the material because of anti-Semitic comments or others assuming that the student will represent the "Jewish per-spective." Finally, *narrative resistance* involves "a failure of the community of learners to arrive at a shared narrative" (p. 42). For instance, a key narrative in early readings in my stereotyping and prejudice course is that prejudice plays out in subtle and unconscious ways. If students resist this fundamental narrative, then important discussions and understanding of later readings are hindered.

Difficulties in Resolution of Disequilibrium Caused by Diversity-Related Courses. Bowman (2010) suggests that it is valuable to situate student resistance in diversity-related courses within Gurin et al.'s (2002) broader developmental framework grounded in fundamental ideas about how people cognitively make sense of new information they are learning (Piaget, 1983). When learning new information, individuals may often seek to maintain their current ideas and assimilate the new information into preexisting ideas (Nickerson, 1998). As applied to the university context, a college student may be learning new information about other groups (e.g., that African American men are overrepresented in the criminal justice system) and bring that information back to knowledge and stereotypes that they already have (e.g., the idea that racism no longer exists [Neville et al., 2013] or that Black men are violent [Devine, 1989]). If the new information fits with previous information, then there is *equilibrium* (Piaget, 1983).

But someone may not be able to make the new information consistent with their existing beliefs. When faced with a discrepancy between their beliefs and the new information, a person experiences a state of *disequilibrium*—contradiction and imbalance (Piaget, 1985). Motivated to resolve this discrepancy, they put effort into either updating their current schemas or developing new ones (Kibler, 2011). Similarly, in his classic writings about *Democracy and Education*, Dewey (1920) proposes that our thinking is prompted "by an *un*settlement and it aims at overcoming a disturbance" (p. 380). For instance, a student reading the book *The New Jim Crow: Mass Incarceration in the Age of Colorblindness* (Alexander, 2010) may be learning new information about the impact of institutional racism on imprisonment. Their previous belief that the criminal justice is fair for all races or that Black men are violent is now called into question. The student is disconcerted, so they could try to resolve this discomfort by actively engaging with the intellectual ideas and having dialogues with diverse peers (Gurin et al., 2004). The student could then show reduced prejudice and more positive intergroup attitudes and behaviors.

Bowman (2010) suggests that this process of disequilibrium resolution, however, may take some time and effort. Taking a single diversity course may not be enough to reap these benefits. He concludes that "first-year students who take two diversity courses experience substantial benefits in comfort with differences, an appreciation of similarities and differences among people, intended and actual contact with diverse peers, and overall well-being" (p. 562). These discomforting and uncertain college experiences can stimulate growth in understanding about other groups (Ruble, 1994), but it may be a long and difficult process.

Hurtado (2005) presents a related challenge, suggesting that the quality of the interactions that students have as they are grappling with discomfort is important. Facilitating positive interactions is critical. Students reporting higher *negative* interactions with diverse student peers demonstrated many negative intergroup outcomes, such as lower cultural awareness and lower support for race-based initiatives. They also reported that their values differed more from other racial groups than did students who did not report negative interactions. Hurtado (2005) concludes that "when left to chance, negative interactions can reinforce differences between groups rather than include a serious exploration of commonalities" (p. 601). In chapter 5, we consider ways to approach these challenging dialogues. Do not leave them to chance.

Reflecting on Your Course to Make the Content More Inclusive
To evaluate your course content to make it more culturally inclusive, Samuels (2014) suggests asking yourself a series of questions, including "Are the texts/readings I use written by authors from diverse backgrounds (different races, sexual orientations, genders, abilities, and so on)?" (p. 71) and "Do the materials I use in my courses help students understand historical, social, and/or political events from diverse perspectives?" (p. 70). The ways that you make the content more inclusive to promote student learning, to accurately represent the knowledge in your field, and to promote positive intergroup relations will vary depending on the specifics of your course and your academic discipline. Yet it is important to infuse inclusive content across the humanities, social sciences, and natural sciences. (See Branche et al., 2007, for a rich set of concrete examples of faculty members integrating diversity into their courses.)

As an example, I provide a recent lab exercise that Carolyn Weisz (2016) created for her psychology research methods course to make the content more inclusive. In Figure 3.1, you can see her learning objectives, readings, and teaching ideas.

I encourage you to use Table 3.5. as a template to mull over possibilities for making one of your current assignments more inclusive.

Methods of Instruction

In addition to including inclusive course content, instructors should also strive to use inclusive pedagogical approaches (Gay, 2018; Higbee et al.,

Figure 3.1.   Example of inclusive lab exercise for a research methods course.

Culturally-Sensitive and Community-Based Research: A Topic Unit for Psychology Research Methods Courses	
Learning Objectives: (1) Gain familiarity with methods, approaches, and practices that characterize culturally-sensitive and community-engaged research in psychology; and (2) Increase your awareness of your own identities, cultural perspectives, and positionality with respect to dynamics of status and power, and consider how these might relate to the processes and products of research.	
Key Concepts and Readings	**Teaching Ideas**

<u>**Warner (2008)**</u>
intersectionality (Cole, 2009)
master category
identification
structural context
grounded theory (Heydarian, 2016)
 	
<u>**Rogler (1989)**</u>
emic/etic
category fallacy
acculturation (Sam & Berry, 2010)
back-translation (Chapman & Carter, 1979)
 	
<u>**Sieber & Sorensen (1992)**</u>
gatekeepers
focus group
participant observation
respect, beneficence, and justice
(National Commission for the Protection of Human Subjects of Biomedical and Behavioral Research, 1979)
 	
<u>**Stoudt, Fox, & Fine (2012)**</u>
Privilege
participatory action research
critical justice scholars (also see Salter & Adams, 2013)
Playback Theatre
 	
<u>**Corrigan, Pickett, Kraus, Burks, & Schmidt (2015)**</u>
community-based participatory research
focus groups
stakeholders
grounded theory (also see Heydarian, 2016)
	• **Reflect on personal identities, privilege, and intersections**
	  o free-writing
	  o identity check-list
	  o pair sharing
	  o include student and researcher identities
	
	• **Class discussion/lecture topics**
	  o students share cross-disciplinary learning, e.g., anthropology/business: emic/etic, participant observation, focus groups
	  o acculturation model and questionnaire
	  o use of methods in research planning phase
	    ▪ e.g., gatekeepers, focus groups, participant observation, back translation
	    ▪ use these methods to develop partnerships, and refine questions and research plans
	  o generate examples of gatekeepers
	    ▪ within institutions (e.g., schools, clinics)
	    ▪ within communities (e.g., cultural, street)
	
	• **Pre-class assignments**
	  o reading (especially Warner, 2008; Rogler, 2008; Sieber & Sorenson, 2008)
	  o type out explanations of concepts
	    ▪ use outside sources and web
	    ▪ e.g., emic/etic, participant observation
	
	• **Lab/class activity**
	  o individuals think of a research question to test in a field setting (free-writing)
	  o small groups share ideas and pick one
	  o groups answer questions to develop a research proposal (apply concepts from readings; take team notes on PowerPoint), e.g.,
	    ▪ who is the population? gatekeepers?
	    ▪ pre-research steps?
	    ▪ potential challenges for you as a researcher and risk for participants?
	    ▪ ideas about ways to address these challenges
	  o teams present proposals to class

Note: Weisz (2016).

TABLE 3.5

Worksheet: Adding More Inclusive Content

Update a current set of readings or a current assignment to make it more inclusive.

Describe a current set of readings or assignment and its learning goals.	In what ways it is inclusive (e.g., multiple perspectives, authors from a range of backgrounds, promotes positive intergroup attitudes and behaviors)?	How could you update the readings/assignment to be more inclusive?

2010; Samuels, 2014). For instance, as discussed in chapter 2, the culture in the United States emphasizes autonomy and uniqueness. Members of more powerful social groups (e.g., White individuals, men, those of higher social class) often have more independent self-construals. Members of more marginalized social groups (e.g., people of color, women, working-class individuals) often have more interdependent self-construals that are less in step with the broader cultural norm of independence (Markus & Kitayama, 1994). Instructional methods stressing communal goals and collaboration help ensure that a broad range of students academically thrive and persist (Diekman et al., 2015; Gay, 2018; Gillies, 2014). Here I focus primarily on collaborative learning approaches (Barkley et al., 2014). I also briefly consider ways to achieve desirable difficulty in your instruction and incorporate high-impact practices.

Collaborative Learning

Following Barkley et al.'s (2014) lead, I use *collaborative learning* as an all-embracing term for a variety of methods in which interacting groups or teams of students collaborate or cooperate on academic tasks. It involves "two or more students laboring together and sharing the workload equitably as they progress toward intended learning outcomes" (Barkley et al., 2014, p. 4). Such approaches have many benefits for students from a range of backgrounds, including enhanced academic engagement, performance, and persistence (Barkley et al., 2014; Chen et al., 2018; Johnson et al., 2014; Springer et al., 1999) and improved intergroup relations (Aronson & Patnoe, 1997; Slavin & Cooper, 1999). To learn concrete steps for implementing collaborative learning, I recommend Barkley et al.'s (2014) *Collaborative Learning Techniques: A Handbook for College Faculty.* Meyers's (1997) summary of 68 articles that present small-group collaborative work in psychology classes is another helpful resource. Careful consideration when setting up, facilitating, and assessing collaborative learning creates more successful experiences. I next consider challenges when using cooperative learning with students from varying backgrounds.

Social Comparison Concerns. A key challenge when teaching students from a range of backgrounds is that students may compare their academic performance to others' and be worried they are not performing as well as their peers (Micari & Drane, 2011). When students are working together collaboratively, there is great potential for learning because they encounter differing perspectives that may challenge them and cause discomfort (Ruble, 1994). However, as considered in chapters 2, 4, and 5, not all discomfort is productive: students may feel worried or threatened. Students may experience social-comparison concerns (Micari & Drane, 2011; Micari & Pazos, 2014) in which they make upward social comparisons (Festinger, 1954) to higher-performing peers they are collaborating with. Micari and Pazos (2014) suggest, "When individuals are faced with others whom they view as more competent at some task, the threat of feeling inferior hinders cognitive engagement, resulting in reduced ability to process information" (p. 251). Indeed, students reporting social-comparison concerns when collaborating with small groups (five to seven peers) in STEM classes expressed being less comfortable offering their ideas in their collaborative group and showed lower persistence and performance (Micari & Drane, 2011). Interestingly, in Micari and Drane's (2011) research, students' academic preparation (measured by grades and standardized tests) did not predict social-comparison concerns. Yet students indicating higher self-efficacy reported lower social-comparison concerns and more comfort in their group. Although this STEM program included more women than men, men reported *more* comfort in their groups than women did. Later research by Eddy et al. (2015) found no gender differences in comfort in small collaborative groups (two to four people) in biology courses. They did find, however, that women reported lower comfort than men during larger, whole-class discussion.

Further research has considered ways to reduce social-comparison concerns through an intervention promoting the following related beliefs: (a) one's intelligence can change and grow (Dweck, 2006), and (b) many students struggle academically and these struggles are due to changeable (e.g., lack of effort) and external (e.g., difficulty of material) factors. Students randomly assigned to receive the intervention showed lower social-comparison concerns (Micari & Pazos, 2014). By encouraging students not to focus on their academic ability to explain their struggles, highlighting that struggle is a normal part of challenging college courses, and emphasizing that one's academic ability can change, students experienced lower social-comparison concerns.

Social Identities and Groupings. Another potential challenge involves student identities and the methods the instructor uses to sort students into collaborative learning groups. Are the members of a group self-selected? Randomly assigned? Selected by the instructor? If they are chosen by the instructor, what are the selection criteria (e.g., maximizing diversity, ensuring that students have some other students of their background in their group)?

Many suggest that it is crucial to create diverse small groups in which students are collaborating with others with a variety of identities, perspectives, and personal histories (e.g., Gay, 2018; Michaelsen & Sweet, 2008). Heterogeneous groups can promote strong learning and group dynamics for students of a range of backgrounds (Channon et al., 2017; Donovan et al., 2018). I encourage you to stop to think through possible ways to assign students to small groups, taking your goals into account.

Students could self-select the members of their group. This assignment strategy supports student autonomy (Ryan & Deci, 2017) and may promote comfort (Brookfield & Preskill, 2005). Students feel more comfortable in groups with friends (Theobald et al., 2017) and see group work as more valuable when working with a friend, especially among female students (Eddy et al., 2015). Barkley et al. (2014) suggest that students regard choosing for themselves as fairer and therefore recommend that instructors sometimes let students self-select (see also Brookfield & Preskill, 2005). A potential downside is that when students choose their own groups, they often select peers similar to themselves in terms of gender, race, and academic ability (Freeman et al., 2017), thereby missing out on potential intergroup benefits (Slavin & Cooper, 1999). Assuming that an instructor includes a variety of informal (e.g., discuss this question in a small group for 10 minutes) and formal (e.g., conduct this project with a group of four people over the next month) collaborative work, I would encourage using self-selection for some of the informal groupings. Let students have the autonomy and comfort that comes from turning to those they typically sit by. When you give students some choices for informal groupings, they may be less resistant to assignment of members for more formal groups.

Similarly, I would suggest sometimes using *random assignment* for these more informal groupings. In this case, you could have students count off in sets. Suppose you had a class with 18 students and you wanted to form 6 groups of 3. You could have them number off so that the first student is a 1, the second is a 2, the third is a 3, the fourth would begin again with

1, and so on, until all students have been assigned to a group. Students see random assignment as fair (Barkley et al., 2014). It also helps students to be in a number of different groups, even if the groups are not necessarily diverse along all dimensions.

Finally, I would recommend thoughtfully considering the ways you create more formal collaborative teams. It is important to bear in mind students' social identities, given their impact on group dynamics and performance. For instance, Eddy et al. (2015) found that in small-group (two to four students) peer discussions, female students preferred being collaborators (both listening and explaining), while male students preferred being leaders/explainers. Students of color and international students were more likely than White students to prefer being listeners. Men and women did not differ in their comfort in participating in small-group discussions, with all reporting being fairly comfortable. For men, the value of the peer discussion did not depend on whether the group included a friend. For women, a friend mattered. Without a friend, they found the peer discussions less valuable than men did, whereas they reported the same high value as men when a friend was part of the group. Overall, Eddy et al. (2015) suggest that small-group peer discussions help make the classroom equally comfortable for female and male students. Promoting friendship and familiarity with one another (possibly through longer projects or structured interactions) could further reduce gender differences.

Dasgupta et al. (2015) and Grover et al. (2017) further argue for taking social identities—particularly gender identities—into account when creating small collaborative groups. Dasgupta et al. (2015) assigned female engineering students to one of three 4-person groups varying in its gender composition (75% women, 50% women, or 25% women) and then examined their feelings of threat and anxiety. Dasgupta and her colleagues found that for first-year students, the gender composition had a major impact on their approach to working with their group: when in the minority, women felt more threatened than in the other two conditions. For upper-level students, gender composition did not predict feelings of threat. Interestingly, for group participation, women in a women-majority group participated more than in the other two groups, irrespective of academic level (first-year versus advanced students). Creating groups that had equal gender representation reduced threat, but to boost participation it was important to have women-majority groups.

Grover et al. (2017) examined the impact of gender composition on interactions of groups of either four women (all-women) or one women with three men (male-majority) completing a group math task. All participants completed a practice tutorial at the beginning of the study. The tutorial for one woman (the expert) in each group was different, giving her specific expertise on doing the math problems. This high expertise was kept constant across the two conditions. Yet the expert woman performed worse in the male-majority group than in the all-women group. In their first two studies, these women also experienced lower belonging in the male groups than in the female groups. Performing worse and not belonging then predicted the expert woman feeling worse about her math ability in the male-majority conditions. In the final study, the experts were women who were math-intensive STEM majors with high standardized math scores. While performing worse in the male-majority conditions (like Inzlicht & Ben-Zeev, 2000), they did not experience lower belonging or lower perceived math ability, suggesting that the previous success may have muted the negative interpersonal impact of majority-male environments.

This line of research provides some suggestions for promoting positive group dynamics and performance. First, when assigning students to groups, try to avoid having only one member of a social group (e.g., only one woman, Grover et al., 2017). Having a more equal distribution improves intergroup relations and performance (Dasgupta et al., 2015). In a class that is one-quarter women, have some groups with no women rather than placing one woman in each group. Second, keep in mind that structures you put in place to promote positive group dynamics once the groups are formed are also important. Building positive relationships and friendships matters.

Minimizing Social Loafing. Finally, when devising collaborative learning assignments, consider how to engage all students at a high level. Many of my students report disliking group assignments because some group members contribute less than others, revealing the challenge of social loafing. In qualitative research, Hall and Buzwell (2013) found that students across a range of disciplines reported that their main concern with collaborative projects was the potential for students putting in less effort to receive the same grade as those contributing more. Students are concerned about others' social loafing, "a reduction in an individual's motivation or effort when working collectively as compared to either working individually or coactively (i.e., individually, but in the presence of others who are working on the same task)" (Hart et al., 2004, pp. 984–985). Karau and Williams (1993, 1995) proposed that people put in less effort on collaborative projects (as compared to individual ones) because they see their effort as less valuable in successfully completing the projects. Karau and Williams (1993) concluded that individuals social-loafed more when projects were not seen as personally engaging or meaningful, when their efforts could not be evaluated, and when they believed other group members would perform well. Instructors must create personally meaningful tasks in which students perceive that their input matters.

There are many ways to try to reduce social loafing on collaborative projects. For instance, Aggarwal and O'Brien (2008) suggested designing smaller cooperative projects (or breaking larger projects into smaller parts) with groups of a small size. Bruffee (1999) suggests groups of about five for classroom groupings, and groups of three for longer term projects, given the logistical difficulties. Individual inputs are evident and identifiable within these smaller groups. Aggarwal and O'Brien (2008) additionally suggested having peers evaluate other group members at multiple times during the project. This evaluation creates accountability. By having many evaluations, students are also given the opportunity to improve over time. Stressing improvement facilitates motivation (Dweck, 2006). Ohland et al. (2012) have validated assessment tools for individuals to use to evaluate themselves and their peers when collaborating on group projects (see CATME, www .catme.org, for resources for using their tools).

I would add a few cautions when using peer assessment. As Ohland et al. (2012) note, students may be reluctant to rate each other, particularly to provide negative ratings. Even if the ratings are conducted confidentially and then averaged across the other group members, students may opt to give high ratings, sacrificing accuracy. Bacon et al.'s (1999) work reveals an additional problem: When reviewing students' best and worst collaborative group experiences, Bacon et al. found that more of the worst group experiences (compared to the best ones) included confidential peer evaluations collected once at the end of the term. They argue against using anonymous peer evaluation as a final summative assessment. However, multiple peer assessments can be valuable. As an example, in work with diverse research teams Cheruvelil et al. (2014) recommend providing each group member with averaged anonymous peer feedback accompanied by concrete research-based suggestions for ways to improve. An emphasis on promoting growth is invaluable if you hope for the peer assessment to provide constructively critical feedback.

Using Table 3.6. as a sample worksheet, I recommend that you reflect on potential ways to add more collaborative learning opportunities into your classroom.

Desirable Difficulties
I turn next to discussing instruction approaches that emphasize creating a desirable level of academic struggle. As Bjork and Bjork (2011) note, academic struggles can be "desirable because they trigger encoding and retrieval processes that support learning, comprehension, and remembering. If,

TABLE 3.6
Worksheet: Adding More Collaborative Learning
Update a current assignment to incorporate collaborative learning.

Describe a current assignment and its learning goals.	In what ways could you update it to include more collaborative small-group learning?	What are potential challenges in including collaborative learning? How would you seek to address them?

however, the learner does not have the background knowledge or skills to respond to them successfully, they become undesirable difficulties" (p. 58). So, when fostering an inclusive classroom where all students are learning and thriving, an instructor should strive to create desirable difficulties in which students are highly challenged but have the necessary tools to successfully meet the challenges. Students will often make lots of mistakes in the short run when learning the material. These mistakes provide opportunities to learn and grow (Bjork et al., 2013). By productively struggling with the material while acquiring knowledge, students have enhanced long-term learning (Bjork & Bjork, 2011).

One challenge of teaching is figuring out how to create a desirable degree of difficulty as students are learning new material. Luckily, there are a number of handy resources. For instance, Bjork and Bjork (2011) propose the following set of four learning strategies:

> varying the conditions of learning, rather than keeping them constant and predictable; interleaving instruction on separate topics, rather than grouping instruction by topic (called blocking); spacing, rather than massing, study sessions on a given topic; and using tests, rather than presentations, as study events. (p. 58)

I walk through specific examples of each of these strategies.

First, I urge you to alter the classroom setting across the term rather than keeping it the same every day. Vary it so students learn under different physical conditions. Students will then develop the skills to be able to apply the ideas they are learning to new situations (Bjork, 1994). For example, you could encourage students to sit in different seats and next to different students. Get them out of their comfort zones. Second, as discussed earlier, use a variety of methods of representation of the course content, so that students' learning occurs in multiple ways (Meyer et al., 2014).

Third, when teaching class material, consider using strategies of both spacing out topics rather than blocking them together (Carpenter et al., 2012) and interleaving different topics as you teach them (Kornell & Bjork, 2008). Although students often feel as though "cramming" is an effective strategy (Kornell, 2009), research consistently demonstrates that spacing out the material is more productive for long-term learning (Carpenter et al., 2012). One way to space out materials is to insert different topics into your teaching so that the ideas are not all blocked together but instead are interspersed. So, for instance, when teaching my research design and data analysis course, I often teach topics in blocks, with students learning about one element of conducting a statistical analysis before moving on to the next one. For their first assignment, students learn about creating histograms (bar graphs presenting the frequencies of various data points). Then, for the third assignment, they learn to conduct *t*-tests comparing the ratings across two conditions. However, before running the *t*-test, they need to create histograms to see whether the *t*-test is an appropriate test to run. They have not created histograms for a few weeks. They therefore need to go back to relearn and practice the earlier work. See Persellin and Daniels (2018, pp. 34–35) for concrete examples of using spacing and interweaving in one's teaching.

The fourth strategy that Bjork and Bjork (2011) suggest is using testing as a way to promote long-term learning. When testing their knowledge, students need to retrieve the information from memory to see if they know the answer. While students often believe that rereading materials is an effective way to study, trying to practice retrieving information is more productive (Kornell & Son, 2009). When rereading, one feels as if they know the material, and one may perform well if testing occurs soon after. Testing oneself is often more effortful and leads to mistakes. In the short run, students may feel as if they are performing poorly. However, these efforts to retrieve information yield better long-term memory (Bjork & Bjork, 2011). My advice about testing is similar to that of Adesope et al. (2017), who

> advocate for the use of frequent low-stakes quizzes, rather than high-stakes tests used only for summative purposes. . . . While we maintain that increased formative practice testing is a good idea, students can benefit from retrieval practice in many other ways. . . . Indeed, retrieval practice need not come in the form of a quiz, and can easily be incorporated during self-directed studying (i.e., flash cards or self-generated questions), during structured learning activities in the classroom, or even lectures. (p. 688)

TABLE 3.7
Worksheet: Adding Desirable Difficulty

Update a current assignment to incorporate desirable difficulties.

Describe a current assignment and its learning goals.	In what ways could you update it to include more desirable difficulties in your class?	What are potential challenges in including desirable difficulties? How would you seek to address them?

Encourage students to test themselves. Persellin and Daniels's (2018) book includes many specific examples of using student testing in one's teaching (see especially pp. 21–24).

When adding desirable difficulties to your teaching approaches, keep your students in mind. This book strives to make your classroom inclusive for all students. I urge you to consider your students' current struggles and how they approach your challenging course material. You may need to cultivate the idea that when a task is difficult, that means that it is important; students might assume that the difficulty is a signal that they are not able to do the task (Oyserman et al., 2018). When making the work more challenging, it may also be important to add structure (e.g., smaller weekly assignments to prepare for class, questions to help students focus as they do class readings, in-class engagement and discussion) to give students the resources to rise to the challenge. Structure encourages students to space out their studying, which increases long-term learning (Eddy & Hogan, 2014).

I recommend that you consider whether there are ways to create desirable difficulties—such as presenting materials under different contexts, interleaving and spacing out different topics, and using testing—to promote students' long-term learning in your courses. Table 3.7 serves as a worksheet as you reflect on ways to update a current assignment to incorporate desirable difficulties.

High-Impact Practices
Finally, as you are choosing your methods of instruction, think through whether you could include some high-impact educational practices in your course in addition to the collaborative learning we have already considered.

Kuh (2008, pp. 9–11) describes the following as high-impact practices leading to positive learning outcomes: first-year seminars and experiences; common intellectual experiences; learning communities; writing-intensive courses; collaborative assignments and projects; undergraduate research; diversity/global learning; service-learning, community-based learning; internships; and capstone courses and projects. The Association of American Colleges & Universities (AAC&U) has added eportfolios to Kuh's original list (see www.aacu.org/resources/high-impact-practices). These practices predict positive academic outcomes such as student engagement and learning and college retention for students from a range of backgrounds (Finley & McNair, 2013; Kuh, 2008) as well as promote positive intergroup relations (Soria & Johnson, 2017; Stebleton et al., 2013). I recommend the AAC&U's many resources on high-impact practices, including a number of examples of how various college and universities have successfully incorporated them (see www.aacu.org/campus-model/3325).

In this chapter I have considered a variety of ways to make the context and content of your course more inclusive. By creating a space that is welcoming to all students, incorporating multiple ways for students to engage with the material and demonstrate their knowledge, integrating inclusive course materials, and including high-impact practices such as collaborative learning, you are building the foundation for students from a range of backgrounds to have difficult conversations about challenging topics.

4

CLASS DYNAMICS I

"Do I value discomfort as a part of learning? . . . I think this is a complicated question . . . because there's sort of two levels to the discomfort. One an intellectual and maybe even emotional discomfort, I expect, right? And I do value and I want that to be something that they become comfortable with because . . . it's not a comfortable thing to attempt to see the gray areas, right? Or to not think of things in terms of black and white. . . . So that's one level, of discomfort that I definitely value. . . . But then there's an environmental sort of sense of discomfort that happens within the classroom space itself. . . . I don't know that I would say that I value that so much. So I want there to be a certain level of discomfort, but I don't want the classroom environment or dynamic to be that of discomfort." —Faculty Member (Oleson, 2017)

"In the classroom . . . you should always be able to question or interrogate someone on an intellectual level. If they are making a claim in the intellectual realm, you should be able to dispute it. That should always be up for grabs. . . . You learn so much from disputing or questioning someone else's claim. But, if what they're sharing or claiming or explaining leaves the realm of intellectualism, that is no longer fair game for attack even if you disagree or if you have had an exactly opposite experience. . . . If somebody says something intellectual, you should always be able to question it. But if someone is relating an intellectual idea to their very personal experience or even their general . . . experiences, I think their experience should be safe. But if they are generalizing out of their experience, then you should always be able to question a generalization." —Student (Oleson, 2017)

"I try to make my classroom a safe space for people to disclose things about their personal lives, to put out opinions that may be controversial or bad, and to create a space where we can say 'that person said something that I think is terrible, but let's step back and talk about it.' So I think maybe we need to get away from the idea of safe space being a space where there is no discomfort, there's nothing that upsets you, and it needs to be a safe space where you can be upset and work your upset through some sort of productive way. But I don't think that's what most people mean when they say safe space." —Faculty Member (Oleson, 2017)

T his chapter is the first of two that focus on classroom dynamics, the heart of the book. It primarily concentrates on *preparation* for having difficult conversations in the classroom. It opens with the idea that a college classroom is a small group in which norms influence the interactions between members of the class (Billson, 1986). As an instructor, you need to consider your desired norms and interactions. For instance, my teaching goal is to set up an inclusive, respectful, and intellectually curious classroom environment where students are having spirited and potentially uncomfortable conversations about controversial topics. Although their ideas are often being challenged, it is important that they are free to take intellectual risks and make mistakes and that students of all backgrounds experience this freedom. This chapter explores ways to produce this type of environment. I think through how instructors can not only create a shared understanding between themselves and their students about course content and values but also facilitate discussions about classroom guidelines. This chapter develops a model of discomfort, focusing on ways to foster a discomfort that is essential to growth and learning. This framework for creating productive discomfort takes into account the role of intellectual safety and bravery.

Classroom as a Small Group: Creating Shared Responsibility

In discussion-based courses, it is reasonable to think of the students as making up a *group*, defined as "two or more interdependent individuals who influence one another through social interaction" (Forsyth, 1990, p. 7). Therefore, applying what we know about conformity, norms, and group processes can help us understand and improve classroom teaching and learning (Billson, 1986; Billson & Tiberius, 1991; Fassinger, 1997). For instance, Billson (1986) begins with the foundational principle that "every participant in a group is responsible for the outcome of the group interaction" (p. 144). Given their position, professors clearly have obligations, but students also play a fundamental role in what happens in the classroom. For effective discussion, instructors should seek to create collective ownership in class members' engagement and learning (Oleson, 2015).

Billson (1986) suggests the following concrete ways to empower students to share their ideas and feedback: (a) discuss shared responsibility at the beginning of the course, considering how it affects various elements of the course; (b) provide a clear and comprehensive syllabus that is transparent about not only your course requirements, assignments, and their assessment but also your expectations; (c) allow students to have autonomy over some elements of the course, such as presentation of some material and possibly even how much some assessments are weighted; and (d) obtain anonymous feedback from students early in the course about the strengths and weaknesses of the course and possible ways to improve it. Importantly, these methods for creating group responsibility also promote students' fundamental needs of autonomy, competence, and belonging (Ryan & Deci, 2017), as discussed in chapter 2. Foster shared faculty–student responsibility when setting up the course (on the syllabus and through early class discussions) and seek to maintain it with ongoing input and feedback from students throughout the term.

Norms and Goals of an Inclusive Classroom Space

The university classroom, like any social context, has a set of implicit rules or norms (Howard, 2015). Instructors must be proactive to establish the norms they desire. Right away you should encourage a supportive and inclusive environment (Saunders & Kardia, 1997), creating the expectation that students are to actively engage in discussion (Fassinger, 1995), particularly in classes about sensitive and discomforting topics (Hyde & Ruth, 2002). A useful step is to create a statement for your syllabus that provides expectations and sets your desired classroom climate. In Figure 4.1 I present an example of such syllabus information. You could use it as a template for tailoring your own "words of welcome (and warning)."

Before we turn to consider concrete ways to develop your desired norms, you should think about your broad goals for the learning environment. One of my primary goals is to create a classroom environment where we can grapple with uncertainty and discomfort around challenging topics, while also providing a respectful and socially equitable space. Here I propose a flexible model of productive discomfort to achieve that goal. To understand

Figure 4.1. Syllabus language: Some words of welcome (and warning).

Some Words of Welcome (and Warning)

Congratulations! By enrolling in this course on the social psychology of prejudice, **you have volunteered to engage with a number of socially sensitive and difficult topics that many of your peers (and mine) prefer to avoid.** For much of the course, we will be engaging these topics via a review of the knowledge gained in psychological science on stereotyping, prejudice, and discrimination which should help and encourage us to maintain an academic perspective on these issues. It would be foolish for us, however, to ignore the fact that many of these topics are personally relevant to us in one way or another and, therefore, will provoke emotional responses in addition to intellectual ones. Rather than shying away from these responses, **I believe that personally engaging with and reflecting on these issues will only help to give you a rich and memorable education in the psychology of prejudice, so we will be tackling these responses when they arise head on.**

Note. Vick (2016).

productive discomfort, I consider the relationship between discomfort and learning within the context of the classroom as a safe or brave space.

Productively Creating and Managing Discomfort in Classroom Dynamics and Learning

At times students and faculty could feel uncomfortable in the university classroom. Some discomfort is an essential part of learning and facilitates long-term growth (Gurin et al., 2002; Schrader, 2004). However, as discussed in chapter 2 and later in this chapter, student discomfort may also serve as an obstacle to learning. We will seek to minimize discomfort disruptive to growth and learning.

Productive Discomfort

Here I focus on creating and managing *productive discomfort*. My conception of discomfort fruitful for learning is similar to Crawford Monde's (2016) positive tension and do Mar Pereira's (2012) didactic discomfort. In her definition of *didactic discomfort*, do Mar Pereira (2012) presents it as "intellectual and/or emotional discomfort felt by students" (p. 129). This chapter's opening quote echoes her as the faculty member notes the value of "an intellectual and maybe even emotional discomfort." do Mar Pereira further suggests that this comfort can be prompted "directly or indirectly by the material covered and/or methods deployed in a course" (p. 129). Finally, she suggests that it "is perceived by teachers (and often also by the students themselves) as an experience that can enable or generate learning" (p. 129).

The elements of do Mar Pereira's definition begin to suggest the richness of discomfort. Recent qualitative interviews of faculty and students conducted by my research team further suggest that it is complicated to understand how discomfort can be productive (Oleson, 2017). Some respondents suggested that it was important to take into account the *magnitude* of discomfort that students were experiencing. Too much discomfort could be problematic. These ideas are reminiscent of the Yerkes-Dodson law (Yerkes & Dodson, 1908), which suggests that for difficult tasks a moderate level of arousal best facilitates performance. Many approaches present learning as involving a set of three concentric circles, with one's comfort zone in the inner circle, the learning edge beginning the next circle, and the danger zone on the outer circle (e.g., www.socialjusticetoolbox.com/activity/comfort-zone-learning-edge-danger-zone/). Learning is promoted when individuals are at the edge of their comfort zones (Adams & Bell, 2016; Gurin et al., 2013).

Other respondents suggested that there were *qualitatively different types* of discomfort. Some types of discomfort were helpful for learning but others could be problematic. Relatedly, in Vinton's (2016) research, a factor analysis revealed the following different types of discomfort in the university classroom: (a) students may feel as if they do not belong or that they are not smart enough; (b) students may experience a distressing environment in which they feel as though the professor is making assumptions based on their identities; and (c) students may experience uncomfortable classroom dynamics that are not useful to learning. Instructors must be prepared to step in to manage these types of discomfort.

Based on relevant research and my experiences as an instructor and faculty developer in higher education, I propose that we consider both the magnitude and the type of discomfort. We should strive to balance the amount of discomfort. But we should also seek to keep the discomfort centered on ideas and learning, while reducing discomfort created by questioning someone's worth, intelligence, personal experience, or identity (see opening quotes and chapter 2). Students' personal experiences (e.g., trauma, oppression) and identities may be relevant to the discussion, but you should work to ensure that members of marginalized groups do not experience extra discomfort. Productive discomfort is a moderate level of intellectual or psychological disturbance that students experience as they engage with difficult materials in a learning environment. Instructors can intentionally create it through certain pedagogical approaches, or it can be a side effect of engaging with controversial topics, especially with a diverse group of students. Creating discomfort that is productive for the learning of *all* students involves instructors thoughtfully considering social justice and equity issues in their classroom.

Cognitive Development and Disequilibrium

Discomfort can be valuable for learning because individuals work to resolve discrepancies and unsettling emotions. In chapter 3, when exploring the positive impact of diversity (including inclusive course materials and interactions with peers across difference), I introduced Gurin et al.'s (2002) developmental framework grounded in basic cognitive ideas about how individuals make sense of new information they are learning (Piaget, 1983; Ruble, 1994). Individuals often assimilate new information into preexisting ideas. However, at times they may not be able to make the new information consistent with their current understanding, so they alter their existing schema to be consistent with the newly learned material. When faced with a discrepancy between their beliefs and the new information, they experience a state of disequilibrium, contradiction, and imbalance (Festinger, 1957; Piaget, 1985) and put effort into resolving the discrepancy, which can lead to change. Nagda and Gurin (2013) suggest that a learning environment with interaction between diverse peers could create a desirable level of difficulty where students need to actively engage and work to learn the material, improving long-term retention of knowledge (Bjork & Bjork, 2011). Without the push of difficulty and discomfort, individuals remain comfortable and learn less.

Pedagogy of Discomfort

As noted earlier, this model for productive discomfort also includes issues of power and social inequity. In a classroom where my students and I are experiencing discomforting emotions, I seek to make sure that all students—including those from underrepresented backgrounds—are able to actively engage and thrive during classroom discussion. It is essential to understand the perspectives of more and less advantaged students (Nagda & Gurin, 2013). A pedagogy of discomfort (Boler, 1999; Boler & Zembylas, 2003) is

> grounded upon the idea that discomforting feelings are valuable in challenging dominant beliefs, social habits, and normative practices that sustain social inequities and thus create openings for individual and social transformation. A major requirement, then, of pedagogy of discomfort is that students and teachers are invited to embrace their vulnerability and ambiguity of self and therefore their dependability [*sic*] on others. (Zembylas, 2015, p. 170)

With this approach, faculty seek to create discomfort in themselves and their students. Students' discomfort likely varies, depending on their position. For instance, the discomforting affective responses (guilt, anger, sadness, defensiveness) resulting from classroom discussion of the negative impact of racial prejudice on students' academic lives are often not the same for White and Black students (e.g., Zembylas, 2012). When collectively experiencing uncertainty and discomfort, students and faculty both step (or are pushed) outside their "comfort zones," which results in transformation.

As a foundation when approaching the creation and management of discomfort in your classroom, I encourage you to ask three questions posed by Zembylas and McGlynn (2012):

1. How appropriate is it to engage students in activities that create discomforting situations;
2. How effective are discomforting pedagogies in creating transformative possibilities for students; and
3. How can a teacher deal with students' discomforting emotions in ways that are ethically and pedagogically acceptable? (p. 54)

Let's consider each of these questions in turn.

Appropriateness of Creating Discomfort. First, classroom discussions and activities about sensitive or controversial topics that are likely to generate discomfort, or positive tension, should be done for clear pedagogical reasons (Crawford Monde, 2016; Zembylas & McGlynn, 2012). A thoughtful instructor "does not promote discomfort for its own sake" (Leonardo & Porter, 2010, p. 153). It is appropriate to create discomfort when it is critical for students' learning. For instance, many instructors of workshops on social justice or academic courses on stereotyping and prejudice ask students to complete a measure of implicit bias, such as the implicit association test (implicit.harvard.edu/implicit/). This pedagogical practice causes students to grapple with and reflect on their stereotypes or prejudices toward other groups (e.g., Nadan & Stark, 2017). Both understanding in a firsthand way how this measure works (including its strengths and limitations) and experiencing discomfort as you reflect on your own potential for bias could greatly enhance students' learning.

Impact of Discomfort. The second question to consider is whether the discomfort you are creating has the intended effect of facilitating student learning and transformation. Certainly discomfort can have a critical impact: intergroup dialogues instigate intellectual and personal growth in students (e.g., Gurin et al., 2002; Hurtado, 2005). Experiencing discomfort that pushes them out of their comfort zones can help students understand perspectives of those who are different from them (Coulter et al., 2013; Leibowitz et al., 2010). Additionally, classroom discomfort may be particularly helpful for students' learning when used in combination with instructors trying to empathize and understand students' perspectives that they find problematic or offensive (Zembylas, 2012; Zembylas & Papmichael, 2017). It is worth striving for the "sweet spot" where you are getting students out of their comfort zone but are not causing them to be overly distressed.

Yet, in practice, managing discomfort can be challenging to do in a pedagogically responsible way, and it is not always successful. As do Mar Pereira (2012) notes, it takes "time, energy, and emotional availability" (p. 133) to manage discomfort in ways productive for learning in the college classroom. Based on her literature review, she argues for building in extra time in class and during office hours to engage with students' discomfort. She further recommends including time for students to dialogue with each other, to personally reflect on their experiences, and to get to know each other. A classroom filled with discomforting emotions can be transformative, but instructors need to approach it responsibly, building in the necessary time, energy, and resources.

To enhance the educational benefits, I would especially encourage time for students to reflect on the discussion (see also Nadan & Stark, 2017).

I recommend Brookfield's (1995) critical incident questionnaire (CIQ, see www.stephenbrookfield.com), where students write down their reactions to classroom dynamics. The standard CIQ contains the following questions:

- At what moment in class this week did you feel most engaged with what was happening?
- At what moment in class this week were you most distanced from what was happening?
- What action that anyone (teacher or student) took this week did you find most affirming or helpful?
- What action that anyone took this week did you find most puzzling or confusing?
- What about the class this week surprised you the most? (This could be about your own reactions to what went on, something that someone did, or anything else that occurs.) (Brookfield, 1995, p. 34)

You could adapt this type of short questionnaire to encourage students to reflect on these items (or a subset of them) when there is classroom discomfort. You could update the wording to foster students' consideration of many perspectives or ask them to research the subject so they are able to integrate different viewpoints into their reflection (see Warren, n.d.).

Ethical Implications of a Pedagogy of Discomfort. Third, you must consider the potentially complicated ethical issues that a pedagogy of discomfort raises, especially if you are explicitly creating (rather than merely responding to) discomfort. As the architect of this discomfort, you are responsible (in collaboration with your students) for constructing a learning environment where students are able to approach and manage the discomforting emotions. For instance, earlier I suggested that it could be pedagogically appropriate to ask students to complete a measure of implicit bias. However, you must consider how to best approach and discuss this exercise, because measures like the implicit association test do not have the precision to diagnose a specific person's bias (e.g., Blanton & Jaccard, 2006; Jost, 2019). Instead think of "the IAT mainly as an educational tool to develop awareness of implicit preferences and stereotypes" (Project Implicit, 2011). Additionally, students often become defensive at the possibility that they are prejudiced (Howell et al., 2015). Inducing this discomfort could backfire.

But if students see biases as open to change (they have a growth mindset toward their biases), then they may be more open to the possibility that they are prejudiced (e.g., Carr et al., 2012; Murphy & Oleson, 2019). In my stereotyping and prejudice course, for instance, I include a TED Talk on the first day of class by Jay Smooth entitled "How I Learned to Stop Worrying and Love Discussing Race" (www.youtube.com/watch?v=MbdxeFcQtaU). Smooth presents the idea of racism using what he calls "the dental hygiene" approach. Rather than thinking of racism as something that a person has or does not have, consider it to be something that one needs to engage with each day, like brushing one's teeth. In this case, letting others know that they said something prejudiced is then shifted from calling them prejudiced people to presenting them as individuals with "something racist stuck in (their) teeth." Finally, you could do an exercise about bias in which you ask students to read case studies, or vignettes, that are not real but capture nuanced variables of interest. Students may be able to discuss a heated topic in this way that is less personal, allowing them to experience a productive level of discomfort (Crawford Monde, 2016).

Both ethically and practically, how should instructors create an inclusive learning environment that promotes students' meaningful and constructive engagement with discomforting materials? To help answer this question, I examine the value of treating the classroom as a safe space yet conclude that there are limits to this approach, given power imbalances and issues of social inequity (MacDonald, 2013). I then examine bravery and propose Verduzco-Baker's (2018) modified brave space as a thoughtful foundation. Before turning to explore safety and bravery, I encourage you to stop to reflect on the discomforting situations that occur in your classroom, answering the three questions posed by Zembylas and McGlynn (2012). Table 4.1 could serve as a template for your reflection. Is the discomfort that you are creating appropriate, effective, and ethical?

The Classroom as an Intellectually Safe Space or Brave Space

Many argue that it is important to make the college classroom an intellectually or psychologically safe space where students feel free to take risks to participate and be challenged in discussions about controversial and identity-relevant topics (e.g., Delano-Oriaran & Parks, 2015; Gayle et al., 2013; Holley & Steiner, 2005; Hyde & Ruth, 2002; Purdie-Vaughns et al., 2008). This learning environment supports students from a range of backgrounds to engage meaningfully with discomforting materials. In her analysis of the classroom as a group, Billson (1986) asserts that "when people feel psychologically safe in a group, their participation levels will increase" (principle 4, p. 145). She encourages faculty to create a safe classroom environment where students can express "unconventional ideas and offbeat solutions" (p. 145). Others argue that there are weaknesses in conceiving of the classroom as a "safe space" and instead recommend a "brave space." I present these various approaches, considering limitations with each.

TABLE 4.1
Creating Discomforting Situations: Appropriate, Effective, and Ethical

Discomfort Created	Appropriateness	Effectiveness	Ethical and Pedagogical Acceptability

Intellectual Safety
Based on student survey data, Schrader (2004) defined *intellectual safety* as

a caring environment in which the professor is open and caring, demonstrates respect, and embraces the uniqueness of students and their perspectives and does so in a classroom format [in which] all are invited to participate actively, engage in personal self-disclosure while trusting the confidentiality of such openness, and where the professor maintains a sense of control and direction to facilitate learning." (p. 98)

Further survey research (Holley & Steiner, 2005) revealed that students see instructors of safe classroom spaces as fair and respectful, self-disclosing, knowledgeable, challenging students and discussing controversial ideas/embracing conflict, and using guidelines for discussion.

As is clear in these descriptions of safe spaces containing conflict, controversy, and challenge (Holley & Steiner, 2005), safe is not equivalent to comfortable (Byron, 2017). Yet as one of this chapter's opening quotes suggests, a safe space can be seen as one *without* conflict, struggle, or pain (Boostrom, 1998; Byron, 2017) where "individuals can retreat from ideas and perspectives at odds with their own" (Ellison, 2016). When the term *safe space* was first introduced in the 1960s, it often indicated a physical space where members of marginalized groups could gather separately and be free from discrimination (Kenney, 2001). More recently, the idea of safety or a safe space has been updated and applied to other contexts, including classrooms, where individuals from a variety of backgrounds can experience discomforting emotions as they respectfully discuss difficult topics. My own qualitative research conducted with faculty and students, however, suggests that there are varying understandings of what it means to have intellectual safety in the classroom and whether safety or a safe space would be valuable (Oleson, 2017). One person could reject the idea of safety because it inhibits students' risk-taking, whereas another could embrace it because it allows one to be able to take risks, free from harassment. While having different responses to the value of "safety," both seek to promote risk-taking. Terms such as *intellectual safety* or *safe space* can each be defined in contradictory and ambiguous ways (e.g., Barrett, 2010), making them problematic terms to use to communicate. In addition, understanding intellectual safety in the classroom becomes more complicated if one takes into account students' approaches to learning.

Intellectual Safety and Students' Approaches to Learning

As discussed in chapter 2, an understanding of how you and your students approach classroom learning may help you assess their safety and discomfort. These approaches to learning can be conceived of as being along a continuum (Schrader, 2004). At one end, students see knowledge as being absolute (true or false); they look to their professors to teach them. In the middle positions, students realize that there are multiple perspectives rather than one absolute one. At the opposite end, students see their knowledge as more dependent on the particular context and the supporting evidence; they begin to see themselves as agents in their own learning. Intellectual safety takes into consideration not only a "fit" between instructors' and students' approaches to learning but also a safe respectful environment (Schrader, 2004). An instructor's goal is often to help students challenge their current assumptions, norms, and ways of learning, which creates discomfort. In response, students could "stretch" and develop, changing their prior ideas, but such changes may occur *only* if instructors and other students support them in this process (Schrader, 2004). Without such support, students may resist change. For discomfort to lead to productive change, students may need a safe environment (Coulter et al., 2013; Zembylas & Glynn, 2012).

Limits With Conceiving of the Classroom as a Safe Space. As noted earlier, however, this notion of a safe space is problematic given its varying definitions. But the chief difficulty is that the concept of safety could implicitly assume colorblindness in which the classroom is safe for everyone, regardless of background (hooks, 1994; Leonardo & Porter, 2010). As Barrett (2010) argues,

> students who belong to racially, socially, or economically marginalized groups live in a world which is inherently unsafe—a world where racialization, sexism, ableism, classism, and heteronormativity pose genuine threats to their psychological, social, material, and physical well-being. To contend that the classroom can be a safe space for these students when the world outside is not, is not only unrealistic, it is dangerous. (p. 7)

Similarly, Leonardo and Porter (2010) argue that "for marginalized and oppressed minorities, *there is no safe space*" (p. 149). By asserting that the classroom *is* a safe space for all students, I am treating everyone as equivalent—potentially reinforcing current power structures and denying the general lack of safety for marginalized students. Additionally, students who are members of dominant groups may question the safety of safe spaces because their privilege is threatened (Ludlow, 2004).

As a student shared in a qualitative interview with my research team, calling a classroom a safe space does not then make it safe for everyone (Oleson, 2017). Instead, the student suggested that saying that it *is* a safe space can prevent people from working to make it safe. Students might feel free to say anything without worrying about the consequences; they do not need to take into account others' perspectives because everything is already set up to be safe. Ludlow (2004) presents an additional concern with designating a classroom a safe space when discussing social justice concerns: threats to one's privilege may be seen as violating safety.

The Classroom as a Risky or Brave Space

Emphasizing safety in the classroom is clearly not enough (Redmond, 2010). A different image of the college classroom would be useful. In response, Arao and Clemens (2013) argue for presenting difficult dialogues about race and other topics as being in *brave spaces* rather than safe ones (see also Singleton & Linton, 2006, who emphasize courage). Being safe, they note, can be seen as free from discomfort. Although many advocates of safe spaces argue that safety is what allows people to be uncomfortable and to take risks, Arao and Clemens suggest that we should instead focus on the bravery that risk-taking entails. When engaging with difficult topics, there are likely to be danger and threats, and one must be daring to respond. Students in a brave space, however, "will have the courage to face that danger and to take risks because they know they will be taken care of—that painful or difficult experiences will be acknowledged and supported, not avoided or eliminated" (Cook-Sather, 2016, p. 1).

Modified Brave Space. Recently, Verduzco-Baker (2018) proposed an updated version of a brave space designed specifically for university classrooms. Her modified brave space takes into account that—similar to the classroom not being equally safe for everyone—it may also demand differing amounts of bravery (Zheng, 2016). For instance, consider my social psychology class on stereotyping and prejudice. In this class I could encourage students to be brave, bringing in their unique perspectives and challenging others' viewpoints. One student could argue for a colorblind approach, suggesting that the United States is a fair place where everyone has access to the American dream—regardless of their racial background or social class. It would take great bravery for a student of color or from a lower socioeconomic background to counteract this argument, potentially based on personal experience in addition to class readings.

To lighten this extra burden to be brave placed on marginalized students, Verduzco-Baker (2018) suggests faculty:

1. integrate first-person "virtual" accounts of personal experiences of oppression in the curriculum to eliminate dependence upon students to do this,
2. practice "calling in" rather than "calling out" to challenge uninformed or biased beliefs, and
3. model being brave in their own response to being "called in" (p. 588).

Verduzco-Baker then describes each of these three strategies in more detail. During her courses on race and ethnicity, over the first few class meetings she includes many resources—blogs, qualitative studies, videos—to provide students with a rich understanding of personal experience of discrimination. She also encourages a classroom culture of "calling in" (Trần, 2013) for herself and her students. She begins with the assumption that members of the class are all trying to understand difficult and challenging issues and that sometimes students or faculty will make mistakes—saying the wrong thing, offending others, and so on. When calling others in, one explains the impact of their behavior to help them understand why it is problematic so that they change it in the future. When I call in others or they call me in, we can care for each other and help one another improve. A productive call-in climate is facilitated by individuals being open to learning new ways to respond. In response to their being called in, instructors should model brave responses (Verduzco-Baker, 2018), similar to modeling a growth mindset (Dweck, 2006). You use the correction as an opportunity to grow and learn. You could ask for additional information as well as stress that you will work to teach yourself.

TABLE 4.2
Role of Discomfort and Safety in Your Classroom

What is the role of discomfort in class? (For example, are you explicitly trying to create it? are you managing comfort that emerges from discomforting topics?)	What is the role of safety or bravery in your classroom? Do either of these metaphors seem relevant to your classroom dynamics? Consider how the classroom might be unequally safe or brave; propose ways to reduce inequity.

Students are then seen as having expertise, yet they know that you do not see it as their responsibility to educate you (Verduzco-Baker, 2018).

I encourage you to take time to consider how discomfort and safety or bravery play out in your classroom (see Table 4.2). What is the role of discomfort? Safety or bravery?

Using Transparency to Create Your Desired Classroom Space

Be clear about the atmosphere that you are attempting to create in your classroom. Early class discussions in which you and your students are transparent about desired norms and values can reduce misperceptions. The popular media often presents faculty and students' viewpoints on discomfort and safety as opposed to each other, with students wanting to be safe and free from discomfort (Friedersdorf, 2015). However, for many years my research team has been collecting data on student and faculty perceptions about the college classroom as a discomforting or safe space, and we have found that what students and faculty perceive to be the case can be different than what they actually report (Oleson, 2019; Oleson, Vinton, Buttrill, Murphy, & Harris, 2018; Oleson, Vinton, Buttrill, Murphy, Harris, & Yang, 2018; Vinton & Oleson, 2017). For instance, the *perceptions* of students and faculty members' values often mirror what is reported in the popular press—students are seen as valuing safety more than faculty members are, whereas professors are perceived as valuing discomfort and challenge more than students do. Their actual responses, however, suggest that these perceptions may at times be *misperceptions*. The value that faculty and students place on discomfort, challenge, and safety are often similar to each other. Importantly, these discrepancies could have implications for how students and faculty approach classroom discussion. I would recommend open conversation to clear up initial misunderstandings and assumptions.

Setting Up Norms for Classroom Discussion

You have now done some work to consider what is important in your desired learning environment. I turn next to concrete ways for you to establish classroom norms and expectations to support discussion in which all students engage and thrive. Recognized approaches for promoting conversations about sensitive topics with diverse groups stress setting guidelines, ground rules, or norms before beginning discussion (e.g., Adams & Bell, 2016; Brookfield & Preskill, 2005; Landis, 2008; Singleton & Linton, 2006).

Let's begin by thinking through some sample guidelines for you to consider. To create a brave space in which one can have dialogues about social justice issues, Arao and Clemens (2013) propose the following guidelines: (a) "controversy with civility," (b) "own your intentions and impact," (c) "challenge by choice," (d) "respect," and (e) "no attacks" (pp. 143–149). They argue that "controversy with civility" is a more useful alternative to a common guideline of "agree to disagree" because it pushes people to continue bravely discussing ideas rather than opting to avoid the discomfort of disagreeing. They also encourage participants to own their intentions and impact, rather than the common guideline of "don't take things personally." One must be brave to take responsibility for one's impact—even it was not what one had intended.

Singleton and Linton (2006) present a set of group commitments to use when facilitating courageous conversations about race. Their group agreements are: (a) "Stay engaged," (b) "Experience discomfort," (c) "Speak your truth," and (d) "Expect and accept non-closure" (p. 58). They stress that participants need to remain involved in the discussion, being honest about what they are thinking, even as they are experiencing the discomfort that comes with conversations about race. Such discussions often take time. Everything is not necessarily going to be resolved; being open to uncertainty is crucial. Hollins and Govan (2015, Appendix C) expand on Singleton and Linton's agreements, adding more: (e) no fixing, (f) take risks, and (g) listen for understanding. They encourage participants in their courageous conversations about race workshops to not try to fix other people, to take risks because these risks offer opportunities for growth, and to actively listen, trying to understand others' experiences "without thinking about how you are going to respond" (p. 148). In a classroom setting, students may have concerns about saying something that is not smart or is offensive, which may lead them to avoid taking risks and to mentally rehearse what they are going to say. Stressing risk-taking and careful active listening is important. When facilitating courageous conversations about race workshops, Hollins and Govan suggest that facilitators furnish these norms, responding to questions and providing clarification, but not encouraging a conversation about updating the norms.

Collaboratively Creating Classroom Guidelines

Difficult conversations with students in a university class likely differ in a number of ways from those happening in workshops on interracial conversations. Workshops are often focused on students from different backgrounds having a difficult dialogue about a specific topic, such as race relations. There are established approaches, for instance, for conducting intergroup dialogues (Nagda & Gurin, 2013; Zúñiga et al., 2007). In a university class there may be some dialogue, but the focus is often on students learning the ideas within an academic discipline, such as the methods and findings about race relations in sociology (Verduzco-Baker, 2018). University classes vary from instructor to instructor and involve a group of students meeting over a long period of time, typically for an academic term. In these varying classes, it may be important to *collaboratively* create norms when teaching about difficult topics, social justice, and diversity (see Adams & Bell, 2016, p. 40; Landis, 2008, p. 12) to promote shared responsibility (e.g., Billson, 1986). For example, Kate Duffly (2015) recommends "working with students to collectively create a set of guidelines unique to that group. These guidelines become our commitment as a group to actively engage in creating a productive and rewarding class together." Although each group of students generates distinctive ground rules, she presents examples of some that classes have generated (see Figure 4.2.).

Students and faculty can together create ground rules in a variety of ways. For instance, Brookfield and Preskill (2005; see also Brookfield, 2013,

Figure 4.2.   Examples of Collectively Created Class Guidelines.

"Let the classroom be a space to test ideas."

"Make space for people to talk: Step up and step aside."

"Disagree compassionately."

"Accept when you are wrong and move on."

"Don't make assumptions about people."

"Recognize the difference between feeling uncomfortable and unsafe."

"Assume the best intentions in others."

Note. Duffly (2015).

2015) have a well-established method in which students start to develop the rules by taking time to consider the best and worst group discussions they have had. Students are then asked to talk with a group of three students about what works and what doesn't work for them in group discussions. As a group, they look for ideas they have in common and develop a list of features of good and bad discussions they agree on. Next they come up with three specific ways to create the features of the best discussions and three specific ways to avoid the features of the worst ones. After creating these concrete proposals, all groups come together to develop an overall set of agreed-upon classroom guidelines. This process allows students to bring in their individual ideas and consider them in a small-group discussion before bringing all the ideas together as an entire class.

Challenges With Classroom Guidelines

Unfortunately, guidelines may inadvertently reinforce power differences and privilege, rather than create an equitable and inclusive environment as intended (Arao & Clemens, 2013; Hackman, 2008; Sensoy & DiAngelo, 2014). When coming up with guidelines, a person is influenced by established societal standards of what a classroom should be like, so a seemingly unbiased set of ground rules may be "White, male, middle-class ideals being disguised as a neutral set of beliefs" (Hackman, 2008, p. 38). Even guidelines commonly used in social justice classes may reinforce inequity (Sensoy & DiAngelo, 2014). For instance, "everyone's opinion matters," "assume good intentions," and "speak from experience" may exacerbate power differentials rather than reduce them by making it seem as though the guidelines have made everyone equal and equally safe, regardless of their background. Instead, Sensoy and DiAngelo (2014) argue for alternative guidelines such as "Differentiate between opinion—which everyone has—and informed knowledge, which comes from sustained experience, study, and practice. Hold your opinions lightly and with humility"; "Recognize how your own social positionality (e.g., race, class, gender, sexuality, ability) informs your perspectives and reactions to your instructor and those whose work you study in the course"; "Differentiate between safety and discomfort. Accept discomfort as necessary for social justice growth" (p. 8). They encourage students to make their claims into questions in order to stimulate new information, enhance their critical thinking, and promote humility.

My reading of the various takes on classroom guidelines suggests a few key ideas. First, you may have a set of guidelines that you think are essential for creating an inclusive classroom environment that promotes your goals, such as goals for productive discussion, engaging with multiple perspectives, active listening to others, or providing a space for students who typically do not feel comfortable talking to feel comfortable. If certain guidelines capture your goals, then you could approach the task, as Hollins and Govan (2015) suggest, by presenting the norms, answering questions and clarifying them, but not encouraging an updating of them. This method can also ensure that guidelines that might prove power-reinforcing (Sensoy & DiAngelo, 2014) are not adopted as central ones. Arao and Clemens (2013), Singleton and Linton (2006), Hollins and Govan (2015), and Sensoy and DiAngelo (2014) provide possible guidelines.

Second, developing ground rules in collaboration with students in your course will create a shared sense of responsibility (Billson, 1986) and take into account the unique constellation of students in your course (Duffly, 2015). Because ground rules may reinforce cultural norms of dominant groups (Hackman, 2008), I first ask students to write down their suggestions *anonymously*. My hope is that they will feel freer to suggest ideas that are outside the established ones. I then bring all suggestions to the whole class to discuss. If guidelines that I felt were important were not suggested, I too could put in a couple anonymous suggestions and let the class know that I also participated.

Third, I encourage you to consider the potential role of confidentiality in your classroom guidelines. In recent years, students and faculty colleagues have noted their concerns when conversations that occurred in the classroom are discussed in contexts outside the classroom, including posts on social media (Oleson, 2017). In recent years, one of my students suggested a classroom guideline of "Vegas rules—what happens here, stays here, no gossiping outside the classroom." Similarly, at a recent faculty development workshop I attended, Dereca Blackmon stressed, "What is said here, stays *here*. What is learned here, leaves here." If students feel that their responses will be kept confidential, they may feel freer to take risks (Schrader, 2004).

Using Table 4.3 as a worksheet, start to develop your classroom guidelines and ways to create them for your courses.

Preparing Students for Discussions About Difficult Content

In addition to setting up classroom norms for discussion that are situated within your broader pedagogical goals, it is also important to provide information and set expectations about the course material.

TABLE 4.3
Worksheet: Developing Classroom Guidelines

First, consider what you see as the goals for productive classroom discussion. Second, consider possible obstacles to reaching those goals, such as student resistance, quiet students, power dynamics, and so on. Third, consider concrete ways to create your classroom guidelines, such as coming in with a set of guidelines, collaboratively creating them, and so forth.

Goals that you have for classroom discussion	Potential obstacles to reaching those goals	Ways to approach coming up with classroom guidelines

Providing Information

We strive to create a space where the increasingly diverse group of undergraduates (Espinosa et al., 2019) have robust discussions about controversial topics such as immigration, sexual assault, discrimination in the criminal justice system, and genocide. Thorpe (2016) argues that this more diverse student body has widened the scope of issues discussed in the university classroom. How do we prepare ourselves and our students to have these wide-ranging, intellectually challenging, and identity-relevant discussions with students from varying backgrounds?

Content Forecasts

One way to help prepare students is through "trigger warnings" (Knox, 2017), or "content forecasts" (Stringer, 2016), which involve informing students about the content of upcoming material that could be considered uncomfortable, offensive, sensitive, or distressing—although there has been much discussion about the pros and cons of using such forewarnings in higher education (e.g., American Association of University Professors [AAUP], 2014; George & Hovey, 2019; Wilson, 2015). Wendy Wyatt (2016) summarizes the spirited debate about trigger warnings, presenting seven arguments opposing their use (e.g., they limit free speech by having a "chilling effect," minimizing discomfort can inhibit learning, instructors cannot predict all triggers) and four arguments in favor (e.g., they facilitate dialogue about difficult topics, they promote transparency and respect). She asks,

> Why such strong responses? It is my contention that, at its essence, the issue is about several of our most cherished ethical commitments: freedom, truth, respect, care for others and avoidance of harm. The challenge is that in the case of trigger warnings, these commitments can conflict; professors can't, in a simple way, honor them all. (Wyatt, 2016, p. 23)

Her analysis rings true to me. When in the classroom, I seek to ensure that students are free to take risks, to disagree, and to experience the discomfort that learning involves. But I also want students to feel respected and not overly distressed. I value creating a socially just space where individuals of all backgrounds—including those traditionally underrepresented in higher education—are actively engaging in discussion (see also Spencer & Kulbaga, 2018).

Framework for Providing Information About Sensitive Content
I present a framework for deciding if, when, and how to provide information about sensitive content. I generally find the phrase "trigger warnings" to be too loaded and therefore often unhelpful. My favorite description of this information about potentially distressing content is "content forecasts," a phrase Stringer (2016) uses given that is it "more benign and approachable" (p. 65). Wyatt's (2016) recent essay on the ethics of trigger warnings serves as my foundation for *if* and *when* to provide warnings. She argues that warnings should not be required and are typically unnecessary. She then proposes three elements for instructors to consider when deciding whether to use warnings for specific course materials: "content, context, and mutual obligations" (p. 31).

   Content. In terms of content, Wyatt advocates a "shared standards" principle in which faculty assess what included course content might be triggering for students. She provides examples of such material that she uses in class, including the video of the beheading of James Foley by members of ISIS. She recommends that professors first consider what *they* think might be distressing. Next, instructors can look to *others'* ideas for what might need forewarning. As an example, she presents her course material of a graphic photo of a woman being sexually assaulted by a crowd; the Seattle *Post-Intelligencer* decided not to print the photo, which was taken by one of its photographers. Wyatt argues that the newspaper's decision not to publish the photo should be considered when determining whether to provide a warning. Finally, she encourages faculty to listen to what their *students* suggest to be disturbing content. Overall, Wyatt contends that the guiding principle is to support all students in preparing for the course material. She makes clear that the goal of using trigger warnings is not to curb one's academic freedom but to create a productive learning environment.

Developing Shared Standards. Recent survey studies may be useful in developing shared standards for when warnings could be useful. A growing body of research has examined students' (Bentley, 2017; Beverly et al., 2018; Boysen et al., 2018; Cares et al., 2018; Lowe, 2015) and professors' (Boysen & Prieto, 2018; Boysen et al., 2016) perceptions of trigger warnings to understand not only how trigger warnings are generally viewed but also what content might merit warnings. Research suggests that students have neutral or mixed (Bentley, 2017; Beverly et al., 2018) to positive perceptions (Boysen et al., 2018; Cares et al., 2018) of trigger warnings. Students believe that such warnings are beneficial for those who have previously experienced trauma (Bentley, 2017); yet surveys of students in victimology courses revealed that students who had previously experienced victimization did not differ in their attitudes toward trigger warnings (Cares et al., 2018). Additional research with adults in an online sample found support for using trigger warnings (Bellet et al., 2018). There has been less systematic study of professors; surveys suggest that instructors have negative to neutral (Boysen et al., 2016) or neutral to slightly positive (Boysen & Prieto, 2018) perceptions of trigger warnings. Recent survey research with a national sample of students and faculty suggests that students generally see content warnings as more important in the classroom than faculty do (Buttrill, 2018).

Studies exploring specific content suggest that students in psychology courses believe that it is necessary to include warnings about the topics of sexual assault, child abuse, and suicide; these were also the three topics that students reported the most discomfort discussing in class (Boysen et al., 2018). Warnings were likewise seen as necessary for violence/trauma and self-harm. Additionally, students noted that it is necessary to include warnings about racial issues, sexuality, and gender, but students indicated that faculty often did not include warnings about these topics. Boysen and his colleagues found that students identifying as female or outside the gender binary found discussing such topics to be more distressing than did those who identified as male. A recent survey of psychology instructors found that they shared students' beliefs about trauma-related topics necessitating warnings: sexual assault, child abuse, violent/catastrophic trauma, and suicide received the highest ratings (Boysen & Prieto, 2018). Both students (Boysen et al., 2018) and faculty (Boysen & Prieto, 2018) felt it was important to

TABLE 4.4
Worksheet: Assessing What Course Content Might Be Distressing or Traumatic

My Intuitions	Perspectives of Others	Student Input

include content about these topics. Both groups also reported that students should realize that they are going to be learning about these sensitive topics and that faculty should not avoid covering them.

I encourage you to consider what material you include that might be distressing for students to discuss in class (see Table 4.4.). In psychology courses, for instance, topics such as sexual assault, child abuse, and suicide might prove traumatic. The goal is not to get rid of material whose subject matter is important for your course but to consider what content—based on your intuitions, others' perspectives, or students' input—might be best presented with forewarning.

Context. This framework next takes into account the classroom context by asking three questions: "What is the course? Who are the students? And what is the structure?" (Wyatt, 2016, p. 27). The instructor is focusing on the norms and expectations about the specific course, the students taking it, and how the class is organized. Some classes (e.g., Psychology of Trauma) clearly contain materials about violence; students are prepared—or at least expect—to learn about sensitive topics. Transparent presentation on the syllabus and during initial class meetings could ensure that students understand the course content. Specific warnings may be unnecessary. Other courses (e.g., Introduction to Art History) might incorporate visual images of violence that a student had not realized would be included. A warning could be useful in this case.

You should additionally consider the students in your course. Are they new to college, to this subject area, to your teaching? Have you interacted with them in previous courses so that you know them well and they are familiar with the kinds of material covered? Also reflect on the identities and self-doubts that they could bring to the class (see chapter 2). Would some student identities make interacting with your material more distressing or make students less prepared about what to expect? Are there student concerns that might make learning about certain material more difficult unless they had time to prepare themselves? With students new to college or to your classes, Wyatt suggests being more open to providing warnings because they might not know what to expect.

Finally, in terms of context, Wyatt (2016) recommends taking into account the course's structure—its size and format (e.g., lecture, small-group discussion). She argues that it is particularly important to consider the negative impact of course material when teaching a large course. As she notes, "the nature of a large class means many details about students are a mystery, and mysteries necessitate care" (pp. 28–29). As an instructor, I am motivated to be clear about expectations. With many unknowns ("mysteries"), it is more important for me to step in, providing additional information and attention.

Wyatt (2016) considers a different approach, however, for courses where you are actively engaging with the material through ongoing classroom discussion, as is the focus of this book. "Giving opportunities for engagement with emotionally hazardous material recognizes its power, and this engagement likely serves as a more useful pedagogical approach than offering a simple warning" (p. 29). Here the focus needs to be on the ways that one grapples deeply with the sensitive material. A professor could decide to provide forewarning (or not) but needs to realize that the specific classroom dynamics are of primary importance. The classroom discussion can go in unpredictable and potentially difficult directions, which there has not been a warning about, because those topics are important to students (see Thorpe, 2016). Warnings could be an additional tool, but they are not a substitute for the hard work of engaging students in respectful discussion about sensitive topics.

Mutual Obligations. Finally, this framework includes mutual obligations (Wyatt, 2016), taking into account the roles that students and faculty bring as active agents in creating the learning environment. It is critical that faculty seek to create an environment of trust and respect where students are empowered to advocate for themselves; students and faculty alike value feeling respected in the college classroom (Oleson, 2019). For instance, on my syllabus I include language about our college honor principle, student accommodations for disability, and the types of difficult and sensitive topics that we are exploring in this class. (See chapter 2 for additional suggestions for information to include on a syllabus.) For my class policies and principles, I encourage students to speak to me if they anticipate any issues. If they talk to me about accommodations for disabilities or if they share potential concerns about engaging with certain materials, it is my job to treat them with respect and, if appropriate, provide accommodations (see Taylor, 2017, for consideration of how trigger warnings can be part of accommodation).

However, as Wyatt (2016) notes, it is also reasonable to expect and encourage students who are dealing with trauma to be working on coping. My role is as a teacher, not a therapist. As an instructor, however, I can be a kind person who assists in students' receiving the help and support they need through the campus health center, trained sexual assault advocates, and other community resources (e.g., financial assistance, campus food pantry). While some advocate for faculty to encourage students to seek treatment instead of using trigger warnings (e.g., Roff, 2014), I do not see these approaches as mutually exclusive. Regardless of your decisions about trigger warnings, you should understand the resources available to students who are struggling.

Impact of Trigger Warnings on Student Distress
This analysis for approaching trigger warnings has considered student and faculty *perceptions*, but it has not examined research on the *actual* impact of warnings. In his review of relevant empirical research on trauma and distress, Boysen (2017) concluded that empirical clinical research supports the following ideas: (a) trauma can trigger distress, so students with post-traumatic stress disorder (PTSD) diagnoses might ask for an accommodation including trigger warnings for their disabilities, and (b) this accommodation might help students regulate their exposure to the distressing material, resulting in lower distress and better functioning. In practice, however, it may be difficult to implement effective warnings, Boysen cautioned, given that students may not have documented diagnoses and triggers might be specific to an individual. Warnings might also lead to expectations of higher distress. Boysen advocated research specifically examining trigger warnings.

Fortunately there is now a growing body of work exploring the effect of trigger warnings on individuals' expectations and feelings of distress. In five separate papers (Bellet et al., 2018; Boysen et al., 2019; Bridgland et al., 2019; Gainsburg & Earl, 2018; Sanson et al., 2019), researchers experimentally manipulated trigger warnings (e.g., "*TRIGGER WARNING: The passage you are about to read contains disturbing content and may trigger an anxiety response, especially in those who have a history of trauma*" [Bellet et al., 2018, p. 137]) to assess their psychological impact. Across these five research papers there was limited support for trigger warnings having a positive effect on individuals' distress. But it is important to note a limitation of these samples:

the participants were often not students and had not necessarily experienced previous trauma. In some studies, being warned raised preemptive negative emotions, suggesting that trigger warnings may lead participants to *expect* more negative affect than having no warning. Being warned also impacted participants' beliefs—for example, they believed that warnings were more necessary (Boysen et al., 2019). There was a little evidence that trigger warnings could reduce negative affect when experiencing the distressing material (Gainsburg & Earl, 2018); however, Bellet et al. (2018) found increased distress for participants who believed words could be harmful. In most of the studies the warnings had limited effect on respondents' experiences of distress. The take-home message of the research is that warnings had little impact; they may not particularly help or harm our students.

Ways to Present Expectations and Information

I encourage us to integrate this empirical research within our broader framework of if, when, and how to approach trigger warnings in the university classroom. As a first step, it is important to consider the specific manipulations used in these studies—participants are often warned that they may experience anxiety or distress. One of the key research findings to come out of social psychology is that one's expectations can have a powerful impact on what individuals see, how they act, and how others react to them (e.g., Darley & Gross, 1983; Klein & Snyder, 2003). Similarly, within the medical field, expectations of a negative outcome can be self-fulfilling, as when expecting pain leads to a higher experience of pain (Benedetti et al., 2007; Petrie & Rief, 2019). Trigger-warning research suggests that telling students they may experience anxiety reactions could lead them to expect to experience anxiety.

Therefore, it seems important to present warnings or information about content in ways that are neutral and designed to minimize negative expectations. In a recent qualitative interview (Oleson, 2017), a student suggested that trigger warnings could be thought of as ingredient lists. It is useful and courteous to let someone know when a food contains peanuts in case they do not like peanuts or are allergic to them (see also LaBossiere, 2014). In a similar vein, Spencer and Kulbaga (2018) argue that supplying information about distressing material is similar to other kinds of information that we provide to help students prepare for class. They note that instructors often make suggestions for ways to approach a reading that is particularly difficult intellectually—"The reading for Wednesday is probably the most challenging piece we read all semester. . . . The beginning where the author explains the theory she uses, is much harder than the rest—so if you feel overwhelmed, keep going, as it does get easier as you go along" (Spencer & Kulbaga, 2018, p. 115). They suggest an analogous approach for distressing material, providing information about content and ways for students to approach the reading and their responses to classroom discussion about it:

> The reading for Monday focuses on sexual assault and includes some graphic descriptions of legal cases of rape and intimate partner violence, so I want you to realize that and be prepared for it. As we discuss the reading on Monday, remember that we expect people to be free to share openly and agree or disagree civilly (with the reading, with the instructor, or with each other). Please be aware that this is a common enough experience that we likely have students in class that have experienced it (or know someone who has). Feel free to do what you need to do during that conversation to take care of yourself. (Spencer & Kulbaga, 2018, p. 116)

Stringer (2016) presents two additional examples of content forecasts:

> In tomorrow's lecture we will be looking at the origins of victimology in the 1940s. Our main task is to see their positivist approach and get a sense of the kind of victimological study they set in motion. But with the early victimologists there is sensitive content about victim-blaming in general, and we will look at an example of victim-blaming in the context of sexual assault.
>
> In one section of tomorrow's lecture there will be some graphs and statistics on victimization through crime in Aotearoa/New Zealand, observing gender and ethnic differences in rates of victimization; and discussion of gender and race-ethnicity in relation to stereotypical depictions of crime, the criminal, and the victim. Forms of crime featured in the graphs include interpersonal violence. (p. 65)

In these examples, students are provided with clear descriptions, yet they are not led to expect that they will experience anxiety or distress, and the descriptions are not labeled as trigger warnings. Providing such information on the syllabus or verbally during class could help students prepare for the class discussion. Unfortunately there is not a body of research examining the impact of providing students with these more neutral descriptions of the content. I encourage you to reflect on a class that you teach to determine if, when, and how to present information about sensitive content. Use Table 4.5. as a template.

In this chapter, I have focused on concrete ways way to prepare yourself and your students to have productive discomfort in the classroom. We next turn the classroom dynamics that play out in the moment as students are engaging with sensitive and controversial materials; facing, witnessing, and carrying out microaggressions; and experiencing hot and cold moments in the classroom.

TABLE 4.5
Worksheet: Determining If, When, and How to Provide Information About Difficult Content

Content	Context	Mutual Obligations	How to Present Information

5

CLASS DYNAMICS II

Robert R. Murphy and Kathryn C. Oleson

I think that discomfort is important for people . . . getting to a situation where you're not allowing people to experience other perspectives leads to group polarization. And that, to me, is more dangerous than students feeling uncomfortable." —Faculty Member (Oleson, 2017)

So your identity will dictate the level of sensitivity that you have around that subject. I think identity will therefore dictate your likeliness to participate in class. I think identity will have an impact on your likelihood to do well in the class, your likelihood to relate the information to your own self . . . wow it's everything." —Student (Oleson, 2017)

This chapter is the second one that focuses on classroom dynamics. We build on chapter 4's discussion about how to prepare for difficulty and discomfort in the classroom, and we consider in-the-moment strategies to manage discomfort and facilitate dialogue on controversial topics in ways that are productive for learning. We describe microaggressions occurring among students and between students and faculty, building on chapter 1's discussion of regulating one's biases in the classroom. Next, the chapter explores ways to approach and respond to "hot" moments and difficult classroom dialogues. Additionally, we consider both the difficulties and the values associated with silence and "cold" moments in the classroom. We intend to enhance understanding of these complex issues while also presenting strategies for facilitating productive discussion. Throughout the chapter we explore the potential impact of individuals' social identities in making sense of the classroom dynamics. Our approach is grounded in research but additionally takes into account practical experiences of faculty developers, educators, and social justice advocates.

Microaggressions

In this section, we explore microaggressions that can occur in the classroom. Pierce (1970) coined the term *microaggression* to describe "subtle, stunning, often automatic, and non-verbal exchanges which are 'put downs'" (Pierce et al., 1978, p. 66). Microaggressions typically target individuals of marginalized groups (West, 2019), can be verbal or nonverbal, and can be "invisible" in nature to the perpetrator and even the target (Solórzano et al., 2000; Sue, Capodilupo et al., 2007). Students can microaggress against students or instructors, and instructors can microaggress against students or other instructors (Suárez-Orozco et al., 2015). You may be familiar with the term *microaggression* as it has become popularized in national conversations about universities, safe spaces, and trigger warnings (Spodek, 2018). Although there has been debate about whether microaggressions are simply a symptom of hypersensitivity (West, 2019) or warrant serious attention (Lilienfeld, 2017), there is evidence that microaggressions frequently occur in higher education classrooms (Minikel-Lacocque, 2013; Perry et al., 2009; Suárez-Orozco et al., 2015) and carry serious consequences (Lui & Quezada, 2019; Williams, 2020). We focus primarily on microaggressions students in your classes might experience to assist you in improving their experience and well-being.

Three Main Types of Microaggressions

There are three classes of microaggressions—microassaults, microinsults, and microinvalidations (Sue, Capodilupo et al., 2007). A *microassault,* the most overt form of microaggression, occurs when one tries to intentionally harm another through acts such as name-calling and purposeful discrimination. Less explicit than microassaults, *microinsults* are rude and/or insensitive comments or actions conveyed about a person's social identity. For example, an instructor may talk to a university student in a wheelchair as if the student were a child. This is a microinsult because the behavior reinforces the stereotype that people with disabilities are less competent than others. Finally, a *microinvalidation* is a message that "excludes, negates, or nullifies [one's] psychological thoughts, feelings, or experiential reality" (Sue, Capodilupo et al., 2007, p. 274). For instance, a male student proclaiming that sexism is not a serious issue is invalidating because it trivializes the instances of prejudice women in the class have experienced.

Helping Instructors Identify Microaggressions

In Table 5.1, we present examples of possible microaggressions that your students may face so that you are better able to recognize them when they occur; increased awareness can help you effectively address them (Burns, 2014).

Intersecting Identities

In addition to the microaggressions about single social identities presented in Table 5.1, individuals also struggle with *intersectional microaggressions*—that is, microaggressions that target the intersection of multiple identities. Let's take the case of LGBTQ+ people with disabilities (Conover & Israel, 2018). People with disabilities are often desexualized—they are seen as nonsexual beings (Kattari et al., 2018). People may therefore react negatively if a student with a disability makes a comment that makes their sexual identity salient. This negative reaction could be exacerbated if the statement carries the message that the student belongs to a marginalized sexual demographic—a transgender person with a disability may elicit more negative reactions when identities are made salient compared to either a transgender person without a disability or a cisgender person with a disability.

To illustrate another example, Asian women face prejudice that Asian men do not face to the same degree. People sexually fetishize Asian women, label Asian women as submissive, and hold that many Asian women physically appear similar to one another (Keum et al., 2018). Similarly, Black women deal with stereotypes that play on both gender and race (e.g., angry Black woman) and report being devalued, ignored, and silenced because of their intersectional identity (Lewis et al., 2016; Wilkins-Yei et al., 2018). It is critical for instructors to consider how microaggressions may play on multiple, intersecting identities.

The Subjective Nature of Microaggressions

Earlier we provided instances of microaggressions that members of different social groups face. However, it is important to point out that microaggressions are subjective in nature—what may offend one person may not offend another. Whether or not a message is considered a microaggression is often determined by the target of the message (Moroz, 2015), microaggressions can also occur without the target realizing they have been aggressed against. Williams (2020) reminds readers that microaggressions are highly context-dependent: "they cannot be defined simply on the basis of the exact behavior performed or the precise words in a given sentence" (p. 39). We encourage

TABLE 5.1
Examples of Microaggressions Different Social Groups May Face

Identity Dimension	Identity Group	Microaggression Examples
Educational background	First-generation college students	• Assuming equality in parents' educational background[1] • Unintentionally criticizing parents' intelligence[1] • Mocking student for their or their parents' limited higher-education knowledge[1]
Gender	Transgender, agender, genderfluid, gender non-binary	• "Misgendering"—referring to one by incorrect gender[2,3] • Asking about one's biological sex[2,3] • Showing discomfort[2,3] • Endorsing transphobic thoughts[2,3]
	Women	• Denying opportunities based on prescribed gender roles[4,5] • Sexually objectifying[4] • Assuming incompetence and/or weakness[5] • Downplaying sexism[4]
Race and ethnicity	African American and Black	• Stereotyping as unintelligent[6] • Expressing low academic expectations[6] • Segregating and excluding[6] • Watching with unnecessary caution/suspicion[6] • Assuming that college acceptance was due to affirmative action[6]
	Latinx	• Sexualizing[7] • "Positive" stereotyping (e.g., they are romantic)[7] • Telling racial jokes[8] • Assuming academic inferiority[8] • Making assumptions regarding citizenship[8]

(Continues)

TABLE 5.1 (*Continued*)

Identity Dimension	Identity Group	Microaggression Examples
	Asian American	• Asserting that Asians do not experience discrimination[9] • Perceiving as "foreigners"[9] • Questioning English abilities[9] • Assuming "harmless" stereotypes (e.g., quiet)[10]
	Native American	• Making culture feel "invisible"[11] • Penalizing absences for ceremonial reasons[11] • Reinforcing stereotypic media portrayals[11] • Assuming academically disinterested[11] • Denying historical trauma[11] • Resenting tribal sovereignty[11]
Sexuality	*LGBTQ+ broadly*	• Using slurs/offensive terms[12] • Making offensive jokes[12] • Making disapproving statements (subtle and overt)[12] • Leaving sexual identity out of conversation (e.g., through lack of representation in course material)[12]
	Bisexual and pansexual	• Denying the existence of bi- and pansexuality[13] • "Othering" from both straight and gay/lesbian groups[13]
Religion	*Atheist and agnostic*	• Assuming low moral standards[14]
	Muslim	• Endorsing "terrorist" stereotypes[15] • Assuming untrustworthiness and maliciousness[15] • Making uninformed and offensive cultural comments (e.g., about hijabs, status of women, marriage)[16]

(*Continues*)

TABLE 5.1 *(Continued)*

Identity Dimension	Identity Group	Microaggression Examples
	Jewish	• Drawing swastikas[17] • Making and endorsing anti-Semitic jokes[18] • Treating with hostility due to assumed political attitudes (e.g., Israel-Palestine conflict)[19]
Disability and illness	*Physical disabilities*	• Neglecting to make classroom an accessible space[20] • Reducing one to their disability status[20] • Critiquing for refusing unsolicited help[20]
	Mental disability and illness	• Minimizing intensity and/or importance of disability or illness[21] • Inappropriately attributing personality or behaviors to disability/illness[21] • Expressing fear of disability/illness[21] • Shaming disability/illness[21]

[1]Ellis et al., 2019; [2]Galupo et al., 2014; [3]Nadal, Davidoff et al., 2014; [4]Nadal et al., 2013; [5]Glick & Fiske, 1996; [6]Solorzano et al., 2000; [7]Mekawi & Todd, 2018; [8]Yosso et al., 2009; [9]Sue, Bucceri et al., 2007; [10]Lin et al., 2005; [11]Johnson-Goodstar & VeLure Rohoit, 2017; [12]Vaccaro & Koob, 2018; [13]Legge et al., 2018; [14]Cheng et al., 2018; [15]Nadal et al., 2012; [16]Haque et al., 2019; [17]Sue, Capodilupo et al., 2007; [18]Weaver, 2013; [19]McCarthy, 2018; [20]Kattari et al., 2018; [21]Gonzales et al., 2015.

you to keep context in mind when considering Table 5.1, detecting microaggressions in your classes, and teaching others about microaggressions.

Unsurprisingly, marginalized group members classify a wider variety of acts as microaggressions compared to members of majority groups (Mekawi & Todd, 2018), not because they are more "sensitive" to them, but because they experience them more regularly (West, 2019). Majority-group members may fail to label behaviors as prejudiced because they typically are less knowledgeable about historical and contemporary discrimination (Eibach & Ehrlinger, 2006; Nelson et al., 2013). For instance, individuals of dominant social groups often do not find exotification, power evasion, and color evasion offensive. *Exotification* refers to microaggressions such as "Native Americans are so fierce" and "Black men are just better in bed" (Mekawi & Todd, 2018). Though these statements appear complimentary, they reinforce stereotypes. Even such "positive" stereotypes have negative consequences for oppressed group members (Czopp & Monteith, 2006). Additionally, *power evasion* microaggressions occur when people deny institutional prejudice, inherent in statements such as "everyone has access to the same resources such as schools and hospitals" (Mekawi & Todd, p. 362). We link power evasion to microinvalidations; denying structural inequities invalidates the struggles that those of marginalized identities may have experienced.

Many majority-group members do not find *color evasion* microaggressions offensive, noting for instance, "I don't care if you're Black, Brown, Purple, Yellow, Green . . . I see all people as the same" (Mekawi & Todd, 2018, p. 361). Although well-intentioned, this statement exemplifies the ideology of "colorblindness." It is harmful when one denies the perception of race because this denial invalidates an important part of many individuals' social identities, negates the experience of racial discrimination that individuals have experienced, and can motivate opposition to policies designed to advance marginalized groups in society (Mekawi & Todd, 2018; Neville et al., 2013).

Impacts of Microaggressions

Because microaggressions are typically more socially sanctioned and less blatantly biased than more "macro" forms of prejudice, they can also be more taxing on the targets of prejudice (Murphy et al., 2013). Often upon experiencing microaggressions, targets feel an immediate sense of *did that really just happen?* (Goodman, 2011). Microaggressions make students feel that they do not belong (Minikel-Lacocque, 2013; Harris, 2019) and as though they are impostors in the classroom (Bernard et al., 2018). The feeling of not-belonging can seriously impede students' overall well-being (Booker & Lim, 2018) and academic performance (Walton & Cohen, 2007). In fact, there is evidence that experiencing microaggressions predicts worsened academic performance and higher depressive symptoms among high school students transitioning to college (Keels et al., 2017). Moreover, experiencing microaggressions is associated with negative mental health outcomes (Nadal, Griffin et al., 2014), negative emotional states such as anger, confusion, frustration, and sadness (Harlow, 2003), and compromised self-esteem (Wong-Padoongpatt et al., 2017). By providing an inclusive classroom experience where prejudice is minimized and dealt with properly, faculty members have the power to better students' college experiences and buffer the downstream consequences of microaggressions, such as underrepresented student retention rates (McClain & Perry, 2017).

Remedying the Effects of Microaggressions: Support Networks and Collectivist Coping

When targets of microaggressions feel that the act of prejudice has not been successfully addressed, they can experience worsened and sometimes chronic psychological distress (Sue et al., 2008). However, these negative effects can be mitigated with productive coping strategies. Strong social support networks in the classroom can encourage more efficacious coping (Holder et al., 2015). For instance, Latinx targets who utilized *collectivistic coping* strategies that,involved group-oriented activities such as discussion were more likely to believe they would persist in their university (Hernandez & Villodas, 2018).

Remedying the Effects of Microaggressions: Intervention

Although assisting in one's coping can be helpful, we recommend doing so *in conjunction with* confrontation strategies. Confronting acts of bias has been shown to reduce subsequent expressions of bias (Chaney & Sanchez, 2018) and provide cues of safety and belonging to target group members (Jusuf et al., 2019).

Teaching About Confronting Bias

Faculty members sometimes avoid teaching about or addressing bias to circumvent stressful situations (Pasque et al., 2013). But because faculty members and students come to class with various implicit biases, we must be prepared to act if prejudice happens. As a precaution, instructors can choose to explicitly teach about microaggressions on a given day or incorporate the topic into a lesson. Making students aware about the ways they might express bias can help them avoid acting in biased ways (Monteith, 1993; Perry et al., 2015).

Pérez Huber and Solórzano (2018) outline a sample way to teach about microaggressions. The instructor begins the class with a *Saturday Night Live* clip in which a woman (played by Queen Latifah) humorously walks audiences through microaggressions she has faced. This clip is used to pique students' interest and introduce the topic. The instructor segues into their lesson by talking about ways people of color often deal with microaggressions and prejudice. Throughout the presentation, they teach a number of critical points: the context and types of microaggressions, implicit bias and institutional prejudice, how to respond to (i.e., "confront") microaggressions, and, importantly, why learning about microaggressions is relevant for the course.

Guidelines for Confronting Microaggressions

We draw on Thurber and DiAngelo's (2018) guidelines for approaching microaggressions in the classroom, Cheung et al.'s (2016) and Souza's (2018) suggestions for addressing bias, and Sue et al.'s (2019) taxonomy of *microinterventions* to inform our take on how to respond to microaggressions in your courses. When there is an act of bias, witnesses should consider not what they have to gain from addressing the act, but rather what would be lost if they did not address it (Thurber & DiAngelo, 2018). It is also important to determine one's goals in confronting bias. What are you hoping to accomplish with your confrontation? Common goals include providing support for the targets, making the perpetrator and bystanders aware of the microaggression, putting a stop to the transgression, using it to illustrate course material, and educating the transgressor and/or bystanders (Sue et al., 2019; Thurber & DiAngelo, 2018). Although these goals may call for different tactics in approaching the transgression, certain tactics undoubtedly can meet several of these listed goals (Sue et al., 2019).

Learning from Bias. We take the position that when a microaggression occurs in the classroom, it often can (and should) be turned into a learning opportunity, reflecting broader classroom goals of learning and developing cultural knowledge, as discussed in chapter 3. Understanding, working through, and addressing one's own biases (Murphy et al., 2018) provide students with the opportunity to learn about complex issues within society and themselves. These steps also help reduce the expression of future bias (Monteith et al., 2002), resulting in a more inclusive classroom and better-informed students and faculty.

Sue et al. (2019) draw on empirical literature and social justice work to provide tactics helpful in educating perpetrators of bias and bystanders after a microaggression has occurred. You or a student should make "the 'invisible' visible" (p. 134) by making the class aware a microaggression has occurred. You could raise awareness in subtler ways, such as talking about the microaggression in broad terms (e.g., "People of all genders can be engineers") or asking for clarification to figure out what the perpetrator meant (Cheung et al., 2016), or more directly by challenging the stereotype or making the biased nature of the comment explicit. Students prefer when others confront with a "moderate" amount of intensity as opposed to low or high intensity (Boysen, 2012). You may therefore choose to "call in" rather than call students out (Verduzco-Baker, 2018, p. 588). As discussed in chapter 4, this "calling in" framework operates with the assumption that all students in class mean no harm in their statements and share a mutual goal to learn from each other. By calling in, class members help one another in meeting this goal by educating each other about bias and identity.

Faculty can facilitate a conversation regarding the transgression. When trying to encourage a productive dialogue following a microaggression, it is useful for instructors to consider the difference between intent and impact (e.g., "I'm sure you meant no harm in what you said, but that statement could be offensive to some because . . .") and frame the confrontation in terms of the perpetrator's values (e.g., "You are an open-minded person, do you see how what you said carries the subtle message that . . . ?") (see Sue et al., 2019). Listen carefully and actively to students' responses to promote open and clear dialogue (Souza, 2018). We also find it helpful to encourage a growth mindset ("It is common for people to make mistakes, but we can learn from these mistakes to do better in the future") while not dismissing the comment as permissible. One can also encourage individuals to take responsibility for the impact of their actions (Arao & Clemens, 2013) ("However, let's make sure we take responsibility for the impact our words have, even if we didn't mean to offend"). The perpetrator and other students must more broadly consider and re-evaluate the biases that underlie microaggressions. Sue et al. (2019) suggest using data-driven tactics such as pointing out commonalities between different individuals or groups (Brewer, 2000) and promoting empathy (Galinsky & Moskowitz, 2000), although we note that empathy can be counterproductive when it leads to expressions of pity (Nario-Redmond et al., 2017) or elicits defensiveness (Sassenrath et al., 2016).

Importance of the Context. Given the positive impacts of addressing biases on learning and intergroup dynamics, we take the position that microaggressions should be confronted and learned from. However, there are of course cases in which confrontation is not the best strategy.

Think about *who* is doing the confronting. Research evidences that dominant group members (e.g., White, cisgender male, heterosexual) are often more receptive to being confronted by "allies" (i.e., socially dominant group members who aid marginalized people in overcoming oppression) compared to target group members (Czopp et al., 2006). Targets of prejudice should not feel pressured to confront the bias; they are already in a vulnerable position and should evaluate their own needs first (Holder et al., 2015). They can consider possibilities for action, whether that is speaking up in the moment, following up with the aggressor later, or talking to the instructor after class. Sue et al. (2019) also advise keeping power dynamics of the situation in mind—for instance, perhaps it is more appropriate in some situations for an instructor to confront and not a student, or vice versa.

Situational factors can also warrant strategies other than confrontation. Time constraints and class dynamics may make a productive discussion unrealistic. One could turn to other "microinterventions" (Sue al., 2019, p. 130) or "microaffirmations" (Ellis et al., 2019, p. 3). Subtle communications, such as a side comment or a facial expression, can transmit affirming messages to the target. For instance, a look of shock can communicate "I can't believe that just happened!" Shaking your head can send the message "That was wrong." Similarly, one could use a short phrase like "Whoa!" or "Ouch!" (Aguilar, 2006) to express disagreement with the statement and support the target (Sue et al., 2019). Sue et al. (2019) point out that

> although some may perceive microinterventions to be small and insignificant actions that potentially trivialize the nature of racism, . . . everyday interventions . . . have a profound positive effect in creating an inclusive and welcoming environment, discouraging negative behavior, and reinforcing a norm that values respectful interactions. (p. 134)

When people who share the target's identity communicate these messages, they can validate the target's experience and make them feel like they are not alone (Holder et al., 2015). When allies provide support to targets, they establish solidarity and help the target feel welcomed in the class (Jusuf et al., 2019).

Finally, although we aim to prepare you for microaggressions and prejudice in the classroom, there can be instances in which you do not know how to respond. It is best to address the transgression, but do not worry if you do not know how to respond. You can speak with the perpetrator and/or target privately after class, send an email out to the class addressing the incident, or bring the microaggression into the discussion the following class period.

We encourage you to take a few minutes to consider how you plan to remedy the microaggressions that your students might be experiencing in class (see Table 5.2). Using the potential microaggressions presented in Table 5.1 and considering the various strategies and approaches discussed previoulsy, how do you propose to approach and try to minimize the negative effects of microaggressions in your classes?

Addressing Microaggressions Toward Faculty Members

As detailed in chapter 1, the social identity of faculty members influences their experience in the classroom, with faculty members of marginalized identities more prone to experiencing microaggressions. Faculty members can experience many of the same microaggressions that students do (e.g., denial of discrimination, insensitivity, messages of inferiority and not-belonging, offensive language or messages, stereotyping; see Harlow, 2003; Sue et al., 2011). For instance, if a student makes a comment that Mexican

TABLE 5.2

Worksheet: Remedying the Effects of Microaggressions in Your Classroom

Consider ways to remedy the microaggressions your students might be experiencing.

Microaggressions	Strategies to remedy the effects of microaggressions: Microaffirmations (including nonverbal communication, support networks, collectivistic coping); Interventions (making the invisible visible, facilitating dialogue, encouraging personal reflection)

Americans should return to Mexico and the instructor is of Latinx and/or Mexican identity, the faculty member could feel frustrated and isolated and experience further negative psychological consequences.

Moreover, marginalized faculty members commonly feel that they have their authority challenged, are perceived as less credible on certain topics, and have to work particularly hard to gain students' respect and trust (Harlow, 2003; Perry et al., 2009). The effects and frequency of microaggressions can be exacerbated if the instructor belongs to multiple stigmatized identities (Pittman, 2010).

Many of the principles we outlined for confronting student-targeted bias also apply for faculty members: Acknowledge the microaggression, confront it in a non-threatening manner, and discuss it. However, it is often more difficult for the target of prejudice to initiate the confrontation (Sue et al., 2011). Faculty may feel caught off guard upon experiencing a microaggression (Sue, Capodilupo et al., 2007). Although negative emotions may prevent some faculty members who are the targets of microaggressions from wanting to confront the bias, research also shows that confronting the bias can be liberating for target-group members (Rasinski et al., 2013). In other words, upon experiencing prejudice, some faculty members may shy away from confronting because they are processing their own negative emotions, but others may use the opportunity to relieve emotional distress.

Moreover, faculty members may be uncomfortable with making their social identity salient in the classroom. In chapter 1 we discussed pros and cons for faculty members bringing their identities into the classroom conversation, which may vary depending on a number of factors (e.g., tenure status, stigma associated with the identity). Instructors who do not wish to underscore their identity can still confront the bias in a productive way. They should point out why the statement was indicative of bias yet do not have to highlight that they identify with the group that the transgression targeted. This strategy may only be useful for concealable identities.

Some faculty members may wait to see if a student confronts the behavior. In this situation, the faculty-target has time to process the microaggression and think how to best respond. The faculty member can then jump in and lead the discussion as necessary. We encourage faculty who experience prejudice in the classroom to seek out support from other trusted faculty; just as students receive support from faculty members, we also need to be supported.

Difficult Discussions, Controversial Topics, and Social Identity

Thus far we have provided examples of and tools for approaching microaggressions to help you identify and manage acts of prejudice in the classroom. We have advocated that instances of bias should be turned into learning opportunities and facilitated discussion when appropriate. In fact, microaggressions often *do* lead to difficult conversations about social identity and bias (Sue, 2015; Sue & Constantine, 2007; Sue et al., 2011; Sue et al., 2009), but how should you best approach discussions centered around an act of bias or conversations on difficult topics more broadly?

We next build on the chapter 4 discussion of how to prepare for difficult conversations by stepping back to consider the benefits of difficult discussions for classroom dynamics and individuals of both dominant and marginalized social groups. We discuss difficult dialogues that are brought about by an act of bias or an offensive comment (Sue, 2015), as well as difficult dialogues that are intentionally planned as part of the class agenda (Dessel et al., 2013; Nagda, 2006; Rabinowitz & McHardy, 2014). In either case, it is important to come prepared to facilitate these difficult dialogues (Harlap, 2014; Landis, 2008; Quaye, 2012). We then explore challenges that students face, such as lacking experience or preparedness (Young, 2003) and reconciling new perspectives with one's personal beliefs (Watt, 2007), as well as issues faculty grapple with, namely tensions or "hot moments" and silence or "cold moments" in difficult dialogues. After providing suggestions to overcome these challenges, we consider how difficult discussions influence and are influenced by individuals' social identities with a focus on why students and faculty may initially struggle with or avoid these conversations (Landis, 2008; Stone et al., 2010). Finally, we provide suggestions on how to approach discussions centered around controversial or sensitive issues.

What Makes a Dialogue Difficult?

Nancy Rabinowitz (2014) raises important questions relevant to understanding classroom dynamics and student identities: "What makes something difficult or sensitive? Are they synonyms? . . . But is it really the issues that are contentious or the people that make them so, because they have different points of views?" (p. 8). Here we consider a variety of topics that might be difficult and discomforting to students including (a) controversial, politically charged topics such as gun control, refugees, and abortion; (b) intellectually challenging material that threatens students' beliefs about their intelligence; (c) material regarding systems of power and social justice; and (d) issues that prompt strong emotional and potentially traumatic responses such as sexual assault. This list is not exhaustive and has somewhat arbitrary separations, but it gives a sense of the kinds of difficult conversations occurring in university classrooms. We additionally keep Rabinowitz's (2014) point in mind that the difficulty of a topic often depends on how personal and important the topic is to students in a given class. We encourage you to consider the topics that are relevant for the courses you teach.

The Positive Impact of Difficult Discussions on Intergroup Dynamics and Bias

Chapters 3 and 4 outline ways that difficulty and discomfort can enhance student learning (e.g., intellectual and personal growth [Gurin et al., 2002; Hurtado, 2005; Piaget, 1985]; long-term learning [Bjork & Bjork, 2011]). Here we turn to consider the profound effects embracing difficult topics can have on intergroup dynamics and personal biases in and out of the classroom to encourage you to approach and instigate difficult conversations when appropriate.

Reducing Identity-Blindness While Not Tokenizing

By tackling controversial subjects, students and faculty are given the opportunity to mitigate their own prejudices. Throughout this book, we have discussed racial colorblindness and the negative consequences of colorblind attitudes for classrooms. It is important to be anti-racist, rather than non-racist (Kendi, 2019). We can think about blindness in terms of identities other than race in the classroom and why such "blind" ideologies could be harmful for members of these identities. For instance, some students in your class might believe that they do not judge others based on their sexual orientation. Individuals who think they are immune to sexual prejudice will likely not take ownership of and apologize for their behavior if they *do* happen to microaggress against students who identify as lesbian, gay, bisexual, pansexual, or queer. By avoiding difficult discussions, instructors encourage blindness. Students learn that these topics are better left undiscussed.

The classroom experience is undoubtedly different for marginalized students—they experience microaggressions (Sue, Capidolupo et al., 2007), are often outnumbered, can be *tokenized* (e.g., be treated as the "token Asian person"; Sax, 1996), and are susceptible to stereotype threat (see chapter 2; Steele & Aronson, 1995). When faculty ignore the struggles oppressed students experience in the classroom, they send the message that these issues are not important in that space. The lack of acknowledgement invalidates these students' experiences and their social identities more broadly. Marginalized identity characteristics are often very important to people (Branscombe et al., 1999), so discouraging identity-related discussions can make students feel unimportant, which could lead to academic and well-being threats (D'Augelli & Hershberger, 1993; Ong et al., 2013).

Rather than perpetuate ideologies of blindness, instructors should work to promote *identity-conscious* or *multicultural* ideologies (Banks, 2016). These ideologies acknowledge and celebrate diversity. Identity is not something to shy away from but rather to appreciate. Multicultural ideologies often correspond with low-prejudiced attitudes (Richeson & Nussbaum, 2004) and can promote a sense well-being among members of marginalized groups (Rattan & Ambady, 2011). Faculty members can promote identity-consciousness by having discussions about identity when appropriate and allowing their own and their students' identities to enter class conversations. You should also frame the conversation to send the message that diversity is valued.

At the same time, instructors must be careful not to ask students to "speak for their group." Some class discussions focus on topics that may be— or are perceived to be—particularly relevant to members of some groups (e.g., affirmative action, gender representation in STEM). When these topics are broached, students who are members of underrepresented groups can feel as though others are looking both *at* them and *to* them to help them interpret the conversation (Crosby et al., 2014; Crosby et al., 2008).

Promoting Self-Regulation

By encouraging discussions centered around sensitive and politically charged topics, you also provide students with the opportunity to think deeply about and work through their personal prejudices. The classroom is a venue for growth and change; students and faculty seek to have their ideas challenged, hear new perspectives, and re-evaluate their own positions through class discussion (Oleson, 2017). When having a conversation on a controversial subject—let's say economic inequality—students are given the unique opportunity to hear the personal experiences of people from a diversity of socioeconomic backgrounds. Upon hearing and considering a variety of perspectives, many students and faculty will re-evaluate their own prejudices. Consciously thinking about their own biases often encourages people to reconsider their beliefs and subsequently act in less biased ways (Chaney & Sanchez, 2018; Monteith, 1993). Moreover, hearing the perspective of someone from an "out-group" (i.e., identity group that is different from one's own) induces people to feel empathy toward members of that group, which in turn results in decreased prejudice for that group (Galinsky & Moskowitz, 2000). Finally, intergroup contact (Pettigrew, 1998; Pettigrew & Tropp, 2006) in class discussions and more specifically intergroup dialogue (Nagda et al., 2012) can encourage bias reductions. In sum, discussions about controversial subjects can actually leave students and faculty with fewer intergroup biases.

Alleviating Intergroup Anxiety

Many people experience *intergroup anxiety*, a feeling of anxiousness when interacting with someone of a different identity (Stephan & Stephan, 1985). In the classroom this anxiety manifests itself in many ways that make students of marginalized groups feel excluded and inferior (Turner et al., 2007). Individuals with intergroup anxiety shy away from interacting with, avoid eye contact with, and fail to acknowledge out-group students. These types of communications send ostracizing messages.

When having difficult dialogues, students may feel anxious about offending out-group students—and even avoid acknowledging identity out of fear of offending (Apfelbaum et al., 2008; Sue & Constantine, 2007). Students could also have intergroup anxiety because they feel uninformed about identity-related topics. But by acknowledging and appreciating diversity and approaching rather than shying away from difficult subjects, students can mitigate their intergroup anxieties. Through open discussions, students learn about people different from themselves, which can facilitate more cohesive and comfortable intergroup dialogue (Nagda, 2006). Such intergroup contact allows students of different identities to see cross-group similarities, which in turn promotes more positive intergroup attitudes (Brewer, 2000).

Minimizing Microaggressions

Confronting difficult topics can reduce the frequency of microaggressions that students experience. Microaggressions are thought to be expressions of implicit bias (Sue, Capodilupo et al., 2007), which can be tamed through conscious regulation (Monteith et al., 2007), as considered in chapter 1. So when students and faculty work through their personal biases, they reduce prejudices that could potentially manifest as microaggressions. Approaching discussions on difficult topics may be particularly helpful in reducing experiences of microinvalidations. Students in nondominant groups experience microinvalidations when course material and discussions cater toward more dominant group members (Johnston-Goodstar & VeLure Roholt, 2017). By engaging inclusive dialogue, however, faculty can prevent this erasure of marginalized experiences.

Why Students and Faculty Sometimes Struggle in Difficult Dialogues

Conversations about controversial subjects can tap into deeply rooted beliefs, such as religious and political ideologies. People's values are core to their self-concept (Hitlin, 2003), and so when their core beliefs are challenged, people may feel personally threatened and become defensive (Watt, 2007). Difficult dialogues can also be challenging because many students and faculty might not know *how* to talk about sensitive issues (Oluo, 2019; Pasque et al., 2013; Young, 2003).

Challenging Views

Because individuals are motivated to maintain positive self-views (Leary et al., 1995), they may avoid conversations centered around sensitive subjects in order to keep their views and values untarnished (Stone et al., 2010). For instance, perhaps a class discussion turns to consider political views associated with conservative Christianity that some consider offensive (e.g., same-sex marriage). As the class criticizes some views and perhaps Christianity more broadly, you can imagine that the situation would be difficult for a Christian student whose religion has played a significant role in their upbringing.

Uninformed on How to Participate in Difficult Dialogues

Many students admit to not having experience with navigating serious conversations about particular sensitive subjects in classroom contexts (Bryan et al., 2012). Classrooms often have unspoken norms that discourage discourse around controversial subjects, namely norms of remaining objective, polite, and colorblind (DeFor, 2019; Sue, 2013). Conversations on difficult topics violate these norms; they often involve emotion and opinion (in conjunction with academic perspectives), spark disagreement rather than politeness, and acknowledge identity rather than avoid it (Sue, 2015). Adherence to these common, unspoken classroom norms may serve as barriers to effectively talk about controversial topics (DeFor, 2019; DeFor & Oleson, 2020), preventing students from learning how to talk about topics like prejudice, religion, and sexual assault. Students can be unsure about conversation norms, such as appropriate speaking time, body language, the degree to which they can convey disagreement, and the amount of emotion that is appropriate to express. Students report being unsure how others would perceive their comments and whether they would face consequences for their comments (e.g., dislike from others; Sue et al., 2009).

Moreover, people might not know how to discuss the topic at hand. For instance, one of this chapter's authors grew up in a predominantly White suburb where race was scarcely spoken about. Upon entering an activist-oriented liberal arts college, they found the language and nuance with which people spoke about race to be foreign and intimidating. It was quite a change coming from an environment that equipped people with few skills on how to talk about race to one where people appeared knowledgeable and articulate when discussing race. It is not hard to imagine that one who feels out of the loop about the issues at hand might shy away from discussing the subject. We would encourage you to stop to reflect on challenges that you have as you approach difficult dialogues in your courses, using Table 5.3 as a template.

Emotions and Hot Moments

We have explored benefits and challenges associated with difficult classroom dialogues. We next turn to the role of emotions and hot moments in these conversations.

TABLE 5.3
Worksheet: Challenges Approaching Difficult Dialogues

Describe sensitive, difficult, or politically charged topics you currently discuss in class.	What challenges do you face?

Emotions

Many instructors avoid conversations about controversial subjects, which can be emotionally charged (Stone et al., 2010), because they fear that they will lose control of the class (Hughes et al., 2010; Sue et al., 2009). Some topics are personal to students and could bring to mind negative and potentially traumatic experiences with prejudice and sexual assault (Bertram & Crowley, 2012; James, 2014; Thakur, 2014). Moreover, difficult dialogues may give rise to microaggressions and prejudice, which can arouse negative emotions amongst targets of bias and allies (Sue et al., 2009; Watt, 2007). As outlined previously, these conversations may also cause one to call aspects of their identity into question; the process of reconsidering views about the self and the world can be inherently emotionally challenging. Finally, students with privileged or majority-group identities can feel threatened, become defensive, and experience intensified emotions and tension during difficult dialogues (Knowles et al., 2014; Watt, 2007). For instance, men might feel targeted during a classroom discussion on sexual assault as women report negative experiences with harassment and/or assault perpetrated by men (Thakur, 2014). Similarly, White students often get defensive when it is suggested they harbor racism (Howell et al., 2015).

If students do begin to show signs of "counterproductive" emotions during a discussion (e.g., defensiveness, hostility), take action. You can encourage students to pause and take a deep breath to let emotions stabilize and provide a chance for students to think (Obear, 2016). You can also remind students of the classroom norms and goals, specifically goals that focus on deep learning and guidelines that center on respect and perspective-taking (Arao & Clemens, 2013). You can acknowledge the emotions that difficulty can arouse, even admitting you find the topic distressing, but also encourage and model open-minded and respectful discourse, despite these emotions (James, 2014; Verduzco-Baker, 2018).

However, certain emotions do have a time and a place in difficult discussions. When discussing their experiences with oppression, members of marginalized groups may express frustration or anger. By allowing these students to express emotion, you provide them with a space to cope with their experiences and give students of other identities an opportunity to understand the gravity of the issues being discussed (Leonardo & Porter, 2010). We distinguish productive "negative" emotionality from cases such as majority-group members expressing anger and defensiveness when learning about oppression (Watt, 2007). It is important for instructors to recognize instances when emotions may hinder class discussions (e.g., hostile personal attacks, Obear, 2016) and when letting emotions enter the conversation may benefit the class.

Hot Moments

Intense emotions in class discussions can lead to hot moments. Warren defines *hot moments* as instances when "people's feelings—often conflictual—rise to a point that threatens teaching and learning" (Warren, n.d., p. 1). These moments are characterized by "hot-button" emotions and "heated" discussion. Though hot moments are thought to be disruptive to learning and classroom dynamics (Harlap, 2014; Warren, n.d., 2005), the relationship between emotion and student learning is more complex. Students and faculty often value the productive discomfort (see chapter 4) that could accompany hot moments. However, discomfort caused by microaggressions, feelings of not belonging, or instances of trauma resurfacing is generally not helpful for student learning.

People differ in how they define *hot moments*, which might influence how they believe these moments relate to learning (Oleson, 2017). Some perceive hot moments to be instances of unproductive discomfort that threatens student learning and well-being (Warren, n.d.), yet others believe that hot moments are when learning can be *most* productive (Crawford Monde, 2016). We suspect that disagreements about hot moments and discomfort in the classroom are in part driven by the ambiguity of the terms themselves. As discussed in chapter 4, there can be an appropriate amount of discomfort, emotions, and tension—"positive tensions" (Crawford Monde, 2016)—that is in fact helpful to learning. Instructors can intentionally promote positive tensions and disagreements, but should address less productive hot moments in their classes, as we discuss in the next section.

Addressing Unproductive Hot Moments

We now turn to addressing hot moments that are generally unproductive for student learning and threaten their feelings of classroom comfort. One needs to understand the potential causes of hot moments. Discussions on topics that students feel particularly strongly about can ignite a hot moment (Warren, n.d.). For instance, an ethics class in which students read philosophical takes on the ethics of abortion, a topic that many feel passionately about, could elicit heated emotion. Classroom dynamics can also inspire "heat." Hot moments are sometimes characterized by personal attacks on individuals rather than critiques of their ideas, and so in a classroom with an already ruptured dynamic, personal attacks and unproductive tension can arise (Warren, n.d.). Microaggressions, if not handled well, may also lead to hot moments (Sue, 2013; Sue et al., 2009). Poorly addressed microaggressions can inspire angry outbursts, personal attacks, and/or unfacilitated argument. Faculty might consider having students write out their thoughts or respond to a question prior to having a discussion that might breed tensions; this lets students more carefully consider their thoughts before contributing something potentially inflammatory or offensive (Thakur, 2014). Through awareness of the antecedents of hot moments, instructors can better equip themselves to navigate tensions in the classroom before they transpire into chaos.

What should you do when a hot moment arises? Warren (n.d., 2005) suggests ways for instructors to manage hot moments. The most important thing is to stay calm. Remember that hot moments can be turned into learning opportunities, but the heat should be turned down to a productive level of discomfort. She uses the metaphor of taking a breather from a hectic party by stepping outside and looking down on the party from a balcony to illustrate that instructors can take a step back to consider the situation from a fresh perspective. Specifically, you might find it useful to consider possible causes of the underlying tension and the heated comments. Why might a student make those comments in a class discussion at that particular point? Students often struggle to coherently convey their thoughts, so you should do some investigative work to read between the lines of what they are saying and why they are saying it.

Instructors can then remind students of their established classroom norms, such as restraining from personal attacks, allowing open discussion, and considering others' perspectives (Warren, n.d.). Moreover, it can be helpful to establish in the beginning of class that understanding others' perspectives is a necessary requirement to learning. Students and faculty in discussion-oriented classes work together to build knowledge, rather than faculty members simply transmitting it to their students (e.g., Schrader, 2004; Vygotsky, 1978). It is therefore critical to consider others' perspectives to best understand the larger topic. Introducing the idea that multiple perspectives enhances understanding of a topic, or even reminding students of it at the onset of a hot moment, may help orient students to a place of perspective-taking and understanding. In some cases, it might help to depersonalize the conversation by talking about the disagreement in broad or vague terms: "some people might think X, but others might believe Y" (Warren, 2005). Another strategy Warren suggests is having students complete a reflective writing activity, which can be calming. One could also adapt Brookfield's (1995) critical incident questionnaire, described in chapter 4, encouraging students to reflect on aspects of the situation when things are heated.

There are of course cases when a student requires special attention. For instance, after using a variety of strategies to diffuse hot moments, you may feel a student does not have a good understanding of why their comment was offensive. Approach them outside of class to discuss their perspective, introduce other perspectives, teach them about the topic more broadly, and help them develop more appropriate ways to express their ideas. In other cases, students might be so emotionally shaken up by the hot moment that it is best for faculty to acknowledge these students and allow them to step outside the classroom to collect their thoughts.

Warren (n.d.) suggests ways to have students "do the work." In the heat of a moment, you can ask students what they think they could learn from the moment. This strategy might help students realize the larger scope of the issues and interpret the meaning of the clash. Consistent with research on growth mindset (Dweck, 2006), students could approach the conversation with the optimistic prospect of learning from one another. You additionally can ask students what they can learn from their reactions in the discussion about the topics at hand.

Silence and Cold Moments

Instructors are tempted to avoid difficult discussions because they anticipate silence from students, leading to a *cold moment* when there is a prolonged silence in the classroom. Traditionally, cold moments are perceived as counterproductive to learning (Fassinger, 1995; Gilmore, 1985). Students and faculty members we have interviewed report feeling awkward, on edge, and uneasy during cold moments (Oleson, 2017). However, cold moments and silence can prove beneficial to teaching and learning (Ollin, 2008).

Causes

Students may not talk and instead censor themselves because they are afraid of sounding racist, sexist, and so on (Sue & Constantine, 2007) and offending other people (Fox, 2017). Interestingly, students more commonly report not speaking up in class because of reasons such as shyness and unpreparedness rather than avoiding seeming prejudiced (Hyde & Ruth, 2002).

Microaggressions can also cause cold moments. Imagine a case in which a student refers to cisgender women as "real women," therefore implying that transgender women are less female than their cisgender counterparts. The class might go silent; nobody knows how to respond. There are a host of reasons why students could avoid speaking, and instructors are faced with the challenge of interpreting the cause of the silence.

Silence and Learning

Many instructors and students perceive silence as an obstacle to learning. They view dialogue as a key indicator that the class is learning. Education systems often reward skills involving speaking (e.g., oral presentation abilities) and fail to reward individual-level learning processes like independent, deep thinking (Markus & Conner, 2013; Ollin, 2008; San Pedro, 2015). However, this silence-as-unproductive principle is rooted in Western values. Alternatively, silence can be an integral value for some Native American students, but when they do not participate verbally, instructors perceive them to be disengaged and disinterested. In reality, they can be practicing silence as a way of engagement (San Pedro, 2015).

In fact, what Ollin (2008) calls *silent pedagogy* can be particularly useful for learning (see also Merculieff & Roderick, 2013). Deep and novel perspectives are often brought to the table during difficult dialogues. These ideas may require deeper-level processing to fully grasp, consider, and form a response (Bowman, 2010; Hurtado, 2005). Silence can allow students time to process. It provides a space away from the noise of others' voices where students can engage in deep learning. Similarly, silence can be used as an "absorption" period. Apart from thinking deeply about others' comments, students sometimes need quiet moments to simply absorb or understand the ideas (Ollin, 2008). Course material and discussion can be too complex to take in quickly and rather necessitates a period of silence to process.

Students differ in the extent to which they need quiet time to absorb and process new information in the classroom (Markus & Conner, 2013).

In a space that discourages silence, students who require more processing time may not have the opportunity to verbally participate to the extent they wish. When instructors encourage students to let silence sit between comments, they are promoting a greater diversity of voices. It is also worth considering the *types* of students who often feel more comfortable jumping into the conversation. People of marginalized identities often are socialized to believe their voices are less valuable and so may not speak up as much as others. Educational institutions often reinforce this pattern of oppression (San Pedro, 2015), leaving those of privileged identities (e.g., White, heterosexual, cisgender men) dominating conversations. Quiet moments allow students whose voices have been previously silenced the opportunity to speak in the conversation.

What to Do About Cold Moments

We next provide tips on how to prepare for and navigate cold moments. We hope that we have demonstrated that silence can sometimes be productive. Faculty members could discuss that silence can be productive and encourage students who typically jump to speak to practice restraining themselves to allow for a diversity of voices (see Chickering, 2008). However, you should also set the norm that it is okay to *break* the silence. Students can be frustrated with others' unwillingness to speak (Hyde & Ruth, 2002), so encouraging an environment where students feel comfortable being the first voice after a bout of silence may progress the conversation as well as mitigate students' frustrations.

Moreover, instructors should take steps to ensure that students feel prepared to discuss the material at hand. Quantitative data (Hyde & Ruth, 2002) as well as qualitative interviews (Oleson, 2017) suggest that students often do not speak because they feel unprepared on the topic. Instructors can take a variety of steps to ensure that students complete the assigned reading, such as making the reading a manageable quantity, assigning engaging material, and asking students to write responses to the reading. In-class activities, including short reflections and partner conversations, also let students gather their thoughts and generate ideas to share with the class. Faculty members should additionally ensure that they are prepared to encounter potential silence. Ask yourself, Do I expect silence? When do I expect it? Can it serve a productive purpose? If silence extends for a prolonged period of time, how will I deal with it?

Faculty members can also take precautionary steps in how they frame the material. Along with individual reflections and partner work, use other opening activities such as having students email definitions or examples.

Photos, videos, audio, and other sources of media can be used as an introductory activity to spark conversation. We also encourage you to begin with a silent board discussion (one of many established active-learning exercises that Alison Cook-Sather shared in a faculty workshop at Reed College). Write a term or phrase on the board and circle it. Then have students come to the board silently to add their thoughts in new circles. Students connect their contributions with lines. They can make connections to the original word/phrase or add connections between students' ideas. Allow all students to come to the board, potentially multiple times. You could then read the responses out loud and use them for a class discussion. This exercise provides an opportunity for all students to contribute, especially those who are typically quiet or need more time to reflect and absorb the material.

You might also consider assigning student "discussion leaders" for certain days. These students are tasked with mastering that day's material, discussing the material together with each other before class, and generating questions for discussion. This way, those students are partially responsible for a successful conversation. The instructor can refer back to the questions generated by discussion leaders if the conversation lulls and ask leaders to explain parts of the material.

As we have argued, silence can promote learning experiences. However, there are certainly cases of conversations being dominated by cold silence when discussion is necessary. So, what happens when a cold moment occurs despite your preparation? First, let it sit. Only if it becomes excessive should you proceed with other strategies. After letting it sit, instructors can reframe or repeat the question. Students might not fully comprehend the question and reframing it can provide an opportunity to better explain your question in terms that are more accessible to students. You may also realize when reframing that the question is "too big," and you can follow up with smaller questions. These smaller questions can eventually nudge students to the original, bigger question that you posed.

If silence persists after letting it sit and re-asking your question, you can have students think about the issue for a few minutes on their own or with a partner. Some faculty reported success with asking students to write briefly or turn to a partner to discuss the material at hand (Oleson, 2017). This allows students to collect their thoughts and generate some ideas to share with the class. Similarly, Fox (2017) suggests having students anonymously write down "one thing I've been reluctant to say" during the discussion (or in previous class meetings; p. 133). You could use some of these responses to generate conversation. You might also consider having the same discussion but in small groups. You can pose a few questions and project them on a board and/or print them out for students to discuss in small groups. Some students thrive in smaller discussion environments.

Varying large-group and small-group discussions can give students a diversity of experiences and skills fruitful for learning.

The Role of Social Identity in Difficult Discussions

The demographic makeup of the students and faculty in the class impacts difficult discussions, microaggressions, and hot and cold moments. Difficult conversations are particularly productive for learning and growth when there are students from varying backgrounds who give unique perspectives (Gurin et al., 2002; Souza et al., 2016). Learning can be likened to a puzzle; each perspective is a puzzle piece, and when many perspectives are provided, students can see the full picture rather than one or two pieces. Difficult conversations are often enhanced when a student or instructor identifies with the issue being discussed because they can provide a more personalized, firsthand account of topics the material has covered (Gurin et al., 2013).

Student Identity

Although these conversations are especially productive with a diversity of students and when there are students who identify with the conversation topic, a diverse class may also engender more cold and hot moments and create difficult dialogues (Rabinowitz, 2014; Young, 2003). For instance, faculty of color teaching at predominantly White institutions reported that dialogues were more difficult in racially diverse classes (Sue et al., 2011). Similarly, Quaye's (2010) interviews with faculty members facilitating dialogues around race revealed that participants "noticed that it was easier to discuss racial realities at a distance when there were few people of color present with whom to engage" (p. 556). Additionally, when classes are diverse, students report being less willing to participate in difficult dialogues when someone has said something controversial about race compared to non-difficult discussions on "a typical day"; in non-diverse classes, students reported being equally likely to participate in non-difficult and difficult dialogues (Cairati et al., 2018).

These challenges could apply to other social identities. For instance, imagine that a student suggests that sex assigned at birth is one's "real gender." Such a comment might strongly impact classroom dynamics if there are transgender students in the class. The negative emotions experienced by targets of this microaggression can elicit a hot moment. However, if there is not a transgender student present, others in the class may not feel obligated to address the comment and a hot moment is avoided. Similarly with cold moments, students might be less likely to engage in the conversation because they do not want to offend the transgender students. In a class with only cisgender individuals, students might feel freer to engage because they have less fear of offending classmates.

Faculty Identity

Professors' identities also have an important impact on classroom dynamics, especially when the course material is seen as relevant to their social identities. As considered in chapter 1, White and Black instructors experience different challenges when teaching about race (see Sue, 2013, 2015), as do male and female instructors when discussing sexual assault (James, 2014; Thakur, 2014). If one is perceived as having expertise on the topic based on their social identity, there are added expectations and pressures. For faculty of color, they feel as if others assume that they are experts on talking about race, and so experience an added pressure that their abilities will be questioned if they cannot successfully facilitate a difficult dialogue about race (Sue et al., 2011). For James (2014), when teaching about sexual assault, students often approach her outside of class to disclose experiences, something she does not think that male faculty members experience as much. Thakur (2014) continues to include readings with violence and rape, but he acknowledges that male faculty members often avoid them, concerned that they will be seen as lacking expertise. Similarly, some White faculty teaching about race worry that, given their lack of personal experience of racism, they may be seen as not having the authority to teach about race (Sue et al., 2009).

Approaching and Navigating Difficult Dialogues

How should faculty members best facilitate difficult dialogues? Chapter 4 explored ways to prepare for facilitating discussions, such as creating and managing discomfort, setting up a brave space, establishing norms, and providing information about upcoming content. We have built on chapter 4's discussion on preparing for difficulty by providing strategies for overcoming obstacles that often accompany difficult discussions: namely, how to deal with prejudice, hostile tensions, and silence in the classroom. Here we propose concrete suggestions for facilitating these discussions more broadly.

In difficult discussions, we want our students to be engaged, open-minded, growth-oriented, respectful, thoughtful, and bias-aware (Mosely & Obear, 2019; Murphy et al., 2018; Obear, 2016; Souza et al., 2016; Sue, 2015; Watt, 2007). Tervalon and Murray-Garcia (1998) encompass these values in their term *cultural humility*, which refers to a process involving persistent "self-reflection and self-critique as lifelong learners" (p. 118) to develop mutual respect among individuals of different social identities. As facilitator and perceived "expert" in the class, you must actively model the qualities you hope to see in your students (Verduzco-Baker, 2018). Both Obear (2016) and Souza et al. (2016) emphasize the important role nonverbal behavior plays in difficult dialogues. As an instructor, you should both be aware of your nonverbal behavior and intentionally use nonverbal signals to express active listening and affirmation, for example by nodding and genuinely smiling (Souza et al., 2016). Supplement your nonverbal affirmation by responding to student comments in ways that communicate you have listened to and processed what has been said. You can do this by paraphrasing a comment, raising a question based on a student comment, and relating the comment back to course content (Souza et al., 2016; Thakur, 2014; Vick, 2016). There may be times when a comment angers or agitates you, but rather than redirecting the conversation or shutting down the comment, maintain a teaching mindset—think about the prospect a diversity of opinions has on learning (Vick, 2016). Mosely and Obear (2019) recommend shifting your attention to your goals and values involving inclusion (e.g., "create space for honest, authentic dialogue" and "encourage identity development and growth") and allow these values to guide how you respond in these situations.

You should also actively monitor the conversation and its dynamics. If the content of the dialogue seems to be unproductive or irrelevant to the material, you should step in and redirect. To encourage thoughtful learning and deep discussion, make an effort to continually pose more difficult but manageable questions. Moreover, if the conversation seems to be dominated by a few students, particularly by students from historically represented groups, you should make direct efforts to encourage new voices (Fisher, 2019; Jaschik, 2019). Depending on the situation and your own comfort, you can take a softer approach such as reminding students that the class benefits from a diversity of perspectives and to allow for all voices to enter the conversations, or a more direct strategy like naming the dynamics as non-inclusive.

The ways that you choose to navigate difficult dialogues will also be contextually based. For instance, the dynamics of these conversations often depend on the perspectives and identities of the students involved (Cairati et al., 2018). Similarly, the presence or absence of hot and cold moments and prejudiced comments will influence the course of discussion.

Other contextual factors certainly will guide how you handle difficult discussions, as well as prepare for and navigate a variety of situations presented throughout the chapter—microaggressions and prejudice, emotions and hot moments, and silence and cold moments. In addition to providing information to enhance your understanding of these topics, we have drawn on the social psychological and educational literatures to suggest a variety of strategies to help you approach challenges you may encounter in your teaching. In Table 5.4, we have compiled many of these suggestions so you can easily refer back to tactics that may be useful to you in preparing and teaching your classes. We share these with you with the goal of helping you create and manage an inclusive, challenging, and respectful classroom space.

TABLE 5.4
Strategies and Specific Suggestions for Navigating Difficulties in the Classroom

Strategy Focus	Specific Suggestions
Confronting Bias	
Make Goals for Confronting Clear	Ask yourself what you are trying to accomplish by confronting. For example, is the goal to terminate the act, support the recipient, educate the transgressor, and/or use it as a chance to demonstrate class material? Let this guide how you intervene.
Make Students Aware of the Biased Statement/Act	Ask questions to clarify what the student meant. Point out that the statement was biased.
Describe Difference Between Intent and Impact	Explain that even if the student may not have intended any harm, they incidentally did or could have hurt or offended.
Frame in Terms of Transgressor's Values	While pointing out the bias, make salient a positive attribute of the perpetrator's to diminish their defensiveness: "You are an open-minded person, aren't you open to the possibility that . . . ?" "You're really respectful, so in order to avoid offending anyone in the future . . . ."
Talking About Microaggressions and Bias	
Teach About Bias	Pique students' interest with media or an activity. Define and provide examples of *implicit bias*, *explicit bias*, and systemic *inequality*. Refer to guides about teaching about and confronting bias (e.g., Pérez Huber & Solórzano, 2018).
Carefully and Actively Listen	Use nonverbal communication to signal active listening, like nodding your head and making eye contact. Build on students' points directly to advance the conversation.

(*Continues*)

TABLE 5.4 (*Continued*)

Strategy Focus	Specific Suggestions
Promote Empathy	Ask students to take the perspective of the target of bias. Ask students to think of the ways that they are similar to people of different groups/targets of bias.
Handling Microaggressions in Other Ways	
Microaffirmations	Use nonverbal communication, like frowning, shaking your head, or raising a hand, to communicate disagreement. Use quick phrases like "Ouch!" to verbally communicate disagreement with the statement and to validate targets. Use warm verbal and nonverbal communication toward the target at later points in the class to signal to them that they belong.
Address at a Later Time	Speak with the perpetrator after class. Engage a dialogue to figure out their perspective and teach them about the meaning and impact of their action. Speak with the target to check in with how they are feeling and to provide affirmation. Send an email out to the class addressing the incident. Address the incident or continue the conversation during the next class period. Seek support from other faculty or staff or use online resources to think about how best to address the act.
Dealing With Emotions and Hot Moments	
Prevent Hot Moments	In the first few minutes of a class before a difficult discussion, ask students to collect and deeply consider their thoughts. State expectations for difficult discussions.

(*Continues*)

TABLE 5.4 (*Continued*)

Strategy Focus	Specific Suggestions
Acknowledge Emotion and Pause	Practice slow breathing to stay calm. Share with the class that you notice that emotions are rising. Encourage the class to pause and breathe. Intervene in the conversation, temporarily putting it to a halt until emotions lighten. Allow students who are feeling emotional to step outside the class to calm down, get water, etc. Have students write down thoughts or respond to a question for a few minutes.
Step Back to Consider Underlying Causes	Consider the cause of the hot moment (e.g., unintentional offensiveness, intentional offensiveness, the way that something was articulated, personal attacks, preexisting tension between students).
Remind Students of Classroom Norms	Bring back relevant classroom guidelines and expectations—no personal attacks, respect, mutual goal of learning and self-improvement. Ask students what they think they can learn from the hot moment.
Depersonalize the Conversation	Remove the students from the comments/ideas to mitigate tensions (e.g., "While some might think this, others might think that"). Relate the student's comments to more abstract ideas underpinning the tension.
Addressing Silence and Cold Moments	
Allow for Silence	Establish a class norm that silence is okay and valuable. If the same students keep breaking the silence, encourage them to allow others to have a chance.

(Continues)

TABLE 5.4 (*Continued*)

Strategy Focus	Specific Suggestions
Ensure Students Feel Prepared	Assign a manageable quantity of work so students have meaningful contributions to the class discussion. Assign engaging material that students are invested in reading and discussing. Assign a short reflection or paper to ensure students are prepared for class. To prepare students for cold moments, establish a norm that it is okay to break the silence. Assign discussion leaders before class.
Use an Activity	During a period of prolonged silence, have students complete an individual or partner reflection so they have something to share. Complete a class-wide activity to stimulate discussion (e.g., silent board activity). Have students complete the majority of the discussion in small groups, then regroup and share at the end of class.
Re-Ask Your Question	Restate the question after a period of silence. Rephrase the question in different terms or provide an example. Ask a "smaller" or less intimidating question that can start the conversation, eventually leading to the "bigger" original question.
Navigating Difficult Dialogues	
Promote Multiculturalism	Explicitly state on syllabus and in class that differences are meant to be recognized and celebrated. Intentionally summarize the benefits of multiculturalism and perils of identity-blindness. Ask questions and generate conversation that recognizes cultural and identity differences. Refrain from putting students of specific identities "under the spotlight" when the topic of conversation is relevant to those identities.

(*Continues*)

TABLE 5.4 (*Continued*)

Strategy Focus	Specific Suggestions
Model Positive Behaviors	Make statements that communicate "cultural humility" (e.g., that you too walk into the class with biases you aim to overcome, and that you have a lot to learn from others). Use positive nonverbal behavior like making eye contact and smiling Approach rather than avoid difficulties. Question others respectfully and refrain from personal attacks.
Focus on Inclusivity Goals	When you feel agitated, redirect your attention to goals such as creating an environment for respectful disagreement and helping students work through their misunderstandings.
Actively Monitor	Listen to comments carefully and assess whether the conversation is continuing in a productive and respectful manner. Monitor all students' verbal and nonverbal behavior for signs of discomfort, disengagement, confusion, or microaggressions. Pay attention to whether the class discussion includes a diversity of student voices or the same students repeatedly.

6

CONCLUSION
Bringing It All Together

Consider for illustrative purposes the following classroom scenario of a White female college instructor, Alex. She is teaching a seminar on stereotyping and prejudice set in a small room where students sit around a table. The class consists of 11 White students, 2 Black students, and 2 Asian students. When discussing racial differences in test scores, a "hot moment" occurs. When one student contends that "maybe White students just work harder than Black students," another student responds angrily. Other students become quiet, seeming reticent to talk.

I n this concluding chapter, I return to the classroom scenario presented in the book's preface. Throughout this book, I have probed each of the situation's elements—the professor's identity, the course content, and so forth—individually and in tandem. Now I pull in material from each of the chapters of the book to provide an overall integration. I then end by encouraging you to collaborate with your students and your faculty colleagues to improve your teaching. As you seek to create inclusive classroom dynamics for your courses, consider your work as a part of a broader system of promoting inclusivity across the campus (Barnett & Felten, 2016) within the larger sociocultural context (Adams et al., 2008). I also describe more general college-wide programs that may be helpful: (a) creating learning communities where faculty together work to create inclusive classrooms (Considine et al., 2014), and (b) developing faculty–student partnerships (Cook-Sather et al., 2014) to help faculty improve their teaching.

Challenging Classroom Scenario

I opened this book with a specific vignette because I wanted to make concrete what we are doing. We have a particular person in a specific classroom. It could be you. It could be me. I have attended many workshops and conferences where we gather in small groups to work through scenarios like this one to make suggestions for what we should do. And in those small-group discussions, I often wonder about all of the elements that we were not told about. What other identities do these students and this professor have? Did this class of students set up a set of guidelines for discussion? What were interactions like in this class the days before this event? Let's bring to bear each of the elements considered in this book to help us understand this scenario.

Instructor

We begin by considering our hypothetical instructor, Alex, who we are told is a White woman. Given that she is White, she may not regularly be aware of or think about her race (Sue, 2003; Tatum 2017). Additionally, as discussed in chapter 1, she may have many other intersecting identities. Some of Alex's identities are visible, while others may be less apparent (e.g., that she has a learning disability) unless Alex has disclosed them. This collection of identities could influence how the instructor sees her students and how her students respond to her.

In addition to her personal and social identities, Alex also brings various biases and stereotypes into the classroom. Although she likely seeks not to act on these prejudiced beliefs, she has been exposed to stereotypes throughout her life and may be impacted in this classroom setting. At some implicit level, Alex may have beliefs that students from different racial groups do not work equally hard in academic settings. She may also implicitly believe in classroom norms such as everyone should be polite and the classroom should be colorblind (Sue, 2013), and therefore she could be upset with the students who disrupted these norms by making an offensive comment or by responding to this comment with anger.

Finally, assuming our hypothetical instructor has been reading this book, she may be trying to promote a growth mindset (Dweck, 2006) in which this hot moment can be used as a learning opportunity. She is seeking to model the idea that everyone makes mistakes as they develop and grow but change is possible. Being transparent about her struggles while learning about sensitive topics can be helpful to students who too are struggling to develop and improve.

Students

Next, let's consider the group of 15 students who were described as 11 White, 2 Black, and 2 Asian students. We have a class that is predominantly White, yet has some racial and ethnic diversity. As discussed in chapter 2, these students bring a variety of needs, intersecting identities, and concerns to the university classroom. To thrive, they need to feel not only that they are competent and autonomous but also that they belong (Ryan & Deci, 2000). A peer voicing reservations about the work ethic of Black students may cause the Black students to feel as though others do not see them as belonging at college. They may question their competence, experience stereotype threat (Steele, 2010), or feel like an impostor (Clance & Imes, 1978), and this instance may not be the first time an offensive comment or situation made them feel inferior during a college class.

Other students may also experience concern based on potentially relevant identities. For instance, students from a working-class background may worry that this peer also sees achievement gaps based on social class as being due to differing work ethics. Effort is also implicated in gender stereotypes concerning achievement. Smith et al. (2013), for example, have found that female students in STEM fields feel as though they need to work harder than others to perform well, which predicts lower belonging in these fields. Male students did not show this pattern of results. Hearing a peer voice stereotypes about how hard Black students work may bring to mind female students' self-doubts about whether they need to work harder to make up for possible lack of ability. Finally, bringing up possible racial or ethnic differences in how hard groups work may raise issues for the Asian students, who could be stereotyped as working hard and succeeding in academic environments. They may worry about the expectations that are being placed on them based on their ethnic group, which may affect them academically (Cheryan & Bodenhausen, 2000).

Context and Content

Now let's focus on the context and content of the course, including the physical and psychological space, course content, and methods of instruction, as discussed in chapter 3. This is a small seminar course on stereotyping and prejudice where students are sitting around a table. We do not have many details, but we can easily imagine circumstances in which the course was set up to be inclusive. The class is small with only 15 students. Presumably students know others' names and they make eye contact and engage with one another as they sit around the table. One hopes that the classroom is inviting, both structurally and symbolically (Cheryan et al., 2014). For example, assume it is well lit, at a comfortable temperature, and accessible to all students. Additionally, imagine the space suggests that everyone belongs and can be successful.

The design, content, and methods of instruction of this course may also impact how Alex and her students react in this hot moment. If some students already felt marginalized in the class before the hot moment, it is likely a very different experience than if all students felt the professor and their peers promoted their thriving. The hot moment in the initial case may be a symptom of broader simmering problems. To build a strong foundation, it is important that these fifteen students felt that they were represented in the course materials, that there were multiple perspectives presented by authors of varying backgrounds, and that inclusive content was incorporated throughout the course rather than tacked on (Trimble et al., 2004). In addition to this course content, the inclusiveness of the course design is significant—we hope that this course included multiple ways for students to engage with the material, presented the material using a variety of methods, and included various methods for students to demonstrate their knowledge (Meyer et al., 2014).

Finally, a better stage would be set for approaching these hot and cold moments if the instructor used inclusive methods of instruction in this discussion-based course. We hope that, before this hot moment, students had been presented with challenging assignments and interactions about difficult topics that pushed them to struggle with desirable levels of difficulty (Bjork & Bjork, 2011). Most importantly, it would be helpful if Alex had included high-impact practices in her course (Kuh, 2008). For instance, students could be engaging in collaborative learning where they are working together with small groups of students in informal and formal ways (Barkley et al., 2014). Alex could number them off into groups of 4 to have them discuss the ideas for 5 to 10 minutes in a small group. She could have them conduct more long-term independent research projects with a group of students. By engaging in collaborative work, including independent research, students would be both strengthening their academic engagement and performance as well as improving their intergroup relations with other students in class. They could have a solid foundation for approaching challenging classroom discussions.

Class Dynamics I: Preparation

To further examine this classroom vignette, we should consider the classroom climate and norms, exploring how the instructor and students have prepared for approaching difficult discussions. Imagine that this instructor's central goal is similar to what I proposed in chapter 4: to create a learning environment where she and her students grapple productively with uncertainty and discomfort around challenging topics, while also providing a respectful and socially equitable space. Throughout the semester she may have sought to create and manage productive discomfort within a space that encouraged her students to take risks and be brave (while also seeking to ensure that students from marginalized groups were not burdened with being extra brave) (Verduzco-Baker, 2018). The discomfort is at a moderate level and is centered around the ideas that are being studied.

The hope is that she created a space where she talked openly and transparently with her students about her expectations and perceptions and that she solicited feedback from her students (including anonymous feedback to ensure that they felt comfortable sharing an idea that might be unpopular). In addition, the foundation would be stronger if she included classroom guidelines or norms, preferably creating them collaboratively with her students (Adams & Bell, 2016). For instance, she and her students may have come up with guidelines such as have controversy with civility, don't make personal attacks, assume the best intentions in others, know the difference between being unsafe and being uncomfortable, and ask questions to understand things. Finally, the instructor could have sought to ensure that students were informed about upcoming topics of discussion so that they were prepared to address controversial topics.

Classroom II: Approaching the Hot and Cold Moments

We now turn to think through the specific incident that occurs in the class. The class is discussing racial differences in test scores, and a hot moment occurs between two students when one contends that "maybe White students just work harder than Black students." Other students become quiet, seeming reticent to talk. The summary table at the end of chapter 5 presents many possible ways to approach these classroom dynamics. I consider some that seem relevant to this particular scenario.

In this example, students in the class seem aware that something has happened, so it is not critical that the instructor make them aware. Another student has already responded, presumably drawing attention to the biased statement. To determine how she wants to intervene, Alex should consider her goals, such as educating the student who made the comment and bringing these ideas back to the course material (Sue et al., 2019; Thurber & DiAngelo, 2018). There is not a particular target for the comment made, although the Black students in class may feel implicated. Alex likely also has a goal of making sure that all students feel supported and that she is not questioning any of their work ethics based on their race or other social identities (e.g., socioeconomic status, gender, first-generation college student status).

In addition to considering her goals, Alex might initially want to assess the emotions in the room to help her decide how to respond. For instance, she might want to pause and take a deep breath (Obear, 2016). She could also acknowledge the emotions in the room and encourage her students to pause and take a deep breath. She could step back and consider the possible underlying issues (Warren, 2005). Maybe this is the first hint of strong disagreement, but possibly there have been tensions brewing for many weeks. Depending on her assessment of how high the emotions are at the moment, she might take different approaches—for instance, asking students to write briefly, or giving students the option to leave the class for a few minutes to get a drink of water and calm down. She wants to reduce the heat so that there is a productive level of discomfort. She also wants to bring the discomforting emotions back to the difficult material about racial achievement gaps and away from students' personal concerns.

Assuming that emotions are at a level where students are ready to have a discussion, the instructor could bring in a variety of different topics from the course to help her meet her goals of educating the student who made the comment while also focusing the discussion on course material. She could talk about how this course examines research evidence. For instance, she could ask what psychology research tells us about why we might want to believe that racial gaps in achievement are due to differences in how hard people work. The students could then consider cultural ideologies such as the Protestant work ethic, the just world hypothesis (Lerner, 1980), and system justification (Jost & Hunyady, 2005) and how they help explain cultural stereotypes about how hard-working different groups are, given that people want to believe that the achievement gaps are fair. She might bring in research about how the media (Ruscher, 2001) or important figures in our life, such as our parents (Miklikowska, 2016), can shape the stereotypes that we have about members of social groups. If it seemed appropriate, the instructor might note that she too has been influenced by these forces. She could then bring in research on other factors that could influence racial gaps in achievement, such as negative stereotypes and stereotype threat (Schmader & Hall, 2014; Walton & Spencer, 2009), environmental factors like neighborhood violence (Sharkey et al., 2014), and socioeconomic status and segregation (Reardon et al., 2019).

As the instructor is bringing in these research examples, she could encourage all students—including those students involved in the hot moment and the students who were quiet earlier—to engage in discussion. She could refer back to classroom norms about having difficult discussions, such as encouraging students to have "controversy with civility" and "respect" (Arao & Clemens, 2013). While facilitating this discussion, she could ask the student who made the original comment to clarify their statement and call on their principles of being open-minded and not wanting to offend their peers (Sue et al., 2019). She should pay close attention to the discussion, listening carefully to students' responses and trying to gauge their verbal and nonverbal reactions (Obear, 2016; Souza, 2018). In this conversation, she should make sure to state that she does not believe that there are racial differences in how hard someone works. Her goal is to reassure her students that she is not biased toward some students. If she feels that the situation has been addressed, she could return to her planned class material. It would also be helpful for her to email the whole class, letting them know that she is happy to talk outside of class. Finally, she might want to have one-on-one conversations outside of class with each of the two students involved in the hot moment.

In this example, it is likely relatively easy for the instructor to bring in ideas from the course, given that it focuses on stereotyping and prejudice. However, one could adapt this scenario to a chemistry course where students start discussing why some groups are more likely to pursue careers in chemistry. A student could suggest that the differential career pursuit could be explained by differences in aptitude or work ethics, sparking a hot moment. An instructor might not have ready research on how stereotypes, environment, and structural factors can affect one's likelihood to persist in various careers. The instructor also might not have set up norms or guidelines at the beginning of the course. In this moment, she could manage the heated class dynamics (as described previously) and then bring in additional research during the next class meeting. Even without additional research, however, she could discuss the ideas of stereotyping and prejudice in general terms, considering how these processes are oversimplified and are treating each person in the group the same rather than taking into account the broad variability of people. She could also set up guidelines at this point to ensure that students feel respected, that they are treated as individuals rather than as members of stereotyped groups, and that their work ethics and ability are not in question.

As an instructor, you need to develop your own toolkit for approaching difficult discussions. There is not one way to do this. Here I have sought to provide you with a variety of options. As has been stressed throughout the book, I recommend that you consider the entire life space of you in your classroom. Doing the work early in the semester to create your desired inclusive space that takes into account you, your students, the course materials, and so forth can help you and your students treat difficulties as learning opportunities in which disagreement and challenge can enrich the learning process.

In addition, I urge you to develop broader networks of faculty, staff, and students to help you in this process. It is important to situate your classes within the broader campus context (Barnett & Felten, 2016) and consider campus programming that could serve as resources to support you as you work to support your students. In particular, I focus on the following possibilities to help you improve: (a) working with a small group of faculty, and (b) partnering with a student.

College-Wide Programs

Throughout this book I have stressed the value of collaboration for growth and learning among students in your courses. Collaboration is just as valuable for you as an instructor who aims to teach courses with inclusive classroom dynamics.

Faculty Learning Communities

I encourage you to engage with a community of faculty peers who support each other in their teaching and who learn together about new pedagogical approaches. When teaching, you may question yourself and your abilities—feeling like an impostor or experiencing burnout. You may feel alone in these experiences, although my guess is that many of your peers are also encountering them (Jaremka et al., 2020). Collaborating with trusted faculty peers can be invaluable in your teaching, not only to help you learn new techniques but also to feel supported in your work. See Cox (2004) to learn more about faculty learning communities in general. Both Petrone (2004) and Considine et al. (2014) provide helpful insights for creating faculty learning communities focused on teaching and learning with an increasingly diverse collection of college students.

Here I focus on a faculty learning community centered on creating and managing classroom discomfort in ways productive for learning that I participated in last year. A faculty member in the Spanish department and I cofacilitated this learning community that included four additional professors. While any faculty member was able to sign up, our community was all women. Our group included two assistant professors, two associate professors, and two full professors from a range of departments in the arts, literature, social sciences, and psychology. We met four times (about once a month) over the spring semester to consider ways to foster a classroom where students of all backgrounds could constructively participate in classes involving challenging topics such as violence, race, gender, and identity. For me, the community was meaningful because I learned about other professors' experiences and possible strategies for approaching tough issues. I felt supported in sharing my personal struggles and realized that others had similar challenges. And this comradery was a great deal of fun. My husband would tease me about how much I looked forward to these gatherings. I urge you to seek to create a community of faculty who are interested in supporting each other to work on their development in creating an inclusive classroom.

Faculty–Student Partnerships

Another promising way to improve your skills in navigating difficult dialogues is to gain pedagogical feedback from a student who is partnering with you. A number of colleges have created faculty–student partnership programs to help faculty develop their teaching, given that students have important insights into our teaching (Cook-Sather et al., 2014). One of these partnership programs, the Student Consultant for Teaching and Learning Program at Reed College, was developed based on Alison Cook-Sather's Students as Learners and Teachers (SaLT) program at Bryn Mawr and Haverford (see Oleson, 2016; Oleson & Hovakimyan, 2017). Faculty members volunteer to participate in this program. Students apply to be consultants and are paid for this position. Alternatively, students could receive academic credit, if that made sense for your academic environment. Student consultants provide an opportunity for faculty members to reflect on their pedagogy, receive feedback from a student not in their course, and work collaboratively to meet their teaching goals. Together, the faculty member and student consultant develop areas to focus on throughout the semester. For instance, a student consultant could keep track of classroom dynamics, such as how much each student talks, how much each student interrupts or is interrupted, and when there are cold or hot moments in class. A student consultant is able to provide a perspective that makes the classroom more inclusive (see Cook-Sather & Agu, 2013; Cook-Sather, 2019). The consultant attends class throughout the semester, takes detailed observation notes that include the timing of all events during class, and meets weekly with their faculty partner to communicate their candid and confidential observations. From these detailed notes, instructors are able to see when there were silences and when many students engaged. The consultant also solicits midterm feedback about what aspects of class are working well and what aspects can be improved. The instructor then makes updates to the course during the second half in response to student feedback.

When I was director of the Center for Teaching and Learning at Reed, I oversaw the student consultants program. I have also participated in it twice, partnering with a student to improve both my social psychology course and my research design and data analysis course. In both roles, the experience had a major impact on my teaching. Student consultants are uniquely positioned to take the perspective of students in the class while also understanding the professor's goals (Oleson & Hovakimyan, 2017). As a team, the faculty member and student consultant are able to come up with ways to improve the class that might not have been seen without the partnership (Wagner-McCoy & Schwartz, 2016). For instance, by keeping detailed logs about students' participation, my student consultant helped me notice ways that not all students were included. We then brainstormed strategies to alter interactions. Quieter students were more apt to talk after having written ideas on the board. Asking students who arrived late to join us at the table (rather than letting them sit to the side because they did not want to draw attention to themselves) engaged them in the on-going conversation. Small changes, developed in collaboration with a student consultant, yielded more inclusive classroom dynamics.

Concluding Thoughts

I encourage you once again to stop to ponder the questions that you were seeking answers for in this book. As a part of your reflection, seek feedback from colleagues and students. I recently attended the annual meeting of the Society for the Psychological Study of Social Issues. The conference theme was "Fighting injustice: The power of research, policy, and activism in challenging times." I would add classroom teaching (in this "radical space of possibility" [hooks, 1994, p. 12]) to that list. It is difficult to foster a learning environment where all students thrive. Discussing controversial and sensitive topics is uncomfortable and may call some of our cherished ideas into questions. We will make mistakes in the process. But it is worth it.

So, are you ready? Go promote inclusive classroom dynamics.

REFERENCES

Acevedo, S. M., Aho, M., Cela, E., Chao, J. -C., Garcia-Gonzales, I., MacLeod, A., Moutray, C., & Olague, C. (2015). Positionality as knowledge: From pedagogy to praxis. *Integral Review, 11*(1), 28–46.

Adams, G., Edkins, V., Lacka, D., Pickett, K. M., & Cheryan, S. (2008). Teaching about racism: Pernicious implications of the standard portrayal. *Basic and Applied Social Psychology, 30*(4), 349–361. https://doi.org/10.1080/01973530802502309

Adesope, O. O., Trevisan, D. A., & Sundararajan, N. (2017). Rethinking the use of tests: A meta-analysis of practice testing. *Review of Educational Research, 87*(3), 659–701. https://doi.org/10.3102/0034654316689306

Aggarwal, P., & O'Brien, C. L. (2008). Social loafing on group projects: Structural antecedents and effect on student satisfaction. *Journal of Marketing Education, 30*(3), 255–264. https://doi.org/10.3102/0034654316689306

Aguilar, L. C. (2006). *Ouch! that stereotype hurts: Communicating respectfully in a diverse world.* International Training and Development.

Aguilar, L., Walton, G., & Wieman, C. (2014). Psychological insights for improved physics teaching. *Physics Today, 67*(5), 43–49. https://doi.org/10.1063/PT.3 .2383

Alemán, S. M., & Gaytán, S. (2017). "It doesn't speak to me": Understanding student of color resistance to critical race pedagogy. *International Journal of Qualitative Studies in Education, 30*(2), 128–146. https://doi.org/10.1080/09518398.2016 .1242801

Alexander, M. (2010). *The new Jim Crow: Mass incarceration in the age of colorblindness.* New Press.

Alter, A. L., Aronson, J., Darley, J. M., Rodriguez, C., & Ruble, D. N. (2010). Rising to the threat: Reducing stereotype threat by reframing the threat as a challenge. *Journal of Experimental Social Psychology, 46*(1), 166–171. https://doi .org/10.1016/j.jesp.2009.09.014

Ambady, N., Paik, S. K., Steele, J., Owen-Smith, A., & Mitchell, J. P. (2004). Deflecting negative self-relevant stereotype activation: The effects of individuation. *Journal of Experimental Social Psychology, 40*(3), 401–408. https://doi.org/10 .1016/j.jesp.2003.08.003

American Association of University Professors. (2014). On trigger warnings. http:// aaup.org/report/trigger-warning

Apfelbaum, E. P., Sommers, S. R., & Norton, M. I. (2008, Oct). Seeing race and seeming racist? Evaluating strategic colorblindness in social interaction. *Journal of Personality and Social Psychology*, *95*(4), 918–932. https://doi.org/10.1037/a0011990

Arao, B., & Clemens, K. (2013). From safe spaces to brave spaces: A new way to frame dialogue around diversity and social justice. In L. Landreman (Ed.), *The art of effective facilitation: Reflections from social justice educators* (pp. 135–150). Stylus.

Arkin, R. M., & Oleson, K. C. (1998). Self-handicapping. In J. M. Darley & J. Cooper (Eds.), *Attribution and social interaction: The legacy of Edward E. Jones* (pp. 313–347). American Psychological Association.

Aronson, E., & Patnoe, S. (1997). *The jigsaw classroom*. Longman.

Aronson, J., Fried, C. B., & Good, C. (2002). Reducing thfe effects of stereotype threat on African American college students by shaping theories of intelligence. *Journal of Experimental Social Psychology*, *38*(2), 113–125. https://doi.org/10.1006/jesp.2001.1491

Atwood, J. (1994). Good intentions, dangerous territory: Student resistance in feminist writing courses. *Journal of Teaching Writing*, *12*(2), 125–143.

Bacon, D. R., Stewart, K. A., Silver, W. S., Acevedo, S. M., Aho, M., Cela, E., Chao, J. -C., Garcia-Gonzales, I., MacLeod, A., Moutray, C., & Olague, C. (1999). Lessons from the best and worst student team experiences: How a teacher can make the difference. *Journal of Management Education*, *23*(5), 467–488. https://doi.org/10.1177/105256299902300503

Banaji, M. R. (2007). Pervasiveness and correlates of implicit attitudes and stereotypes. *European Review of Social Psychology*, *18*, 36–88.

Banks, J. A. (1993). Multicultural education: Historic development, dimensions, and practice. *Review of Research in Education*, *19*, 3–49. https://doi.org/https://www.jstor.org/stable/1167339

Banks, J. A. (2016). *Cultural diversity and education: Foundations, curriculum, and teaching* (6th ed.). Routledge.

Bargh, J. A. (1999). The cognitive monster: The case against the controllability of automatic stereotype effects. In S. Chaiken & Y. Trope (Eds.), *Dual process theories in social psychology* (pp. 361–382). Guilford.

Barkley, E. F., Major, C. H., & Cross, K. P. (2014). *Collaborative learning techniques: A handbook for college faculty* (2nd ed.). Jossey-Bass.

Barnett, B., & Felten, P. (Eds.). (2016). *Intersectionality in action: A guide for faculty and campus leaders for creating inclusive classrooms and institutions*. Stylus.

Barrett, B. J. (2010). Is "safety" dangerous? A critical examination of the classroom as a safe space. *Canadian Journal for the Scholarship of Teaching and Learning*, *1*(9). https://doi.org/10.5206/cjsotl-rcacea.2010.1.9

Baumeister, R. F. (2010). The self. In R. F. Baumeister & E. J. Finkel (Eds.), *Advanced social psychology: The state of the science* (pp. 139–175). Oxford University Press.

Baumeister, R. F., & Leary, M. R. (1995, May). The need to belong: Desire for interpersonal attachments as a fundamental human motivation. *Psychological Bulletin, 117*(3), 497–529. https://doi.org/10.1037/0033-2909.117.3.497

Baxter Magolda, M. B. (1992). *Knowing and reasoning in college: Gender-related patterns in students' intellectual development.* Jossey-Bass.

Baxter Magolda, M. B. (2001). *Making their own way: Narratives to transform higher education to promote self-development.* Stylus.

Beck, K., Daniel, E., DeFor, M., Hayworth, K., Peterson, M., & Oleson, K. C. (2019, June). *Politics in the classroom: Exploring faculty self-disclosure of political ideology.* [Poster presentation]. 15th Meeting of the Society for the Psychological Study of Social Issues, San Diego, CA.

Belenky, M. F., Clinchy, B. M., Goldberger, N. R., & Tarule, J. M. (1986). *Women's ways of knowing.* Basic Books.

Bellet, B. W., Jones, P. J., & McNally, R. J. (2018). Trigger warning: Empirical evidence ahead. *Journal of Behavior Therapy and Experimental Psychiatry, 61,* 134–141. https://doi.org/10.1016/j.jbtep.2018.07.002

Benedetti, F., Lanotte, M., Lopiano, L., & Colloca, L. (2007). When words are painful: Unraveling the mechanisms of the nocebo effect. *Neuroscience, 147*(2), 260–271. https://doi.org/10.1016/j.neuroscience.2007.02.020

Bentley, M. (2017). Trigger warnings and the student experience. *Politics, 37*(4), 470–485. https://doi.org/10.1177/0263395716684526

Benware, C. A., & Deci, E. L. (1984). Quality of learning with an active versus passive motivational set. *American Educational Research Journal, 21*(4), 755–765. https://doi.org/10.3102/00028312021004755

Bernard, D. L., Hoggard, L. S., & Neblett, E. W. (2018). Racial discrimination, racial identity, and impostor phenomenon: A profile approach. *Cultural Diversity and Ethnic Minority Psychology, 24*(1), 51–61. https://doi.org/10.1037/cdp0000161

Bernard, D. L., Lige, Q. M., Willis, H. A., Sosoo, E. E., & Neblett, E. W. (2017, Mar). Impostor phenomenon and mental health: The influence of racial discrimination and gender. *Journal of Counseling Psychology, 64*(2), 155–166. https://doi.org/10.1037/cou0000197

Bernard, D., & Neblett, E. (2018). A culturally informed model of the development of the impostor phenomenon among African American youth. *Adolescent Research Review, 3*(3), 279–300. https://doi.org/10.1007/s40894-017-0073-0

Berrett, D. (2015, September 21). The unwritten rules of college. *The Chronicle of Higher Education.* https://www.chronicle.com/article/The-Unwritten-Rules-of/233245

Bertram,C., & Crowley, S. M. (2012). Teaching about sexual violence in higher education: Moving from concern to conscious resistance. *Frontiers: A Journal of Women Studies, 33*(1), 63–82. https://doi.org/10.5250/fronjwomestud.33.1.0063

Beverly, E. A., Díaz, S., Kerr, A. M., Balbo, J. T., Prokopakis, K. E., & Fredricks, T. R. (2018, January–March). Students' perceptions of trigger warnings in medical education. *Teaching and learning in medicine, 30*(1), 5–14. https://doi.org/10.1080/10401334.2017.1330690

Bezrukova, K., Spell, C. S., Perry, J. L., & Jehn, K. A. (2016). A meta-analytical integration of over 40 years of research on diversity training evaluation. *Psychological Bulletin, 142*(11), 1227–1274. https://doi.org/10.1037/bul0000067

Billson, J. M. (1986). The college classroom as a small group: Some implications for teaching and learning. *Teaching Sociology, 14*(3), 143–151. https://doi.org/10.2307/1318467

Billson, J. M., & Tiberius, R. G. (1991). Effective social arrangements for teaching and learning. In R. J. Mengus & M. Svinicki (Eds.), *College teaching: From theory to practice* (New Directions for Teaching and Learning, No. 45, pp. 87–109). Jossey-Bass. https://doi.org/10.1002/tl.37219914510

Bjork, E. L., & Bjork, R. A. (2011). Making things hard on yourself, but in a good way: Creating desirable difficulties to enhance learning. In M. A. Gernsbacher, R. W. Pew, L. M. Hough, & J. R. Powertantz (Eds.), *Psychology and the real world: Essays illustrating fundamental contributions to society* (pp. 56–64). Worth.

Bjork, R. A. (1994). Memory and metamemory considerations in the training of human beings. In J. Metcalfe & A. Shimamura (Eds.), *Metacognition: Knowing about knowing* (pp. 185–205). MIT Press.

Bjork, R. A., Dunlosky, J., & Kornell, N. (2013). Self-regulated learning: Beliefs, techniques, and illusions. *Annual Review of Psychology, 64*(1), 417–444. https://doi.org/10.1146/annurev-psych-113011-143823

Black, A. E., & Deci, E. L. (2000). The effects of instructors' autonomy support and students' autonomous motivation on learning organic chemistry: A self-determination theory perspective. *Science Education, 84*(6), 740–756. https://doi.org/10.1002/1098-237X(200011)84:6<740::AID-SCE4>3.0.CO;2-3

Blanton, H., & Jaccard, J. (2006, January). Arbitrary metrics in psychology. *American Psychologist, 61*(1), 27–41. https://doi.org/10.1037/0003-066X.61.1.27

Block, C. J., Cruz, M., Bairley, M., Harel-Marian, T., & Roberson, L. (2019). Inside the prism of an invisible threat: Shining a light on the hidden work of contending with systemic stereotype threat in stem fields. *Journal of Vocational Behavior, 113*, 33–50. https://doi.org/10.1016/j.jvb.2018.09.007

Boler, M. (1999). *Feeling power: Emotions and education.* Routledge.

Boler, M., & Zembylas, M. (2003). Discomforting truths: The emotional terrain of understanding difference. In P. Trifonas (Ed.), *Pedagogies of difference: Rethinking education for social change* (pp. 110–135). Routledge.

Booker, K. C., & Lim, J. H. (2018). Belongingness and pedagogy: Engaging African American girls in middle school mathematics. *Youth & society, 50*(8), 1037–1055. https://doi.org/10.1177/0044118X16652757

Boostrom, R. (1998). "Safe spaces": Reflections on an educational metaphor. *Journal of Curriculum Studies, 30*(4), 397–408. https://doi.org/10.1080/002202798183549

Boren, J. P., & McPherson, M. B. (2018). Is coming out in the classroom still an occupational hazard? A replication of Russ, Simonds, and Hunt (2002).

Communication Studies, 69(3), 242–250. https://doi.org/10.1080/10510974 .2018.1466719

Borshuk, C. (2017). Managing student self-disclosure in class settings: Lessons from feminist pedagogy. *Journal of the Scholarship of Teaching and Learning, 17*(1), 78–86. https://doi.org/10.14434/v17i1.20070

Bowman, N. A. (2010). Disequilibrium and resolution: The nonlinear effects of diversity courses on well-being and orientations toward diversity. *Review of Higher Education, 33*(4), 543–568. https://doi.org/10.1353/rhe.0.0172

Boysen, G. A. (2012). Teacher's responses to bias in the classroom: How response and situational factors affect student perceptions. *The Journal of applied psychology, 42*(2), 506–534. https://doi.org/10.1111/j.1559-1816.2011 .00784.x

Boysen, G. A. (2017). Evidence-based answers to questions about trigger warnings for clinically-based distress: A review for teachers. *Scholarship of Teaching and Learning in Psychology, 3*(2), 163–177. https://doi.org/10.1037/stl0000084

Boysen, G. A., Isaacs, R. A., Tretter, L., & Markowski, S. (2019). Trigger warning efficacy: The impact of warnings on affect, attitudes, and learning. *Scholarship of Teaching and Learning in Psychology.* https://doi.org/10.1037/stl0000150 (Advance online publication).

Boysen, G. A., & Prieto, L. R. (2018). Trigger warnings in psychology classes: Psychology teachers' perspectives and practices. *Scholarship of Teaching and Learning in Psychology, 4*(1), 16–26. https://doi.org/10.1037/stl0000105

Boysen, G. A., Prieto, L. R., Holmes, J. D., Landrum, R. E., Miller, R. L., Taylor, A. K., White, J. N., & Kaiser, D. J. (2018). Trigger warnings in psychology classes: What do students think? *Scholarship of Teaching and Learning in Psychology, 4*(2), 69–80. https://doi.org/10.1037/stl0000106

Boysen, G. A., & Vogel, D. L. (2009). Bias in the classroom: Types, frequencies, and responses. *Teaching of Psychology, 36*(1), 12–17. https://doi.org/10.1080/ 00986280802529038

Boysen, G. A., Wells, A. M., & Dawson, K. J. (2016). Instructors' use of trigger warnings and behavior warnings in Abnormal Psychology. *Teaching of Psychology, 43*(4), 334–339. https://doi.org/10.1177/0098628316662766

Branche, J., Mullennix, J., & Cohn, E. R. (Eds.). (2007). *Diversity across the curriculum: A guide for faculty in higher education.* Jossey-Bass.

Branscombe, N. R., Schmitt, M. T., & Harvey, R. D. (1999). Perceiving pervasive discrimination among African Americans: Implications for group identification and well-being. *Journal of Personality and Social Psychology, 77*(1), 135–149. https://doi.org/10.1037/0022-3514.77.1.135

Braslow, M. D., Guerretaz, J., Arkin, R. M., & Oleson, K. C. (2012). Self-doubt. *Social and Personality Psychology Compass, 6*(6), 470–482. https://doi.org/10 .1111/j.1751-9004.2012.00441.x

Brewer, M. B. (1991). The social self: On being the same and different at the same time. *Personality and Social Psychology Bulletin, 17*(5), 475–482. https://doi.org/ 10.1177/0146167291175001

Brewer, M. B. (2000). Reducing prejudice through cross-categorization: Effects of multiple social identities. In S. Oskamp (Ed.), *Reducing prejudice and discrimination* (pp. 165–183). Lawrence Erlbaum.

Bridgland, V. M. E., Green, D. M., Oulton, J. M., & Takarangi, M. K. T. (2019). Expecting the worst: Investigating the effects of trigger warnings on reactions to ambiguously themed photos. *Journal of experimental psychology. Applied, 25*(4), 602–617. https://doi.org/10.1037/xap0000215

Brief of Experimental Social Psychologists. (2012). Jerry Kang website. http://jerrykang.net/2012/08/13/stereotype-threat-amicus-brief-fisher-v-texas/

Brookfield, S. (1995). *Becoming a critically reflective teacher.* Jossey-Bass.

Brookfield, S. D. (2013). *Powerful techniques for teaching adults.* Jossey-Bass.

Brookfield, S. D. (2015). *The skillful teacher: On technique, trust, and responsiveness in the classroom* (3rd ed.). Jossey-Bass.

Brookfield, S. D., & Preskill, S. (2005). *Discussion as a way of teaching: Tools and techniques for democratic classrooms* (2nd ed.). Jossey-Bass.

Bruffee, K. A. (1999). *Collaborative learning: Higher education, interdependence, and the authority of knowledge* (2nd ed.). The Johns Hopkins University Press.

Bryan, M. L., Wilson, B. S., Lewis, A. A., & Wills, L. E. (2012). Exploring the impact of "race talk" in the education classroom: Doctoral student reflections. *Journal of Diversity in Higher Education, 5*(3), 123–137. https://doi.org/10.1037/a0029489

Burgess, B., & Kaya, N. (2007). Gender differences in student attitude for seating layout in college classrooms. *College Student Journal, 41*(4), 940–946.

Burns, K. A. (2014). Minimizing and managing microaggressions in the philosophy classroom. *Teaching philosophy, 37*(2), 131–152. https://doi.org/10.5840/teachphil20144111

Buttrill, S. (2018). *Student and faculty values of classroom dynamics in higher education* [Unpublished senior thesis]. Reed College.

Byron, K. (2017). From infantilizing to world making: Safe spaces and trigger warnings on campus. *Family Relations, 66*(1), 116–125. https://doi.org/10.1111/fare.12233

Cairati, R., DeFor, M., Ge, X., Marsh, K., Yang, T., & Oleson, K. C. (2018, June). *The effects of classroom dynamics on participation in difficult dialogues* [Poster presentation]. 14th Meeting of the Society for the Psychological Study of Social Issues.

Cameron, C. D., Brown-Iannuzzi, J. L., & Payne, B. K. (2012, Nov). Sequential priming measures of implicit social cognition: A meta-analysis of associations with behavior and explicit attitudes. *Personality and Social Psychology Review, 16*(4), 330–350. https://doi.org/10.1177/1088868312440047

Cares, A. C., Franklin, C. A., Fisher, B. S., & Bostaph, L. G. (2018). "They were there for people who needed them": Student attitudes toward the use of trigger warnings in victimology classrooms. *Journal of Criminal Justice Education, 30*(1), 22–45. https://doi.org/10.1080/10511253.2018.1433221

Carpenter, S. K., Cepeda, N. J., Rohrer, D., Kang, S. H. K., & Pashler, H. (2012). Using spacing to enhance diverse forms of learning: Review of recent research and implications for instruction. *Educational Psychology Review, 24*(3), 369–378. https://doi.org/10.1007/s10648-012-9205-z

Carr, P. B., Dweck, C. S., & Pauker, K. (2012). "Prejudiced" behavior without prejudice? Beliefs about the malleability of prejudice affect interracial interactions. *Journal of Personality and Social Psychology, 103*(3), 452–471. https://doi.org/10.1037/a0028849

Carrell, S. E., Page, M. E., & West, J. E. (2010). Sex and science: How professor gender perpetuates the gender gap. *Quarterly Journal of Economics, 125*(3), 1101–1144. https://doi.org/10.1162/qjec.2010.125.3.1101

Case, K. A. (Ed.). (2013). *Deconstructing privilege: Teaching and learning as allies in the classroom.* Routledge.

Case, K. A., & Cole, E. R. (2013). Deconstructing privilege when students resist: The journey back into a community of engaged learners. In K. A. Case (Ed.), *Deconstructing privilege: Teaching and learning as allies in the classroom* (pp. 34–48). Routledge.

Case, K. A., Iuzzini, J., & Hopkins, M. (2012). Systems of privilege: Intersections, awareness, and applications. *Journal of Social Issues, 68*(1), 1–10. https://doi.org/10.1111/j.1540-4560.2011.01732.x

CAST. (2018). *Universal Design for Learning Guidelines version 2.2.* http://udlguidelines.cast.org

Cayanus, J. L., & Martin, M. M. (2008). Teacher self-disclosure: Amount, relevance, and negativity. *Communication Quarterly, 56*(3), 325–341. https://doi.org/10.1080/01463370802241492

Cayanus, J. L., Martin, M. M., & Goodboy, A. K. (2009). The relation between teacher self-disclosure and student motives to communicate. *Communication Research Reports, 26*(2), 105–113. https://doi.org/10.1080/08824090902861523

Chaney, K. E., & Sanchez, D. T. (2018). The endurance of interpersonal confrontations as a prejudice reduction strategy. *Personality and Social Psychology Bulletin, 44*(3), 418–429. https://doi.org/10.1177/0146167217741344

Chang, G. (2012). Where's the violence? The promise and perils of teaching women-of-color studies. In G. Gutierrez y Muhs, Y. F. Niemann, C. G. Gonzalez, & A. P. Harris (Eds.), *Presumed incompetent: The intersections of race and class for women in academia* (pp. 198–218). University Press of Colorado.

Channon, S. B., Davis, R. C., Goode, N. T., & May, S. A. (2017). What makes a 'good group'? Exploring the characteristics and performance of undergraduate student groups. *Advances in Health Sciences Education, 22*(1), 17–41. https://doi.org/10.1007/s10459-016-9680-y

Chapman, D. W., & Carter, J. F. (1979). Translation procedures for the cross cultural use of measurement instruments. *Educational Evaluation and Policy Analysis, 1*(3), 71–76. https://doi.org/10.3102/01623737001003071

Chaudoir, S. R., & Fisher, J. D. (2010). The disclosure processes model: Understanding disclosure decision-making and post-disclosure outcomes among people living with a concealable stigmatized identity. *Psychological Bulletin, 136*(2), 236–256. https://doi.org/10.1037/a0018193

Chen, J., Wang, M., Kirschner, P. A., & Tsai, C. (2018). The role of collaboration, computer use, learning environments, and supporting strategies in CSCL: A meta-analysis. *Review of Educational Research, 88*(6), 799–843. https://doi.org/10.3102/0034654318791584

Cheng, Z. H., Pagano, L. A., & Shariff, A. F. (2018). The development and validation of the microaggressions against non-religious individuals scale (MANRIS). *Psychology of Religion and Spirituality, 10*(3), 254–262. https://doi.org/10.1037/rel0000203

Cheruvelil, K. S., Soranno, P. A., Weathers, K. C., Hanson, P. C., Goring, S. J., Filstrup, C. T., & Read, E. K. (2014). Creating and maintaining high-performing collaborative research teams: The importance of diversity and interpersonal skills. *Frontiers in Ecology and the Environment, 12*(1), 31–38. https://doi.org/10.1890/130001

Cheryan, S., & Bodenhausen, G. V. (2000). When positive stereotypes threaten intellectual performance: The psychological hazards of "model minority" status. *Psychological Science, 11*(5), 399–402. https://doi.org/10.1111/1467-9280.00277

Cheryan, S., Plaut, V. C., Davies, P. G., & Steele, C. M. (2009). Ambient belonging: How stereotypical cues impact gender participation in computer science. *Journal of Personality and Social Psychology, 97*(6), 1045–1060. https://doi.org/10.1037/a0016239

Cheryan, S., Ziegler, S. A., Plaut, V. C., & Meltzoff, A. N. (2014). Designing classrooms to maximize student achievement. *Policy Insights from the Behavioral and Brain Sciences, 1*(1), 4–12. https://doi.org/10.1177/2372732214548677

Cheung, F., Ganote, C. M., & Souza, T. J. (2016). Microaggressions and microresistance: Supporting and empowering students. In *Faculty Focus special report: Diversity and inclusion in the college classroom*. Magna.

Chickering, A. W. (2008). A senior administrator's systemic view on facilitating moral conversations across campus. In R. J. Nash, D. L. Bradley, & A. W. Chickering (Eds.), *How to talk about hot topics on campus: From polarization to moral conversation* (pp. 133–174). Jossey-Bass.

Cialdini, R. B., & Sagarin, B. J. (2005). Principles of interpersonal influence. In T. Brock & M. Green (Eds.), *Persuasion: Psychological insights and perspectives* (pp. 143–169). Sage.

Clance, P. R. (1985). *The impostor phenomenon: When success makes you feel like a fake*. Bantam Books.

Clance, P. R., & Imes, S. A. (1978). The imposter phenomenon in high achieving women: Dynamics and therapeutic intervention. *Psychotherapy: Theory, Research and Practice, 15*(3), 241–247. https://doi.org/10.1037/h0086006

Cohen, G. L., & Garcia, J. (2008). Identity, belonging, and achievement: A model, interventions, implications. *Current Directions in Psychological Science, 17*(6), 365–369.

Cohen, G. L., Purdie-Vaughns, V., & Garcia, J. (2012). An identity threat perspective on intervention. In M. Inzlicht & T. Schmader (Eds.), *Stereotype threat: Theory, process, and application* (pp. 280–296). Oxford University Press.

Cohen, G. L., Steele, C. M., & Ross, L. D. (1999). The mentor's dilemma: Providing critical feedback across the racial divide. *Personality and Social Psychology Bulletin, 25*(10), 1302–1318. https://doi.org/10.1177/0146167299258011

Cokley, K., Awad, G., Smith, L., Jackson, S., Awosogba, O., Hurst, A., Stone, S., Blondeau, L., & Roberts, D. (2015). The roles of gender stigma consciousness, impostor phenomenon and academic self-concept in the academic outcomes of women and men. *Sex Roles, 73*(9), 414–426. https://doi.org/10.1007/s11199-015-0516-7

Cokley, K., Smith, L., Bernard, D., Hurst, A., Jackson, S., Stone, S., Awosogba, O., Saucer, C., Bailey, M., & Roberts, D. (2017). Impostor feelings as a moderator and mediator of the relationship between perceived discrimination and mental health among racial/ethnic minority college students. *Journal of Counseling Psychology, 64*(2), 141–154. https://doi.org/10.1037/cou0000198

Cole, E. R. (2009). Intersectionality and research in psychology. *American Psychologist, 64*(3), 170–180. https://doi.org/10.1037/a0014564

Cólon García, A. (2017). Building a sense of belonging through pedagogical partnership. *Teaching and Learning Together in Higher Education, 1*(22), 1–5. https://doi.org/https://repository.brynmawr.edu/tlthe/vol1/iss22/2

Conover, K. J., & Israel, T. (2018). Microaggressions and social support among sexual minorities with physical disabilities. *Rehabilitation Psychology, 64*(2), 167–178. https://doi.org/10.1037/rep0000250

Considine, J. R., Mihalick, J. E., Mogi-Hein, Y. R., Penick-Parks, M. W., & Van Auken, P. M. (2014). "Who am I to bring diversity into the classroom?" Learning communities wrestle with creating inclusive college classrooms. *Journal of the Scholarship of Teaching and Learning, 14*, 18–30. https://doi.org/10.14434/v14i4.3895

Cook-Sather, A. (2016). Creating brave spaces within and through student-faculty pedagogical partnerships. *Teaching and Learning Together in Higher Education, 1*(18). https://doi.org/http://repository.brynmawr.edu/tlthe/vol1/iss18

Cook-Sather, A. (2019). Gaining perspective on inclusion: What faculty see in what students see. *Teaching and Learning Together in Higher Education, 1*(28). https://repository.brynmawr.edu/tlthe/vol1/iss28/1/

Cook-Sather, A., & Agu, P. (2013). Students of color and faculty members working together toward culturally sustaining pedagogy. In J. E. Groccia & L. Cruz (Eds.), *To improve the academy: Resources for faculty, instructional, and organizational development* (Vol. 32, pp. 271–285). Jossey-Bass. https://doi.org/10.1002/j.2334-4822.2013.tb00710.x

Cook-Sather, A., Bovill, C., & Felten, P. (2014). *Engaging students as partners in teaching and learning: A guide for faculty.* Jossey-Bass.

Corpus, J. H. (2015). Learning from the inside out. *Reed Magazine, 94*(3). https://www.reed.edu/reed_magazine/september2015/articles/features/conferences/conferences.html

Corrigan, P., Pickett, S., Kraus, D., Burks, R., & Schmidt, A. (2015). Community-based participatory research examining the health care needs of African Americans who are homeless with mental illness. *Journal of Health Care for the Poor and Underserved, 26*(1), 119–133. https://doi.org/10.1353/hpu.2015.0018

Couillard, E., & Higbee, J. (2018). Expanding the scope of universal design: Implications for gender identity and sexual orientation. *Education Sciences, 8*(3), 147. https://doi.org/10.3390/educsci8030147

Coulter, S., Campbell, J., Duffy, J., & Reilly, I. (2013, 06). Enabling social work students to deal with the consequences of political conflict: Engaging with victim/survivor service users and a "pedagogy of discomfort. *Social Work Education, 32*(4), 439–452. https://doi.org/10.1080/02615479.2012.668180

Cox, M. D. (2004). Introduction to faculty learning communities. In M. D. Cox & L. Richlin (Eds.), *Building faculty learning communities* (New Directions for Teaching and Learning, No. 97, pp. 5–23). Jossey-Bass. https://doi.org/10.1002/tl.129

Crandall, C. S., Eshleman, A., & O'Brien, L, O'Brien, L. T. (2002). Social norms and the expression and suppression of prejudice: The struggle for internalization. *Journal of Personality and Social Psychology, 82*(3), 359–378. https://doi.org/10.1037/0022-3514.82.3.359

Crandall, C. S., Miller, J. M., & White, M. H. (2018). Changing norms following the 2016 U.S. presidential election: The Trump effect on prejudice. *Social psychological and personality science, 9*(2), 186–192. https://doi.org/10.1177/1948550617750735

Crawford Monde, G. (2016). Embracing tension in the classroom. *The teaching professor, 30*(7), 1–8. https://doi.org/https://www.wcupa.edu/tlac/documents/september2016issue.pdf

Crenshaw, K. (1989). Demarginalizing the intersection of race and sex: A black feminist critique of antidiscrimination doctrine, feminist theory and antiracist politics. *The University of Chicago legal forum, 14*, 139–167. https://doi.org/https://chicagounbound.uchicago.edu/cgi/viewcontent.cgi?article=1052&context=uclf

Crenshaw, K., Gotanda, N., Peller, G., & Thomas, K. (Eds.). (1995). *Critical race theory: The key writings that formed the movement.* New Press.

Crosby, J. R., King, M., & Savitsky, K. (2014). The minority spotlight effect. *Social Psychological & Personality Science, 5*(7), 743–750. https://doi.org/10.1177/1948550614527625

Crosby, J. R., Monin, B., & Richardson, D. (2008). Where do we look during potentially offensive behavior? *Psychological Science, 19*(3), 226–228. https://doi.org/10.1111/j.1467-9280.2008.02072.x

Czopp, A. M., & Monteith, M. J. (2006). Thinking well of African Americans: Measuring complimentary stereotypes and negative prejudice. *Basic & Applied Social Psychology, 28*(3), 233–250. https://doi.org/10.1207/s15324834basp2803_3

Czopp, A. M., Monteith, M. J., & Mark, A. Y. (2006). Standing up for a change: Reducing bias through interpersonal confrontation. *Journal of Personality and Social Psychology, 90*(5), 784–803. https://doi.org/10.1037/0022-3514.90.5.784

Danaher, K., & Crandall, C. S. (2008). Stereotype threat in applied settings re-examined. *Journal of Applied Social Psychology, 38*(6), 1639–1655. https://doi.org/10.1111/j.1559-1816.2008.00362.x

Darley, J. M., & Gross, P. H. (1983). A hypothesis-confirming bias in labeling effects. *Journal of Personality and Social Psychology, 44*(1), 20–33. https://doi.org/10.1037/0022-3514.44.1.20

Dasgupta, N., Scircle, M. M., & Hunsinger, M. (2015). Female peers in small work groups enhance women's motivation, verbal participation, and career aspirations in engineering. *Proceedings of the National Academy of Sciences, 112*(16), 4988–4993. https://doi.org/10.1073/pnas.1422822112

D'Augelli, A. R., & Hershberger, S. L. (1993, Aug). Lesbian, gay, and bisexual youth in community settings: Personal challenges and mental health problems. *American Journal of Community Psychology, 21*(4), 421–448. https://doi.org/10.1007/BF00942151

de Charms, R. (1968). *Personal causation: The internal affective determinants of behavior.* Academic Press.

DeFor, M. (2019). *Why (don't) we talk about race: Exploring the relationship between academic social norms and faculty members' perceptions of conducting race talk in the college classroom* [Unpublished senior thesis]. Portland, OR: Reed College.

DeFor, M., & Oleson, K. C. (2020, February). *Why (don't) we talk about race: Exploring the relationship between academic social norms and faculty members' perceptions of conducting race talk in the college classroom.* [Poster presentation]. 21st Annual Meeting of the Society for Personality and Social Psychology.

Delano-Oriaran, O. O., & Parks, M. W. (2015). One black, one white: Power, white privilege, and creating safe spaces. *Multicultural Education, 22*(3-4), 15–19. https://doi.org/https://pdfs.semanticscholar.org/2204/090b2307702c8258e3d854b43aed8dc19aed.pdf

Denson, N., & Bowman, N. A. (2017). Do diversity courses make a difference? A critical examination of college diversity coursework and student outcomes. In M. B. Paulsen (Ed.), *Higher Education: Handbook of Theory and Research* (pp. 35–84). Springer.

Dessel, A., Massé, J., & Walker, L. (2013). Intergroup dialogue pedagogy: Teaching about intersectional and under examined privilege in heterosexual, Christian, and Jewish identities. In K. Case (Ed.), *Deconstructing privilege: Teaching and learning as allies in the classroom* (pp. 132–148). Routledge.

Devine, P. G. (1989). Stereotypes and prejudice: Their automatic and controlled components. *Journal of Personality and Social Psychology, 56*(1), 5–18. https://doi.org/10.1037/0022-3514.56.1.5

Devine, P. G., Forscher, P. S., Austin, A. J., & Cox, W. T. L. (2012). Long-term reduction in implicit race bias: A prejudice habit-breaking intervention. *Journal of Experimental Social Psychology, 48*(6), 1268–1278. https://doi.org/10.1016/j .jesp.2012.06.003

Dewey, J. (1920). *Democracy and education: An introduction to the philosophy of education.* [ebook]. Macmillan.

Diekman, A. B., Weisgram, E. S., & Belanger, A. L. (2015). New routes to recruiting and retaining women in STEM: Policy implications of a communal goal congruity perspective. *Social Issues and Policy Review, 9*(1), 52–88. https://doi.org/10.1111/ sipr.12010

do Mar Pereira, M. (2012). Uncomfortable classrooms: Rethinking the role of student discomfort in feminist teaching. *European Journal of Women's Studies, 19*(1), 128–135. https://doi.org/10.1177/1350506811426237c

Donovan, D. A., Connell, G. L., & Grunspan, D. Z. (2018). Student learning outcomes and attitudes using three methods of group formation in a nonmajors biology class. *CBE—Life Sciences Education, 17*(4), 1–14. https://doi.org/10 .1187/cbe.17-12-0283

Dover, T. L., Major, B., & Kaiser, C. R. (2016). Members of high-status groups are threatened by organizational diversity messages. *Journal of Experimental Social Psychology, 62*(1), 58–67. https://doi.org/10.1016/j.jesp.2015.10.006

Dovidio, J. F., & Gaertner, S. L. (2000, 07). Aversive racism and selection decisions: 1989 and 1999. *Psychological Science, 11*(4), 315–319. https://doi.org/10.1111/ 1467-9280.00262

Dovidio, J. F., & Gaertner, S. L. (2004). Aversive racism. In M. P. Zanna (Ed.), *Advances in experimental social psychology* (Vol. 36, pp. 1–52). Elsevier.

Dovidio, J. F., Gaertner, S. E., Kawakami, K., & Hodson, G. (2006). Why can't we just get along? Interpersonal biases and interracial distrust. *Cultural Diversity and Ethnic Minority Psychology, 8*(2), 88–102. https://doi.org/10.1037/1099-9809.8 .2.88

Dovidio, J. F., Gaertner, S. L., & Pearson, A. R. (2016). Aversive racism and contemporary bias. In C. G. Sibley & F. K. Barlow (Eds.), *The Cambridge handbook of the psychology of prejudice* (pp. 267–294). Cambridge University Press.

Duffly, K. M. T. (2015). Each class is unique. *Reed Magazine, 94*(3). https:// www.reed.edu/reed_magazine/september2015/articles/features/conferences/ conferences.html

Dutt, K., Pfaff, D. L., Bernstein, A. F., Dillard, J. S., & Block, C. J. (2016). Gender differences in recommendation letters for postdoctoral fellowships in geoscience. *Nature Geoscience, 9*(11), 805–808. https://doi.org/10.1038/ngeo2819

Dweck, C. S. (2006). *Mindset: The new psychology of success.* Random House.

Eddy, S. L., Brownell, S. E., Thummaphan, P., Lan, M.-C., & Wenderoth, M. P. (2015). Caution, student experience may vary: Social identities impact a student's experience in peer discussions. *CBE—Life Sciences Education, 14*(4), 1–17. https://doi.org/10.1187/cbe.15-05-0108

Eddy, S. L., & Hogan, K. A. (2014). Getting under the hood: How and for whom does increasing course structure work? *CBE—Life Sciences Education*, *13*(3), 453–468. https://doi.org/10.1187/cbe.14-03-0050

Eibach, R. P., & Ehrlinger, J. (2006). "Keep your eyes on the prize": Reference points and racial differences in assessing progress toward equality. *Personality and Social Psychology Bulletin*, *32*(1), 66–77. https://doi.org/10.1177/0146167205279585

Elbow, P. (1973). *Writing without teachers*. Oxford University Press.

Elliot, A. J., & McGregor, H. A. (2001). A 2 × 2 achievement goal framework. *Journal of Personality and Social Psychology*, *80*(3), 501–519. https://doi.org/10.1037/0022-3514.80.3.501

Ellis, J. M., Powell, C. S., Demetriou, C. P., Huerta-Bapat, C., & Panter, A. T. (2019). Examining first-generation college student lived experiences with microaggressions and microaffirmations at a predominately White public research university. *Cultural Diversity and Ethnic Minority Psychology*, *25*(2), 266–279. https://doi.org/10.1037/cdp0000198

Ellison, J. (2016). *Dear class of 2020 student*. University of Chicago. https://news.uchicago.edu/sites/default/files/attachments/Dear_Class_of_2020_Students.pdf

Espinosa, L. L., Turk, J. M., Taylor, M., & Chessman, H. M. (2019). *Race and ethnicity in higher education: A status report*. American Council on Education.

Evans, N. J., Broido, E. M., Brown, K. R., & Wilke, A. K. (2017). *Disability in higher education: A social justice approach*. Jossey-Bass.

Fairlie, R. W., Hoffmann, F., & Oreopoulos, P. (2014). A community college instructor like me: Race and ethnicity interactions in the classroom. *American Economic Review*, *104*(8), 2567–2591. https://doi.org/10.1257/aer.104.8.2567

Fassinger, P. A. (1995). Understanding classroom interaction: Students' and professors' contributions to students' silence. *The Journal of higher education*, *66*(1), 82–96. https://doi.org/https://www.jstor.org/stable/2943952

Fassinger, P. A. (1997). Classes are groups: Thinking sociologically about teaching. *College Teaching*, *45*(1), 22–25. https://doi.org/10.1080/87567559709596184

Fassiotto, M., Hamel, E. O., Ku, M., Correll, S., Grewal, D., Lavori, P., Periyakoil, V. J., Reiss, A., Sandborg, C., Walton, G., Winkleby, M., & Valantine, H. (2016). Women in academic medicine: Measuring stereotype threat among junior faculty. *Journal of Women's Health*, *25*(3), 292–298. https://doi.org/10.1089/jwh.2015.5380

Festinger, L. (1954). A theory of social comparison processes. *Human Relations*, *7*(2), 117–140. https://doi.org/10.1177/001872675400700202

Festinger, L. (1957). *A theory of cognitive dissonance*. Stanford University Press.

Fink, L. D. (2013). *Creating significant learning experiences: An integrated approach to designing college courses* (2nd ed.). Jossey-Bass.

Finkelstein, A., Ferris, J., Weston, C., & Winer, L. (2016). Research-informed principles for (re)designing teaching and learning spaces. *Journal of Learning Spaces*, *5*(1), 26–40. https://doi.org/https://pdfs.semanticscholar.org/da98/368935cf519e62f6f8ce23357bf57f466e94.pdf?_ga=2.240691203.1467330128.1587992957-346123328.1587992957

Finley, A., & McNair, T. (2013). *Assessing underserved students' engagement in high-impact practices*. Association of American Colleges & Universities.

Fisher, L. (2019, February 2). Should White boys still be allowed to talk? The Dickinsonian. https://thedickinsonian.com/opinion/2019/02/07/should-white-boys-still-be-allowed-to-talk/

Forscher, P. S., Mitamura, C., Dix, E. L., Cox, W. T. L., & Devine, P. G. (2017). Breaking the prejudice habit: Mechanisms, timecourse, and longevity. *Journal of Experimental Social Psychology, 72*, 133–146. https://doi.org/10.1016/j.jesp.2017.04.009

Forsyth, D. R. (1990). *Group dynamics* (2nd ed.). Brooks/Cole.

Fox, H. (2017). *When race breaks out": Conversations about race and racism in collegeclassrooms* (3rd revised ed.). Peter Lang https://doi.org/10.1177/1469787417707614

Freeman, S., Theobald, R., Crowe, A. J., & Wenderoth, M. P. (2017). Likes attract: Students self-sort in a classroom by gender, demography, and academic characteristics. *Active Learning in Higher Education, 18*(2), 115–126. https://doi.org/10.1177/1469787417707614

Friedersdorf, C. (2015, November). The new intolerance of student activism. *The Atlantic*. http://www.theatlantic.com/politics/archive/2015/11/the-new-intolerance-of-student-activism-at-yale/414810/ https://doi.org/10.1177/1469787417707614

Fryberg, S. A., Markus, H. R., Oyserman, D., & Stone, J. M. (2008). Of warrior chiefs and Indian princesses: The psychological consequences of American Indian mascots on American Indians. *Basic and Applied Social Psychology, 30*(3), 208–218. https://doi.org/10.1080/01973530802375003

Gainsburg, I., & Earl, A. (2018). Trigger warnings as an interpersonal emotion-regulation tool: Avoidance, attention, and affect depend on beliefs. *Journal of Experimental Social Psychology, 79*, 252–263. https://doi.org/10.1016/j.jesp.2018.08.006

Galinsky, A. D., & Moskowitz, G. B. (2000). Perspective-taking: Decreasing stereotype expression, stereotype accessibility, and in-group favoritism. *Journal of Personality and Social Psychology, 78*(4), 708–724. https://doi.org/10.1037/0022-3514.78.4.708

Galliher, R. V., McLean, K. C., & Syed, M. (2017). An integrated developmental model for studying identity content in context. *Developmental Psychology, 53*(11), 2011–2022. https://doi.org/10.1037/dev0000299

Galupo, M. P., Henise, S. B., & Davis, K. S. (2014). Transgender microaggressions in the context of friendship: Patterns of experience across friends' sexual orientation and gender identity. *Psychology of Sexual Orientation and Gender Diversity, 1*(4), 461–470. https://doi.org/10.1037/sgd0000075

Gay, G. (2018). *Culturally responsive teaching: Theory, research, and practice* (3rd ed.). Teacher's College Press.

Gayle, B. M., Cortez, D., & Preiss, R. (2013). Safe spaces, difficult dialogues, and critical thinking. *International Journal for the Scholarship of Teaching and Learning, 7*(2), 1–8. https://doi.org/10.20429/ijsotl.2013.070205

George, E., & Hovey, A. (2019). Deciphering the trigger warning debate: A qualitative analysis of online comments. *Teaching in Higher Education, 35*(9), 1–17. https://doi.org/10.1080/13562517.2019.1603142

Gilbert, D. T. (1989). Thinking lightly about others: Automatic components of the social inference process. In J. S. Uleman & J. A. Bargh (Eds.), *Unintended thought* (pp. 189–211). Guilford.

Gillies, R. M. (2014). Cooperative learning: Developments in research. *International Journal of Educational Psychology, 3*(2), 125–140. https://doi.org/10.4471/ijep .2014.08

Gilmore, P. (1985). "Gimme room": School resistance, attitude, and access to literacy. *Journal of education, 167*(1), 111–128. https://doi.org/10.1177/ 002205748516700108

Glaser, J., Spencer, K., & Charbonneau, A. (2014). Racial bias and public policy. *Policy insights from the behavioral and brain sciences, 1*(1), 88–94. https://doi.org/ 10.1177/2372732214550403

Glick, P., & Fiske, S. T. (1996). The ambivalent Sexism inventory: Differentiating hostile and Benevolent Sexism. *Journal of Personality and Social Psychology, 70*(3), 491–512. https://doi.org/http://doi.org/10.1037/0022-3514.70.3.491

Goff, E., & Higbee, J. L. (2008). Introduction. In J. L. Higbee & E. Goff (Eds.), *Pedagogy and student services for institutional transformation: Implementing universal design in higher education* (pp. 1–8). Center for Research on Developmental Education and Urban Literacy.

Goff, P. A., Steele, C. M., & Davies, P. G. (2008). The space between us: Stereotype threat and distance in interracial contexts. *Journal of personality and social psychology, 94*(1), 91–107. https://doi.org/10.1037/0022-3514.94.1.91

Goldin, C., & Rouse, C. (2000). Orchestrating impartiality: The impact of "blind" auditions on female musicians. *The American economic review, 90*(4), 715–741. https://doi.org/http://doi.org/10.1257/aer.90.4.715

Gonzales, L., Davidoff, K. C., Nadal, K. L., & Yanos, P. T. (2015). Microaggressions experienced by persons with mental illnesses: An exploratory study. *Psychiatric rehabilitation journal, 38*(3), 234–241. https://doi.org/10.1037/prj0000096

Good, C., Rattan, A., & Dweck, C. S. (2012). Why do women opt out? Sense of belonging and women's representation in mathematics. *Journal of personality and social psychology, 102*(4), 700–717. https://doi.org/10.1037/a0026659

Goodman, D. (2011). *Promoting diversity and social justice: Educating people from privileged groups.* Routledge.

Grover, S. G., Ito, T. A., & Park, B. (2017). The effects of gender composition on women's experience in math work groups. *Journal of personality and social psychology, 112*(6), 877–900. https://doi.org/10.1037/pspi0000090

Gummadam, P., Pittman, L. D., & Ioffe, M. (2015). School belonging, ethnic identity, and psychological adjustment among ethnic minority college students. *Journal of experimental education, 84*(2), 289–306. https://doi.org/10.1080/ 00220973.2015.1048844

Gurin, P., Dey, E. L., Hurtado, S., & Gurin, G. (2002). Diversity and higher education: Theory and impact on educational outcomes. *Harvard educational review*, *72*(3), 330–366. https://doi.org/10.17763/haer.72.3.01151786u134n051

Gurin, P., Nagda, B. (R.) A., & Zúñiga, X. (2013). *Dialogue across difference: Practice, theory, and research on intergroup dialogue*. Russell Sage Foundation.

Gurin, P., Nagda, B. R. A., & Lopez, G. E. (2004). The benefits of diversity in education for Democratic citizenship. *The Journal of social issues*, *60*(1), 17–34. https://doi.org/10.1111/j.0022-4537.2004.00097.x

Gust, S. W. (2007). "Look out for the football players and the frat boys": Autoethnographic reflections of a gay teacher in a gay curricular experience. *Educational studies*, *41*(1), 43–60. https://doi.org/10.1080/00131940701308999

Hackman, H. W. (2008). Broadening the pathway to academic success: The critical intersections of social justice education, multicultural design, and universal instruction design. In J. L. Higbee & E. Goff (Eds.), *Pedagogy and student services for institutional transformation: Implementing universal design in higher education* (pp. 61–77). University of Minnesota Press.

Hall, D., & Buzwell, S. (2013). The problem of free-riding in group projects: Looking beyond social loafing as a reason for non-contribution. *Active Learning in Higher Education*, *14*(1), 37–49. https://doi.org/10.1177/1469787412467123

Haque, A., Tubbs, C. Y., Kahumoku-Fessler, E. P., & Brown, M. D. (2019). Microaggressions and islamophobia: Experiences of Muslims across the United States and clinical implications. *Journal of Marital and Family Therapy*, *45*(1), 76–91. https://doi.org/10.1111/jmft.12339

Harackiewicz, J. M., Canning, E. A., Tibbetts, Y., Giffen, C. J., Blair, S. S., & Hyde, J. S. (2014). Closing the social class achievement gap for first-generation students in undergraduate biology. *Journal of educational psychology*, *106*(2), 375–389. https://doi.org/10.1037/a0034679

Harlap, Y. (2014). Preparing university educators for hot moments: Theater for educational development about difference, power, and privilege. *Teaching in Higher Education*, *19*(3), 217–228. https://doi.org/10.1080/13562517.2013.860098

Harlow, R. (2003). "Race doesn't matter, but . . .": The effect of race on professors' experiences and emotion management in the undergraduate college classroom. *Social Psychology Quarterly*, *66*(4), 348–363. https://doi.org/10.2307/1519834

Harris, A. (2019). *The effects of microaggressions on predictors of academic success* [Unpublished senior thesis]. Portland, OR: Reed College.

Hart, J. W., Karau, S. J., Stasson, M. F., & Kerr, N. A. (2004). Achievement motivation, expected coworker performance and collective task motivation: Working hard or hardly working? *Journal of applied social psychology*, *34*, 984–1000. https://doi.org/10.1111/j.1559-1816.2004.tb02580.x

Hausmann, L. R. M., Schofield, J. W., & Woods, R. L. (2007). Sense of belonging as a predictor of intentions to persist among African American and white first-year college students. *Research in higher education*, *48*(7), 803–839. https://doi.org/10.1007/s11162-007-9052-9

Henderson, M. G. (1994). What it means to teach the other when the other is the self. *Callaloo, 17*(2), 432–438.

Henshaw, R. G., & Reubens, A. (2013). Evaluating design enhancements to the tablet arm chair in language instruction classes at unc chapel Hill. *Journal of Learning Spaces, 2*(2). https://doi.org/http://libjournal.uncg.edu/jls/article/view/574/488

Hernández, R. J., & Villodas, M. (2018). Collectivistic coping responses to racial microaggressions associated with Latina/o College persistence attitudes. *Journal of Latina/o psychology, 7*(1), 76–90. https://doi.org/10.1037/lat0000107

Herne, C., & Morgan, S. (2013, May). *Faculty self-disclosure of identities: Decision strategies.* [Paper presentation] Lilly Conference on College and University Teaching.

Heydarian, N. M. (2016). Developing theory with the grounded-theory approach and thematic analysis. *Observer, 29*(4), 38–39. https://doi.org/https://www.psychologicalscience.org/observer/developing-theory-with-the-grounded-theory-approach-and-thematic-analysis

Higbee, J. L., Chung, C. J., & Hsu, L. (2008). Enhancing the inclusiveness of first-year courses through universal instruction design. In J. L. Higbee & E. Goff (Eds.), *Pedagogy and student services for institutional transformation: Implementing universal design in higher education* (pp. 61–77). University of Minnesota Press.

Higbee, J. L., & Goff, E. (Eds.). (2008). *Pedagogy and student services for institutional transformation: Implementing universal design in higher education.* Center for Research on Developmental Education and Urban Literacy.

Higbee, J. L., Schultz, J. L., & Goff, E. (2010). Pedagogy of inclusion: Integrated multicultural instructional design. *Journal of College Reading and Learning, 41*(1), 49–66. https://doi.org/10.1080/10790195.2010.10850335

Hilarides, B. D., & Oleson, K. C. (2008, February). *Coming out and passing: Disability identity management in higher education* [Poster presentation]. 9th Annual Meeting of the Society for Personality and Social Psychology.

Hitlin, S. (2003). Values as the core of personal identity: Drawing links between two theories of self. *Social psychology quarterly, 66*(2), 118–137. https://doi.org/https://www.jstor.org/stable/1519843

Hofer, B. K., & Pintrich, P. R. (1997). The development of epistemological theories: Beliefs about knowledge and knowing and their relation to learning. *Review of educational research, 67*(1), 88–140. https://doi.org/https://www.jstor.org/stable/1170620

Holder, A. M. B., Jackson, M. A., & Ponterotto, J. G. (2015). Racial microaggression experiences and coping strategies of black women in corporate leadership. *Qualitative psychology, 2*(2), 164–180. https://doi.org/10.1037/qup0000024

Holley, L. C., & Steiner, S. (2005). Safe space: Student perspectives on classroom environment. *Journal of social work education, 41*(1), 49–64. https://doi.org/10.5175/JSWE.2005.200300343

Hollins, C., & Govan, I. (2015). *Diversity, equity, and inclusion: Strategies for facilitating conversations on race.* Rowman & Littlefield..

hooks, b. (1994). *Teaching to transgress: Education as a practice of freedom*. Routledge.

Howard, J. (2015). *Discussion in the college classroom: Getting your students engaged and participating in person and online*. Jossey-Bass.

Howell, J. L., Gaither, S. E., & Ratliff, K. A. (2015). Caught in the middle: Defensive responses to IAT feedback among whites, blacks, and biracial Black/Whites. *Social psychological and personality science, 6*(4), 373–381. https://doi.org/10.1177/1948550614561127

Hughes, B., Houston, T., & Stein, J. (2010). Using case studies to help faculty navigate difficult classroom moments. *College teaching, 59*(1), 7–12. https://doi.org/http://doi.org/10.1080/87567555.2010.489076

Hurtado, S. (2005). The next generation of diversity and intergroup relations research. *The Journal of social issues, 61*(3), 595–610. https://doi.org/10.1111/j.1540-4560.2005.00422.x

Hurtado, S., Ruiz-Alvarado, A., & Guillermo-Wann, C. (2016). Thinking about race: The salience of racial identity at two- and four-year colleges and the climate for diversity. *The Journal of higher education, 86*(1), 127–155. https://doi.org/http://doi.org/10.1353/jhe.2015.0000

Hussar, W. J., & Bailey, T. M. (2014). *Projections of education statistics to 2022 (NCES 2014-051)*. U.S. Department of Education, National Center for Education Statistics. U.S. Government Printing Office.

Hussey, H. D., Fleck, B. K. B., & Warner, R. M. (2010). Reducing student prejudice in diversity-infused core psychology classes. *College teaching, 58*(3), 85–92. https://doi.org/10.1080/87567550903418560

Hutchins, H. M. (2015). Out the imposter: A study exploring imposter phenomenon among higher education faculty. *New Horizons in Adult Education & Human Resource Development, 27*(2), 3–12. https://doi.org/10.1002/nha3.20098

Hyde, C. A., & Ruth, B. J. (2002). Multicultural content and class participation: Do students self-censor? *Journal of social work education, 30*(2), 241–256. https://doi.org/https://www.jstor.org/stable/23043864

Inzlicht, M., & Ben-Zeev, T. (2000). A threatening intellectual environment: Why females are susceptible to experiencing problem-solving deficits in the presence of males. *Psychological science, 11*(5), 365–371. https://doi.org/10.1111/1467-9280.00272

Jacoby-Senghor, D. S., Sinclair, S., & Shelton, J. N. (2016). A lesson in bias: The relationship between implicit racial bias and performance in pedagogical contexts. *Journal of experimental social psychology, 63*, 50–55. https://doi.org/10.1016/j.jesp.2015.10.010

James, S. L. (2014). Talking rape in the classics classroom: Further thoughts. In N. Rabinowitz & F. McHardy (Eds.), *From abortion to pederasty: Addressing difficult topics in the classics classroom* (pp. 171–186). The Ohio State University Press.

Jamieson, J., Mendes, W. B., Blackstock, R., & Schmader, T. (2010). Turning the knots in your stomach into bows: Reappraising arousal improves performance on the GRE. *Journal of experimental social psychology, 46*(1), 208–212. https://doi.org/10.1016/j.jesp.2009.08.015

Jaremka, L. M., Ackerman, J. M., Gawronski, B., Rule, N. O., Sweeny, K., Tropp, L. R., Metz, M. A., Molina, L., Ryan, W. S., & Vick, S. B. (2020). Common academic experiences no one talks about: Repeated rejection, impostor syndrome, and burnout. *Perspectives on Psychological Science, 15*(3), 519–543.

Jaschik, S. (2019, February 18). Essay about how White male students dominate discussions sets off debate at Dickinson and beyond. *Inside Higher Ed*. https://www.insidehighered.com/news/2019/02/18/essay-about-how-white-male-students-dominate-discussions-sets-debate-dickinson-and

Jennings, K2016Overcoming racial tension: Using student voices to create safe spaces in the classroom*Faculty Focus special report: Diversity and inclusion in the college classroom*. Magna.

Jennings, T. (2010). Teaching "out" in the university: An investigation of the effects of lesbian, bisexual, and transgender faculty self-disclosure upon student evaluations of faculty teaching effectiveness. *International Journal of Inclusive Education, 14*(4), 325–339. https://doi.org/10.1080/13603110802504556

Johns, J., Inzlicht, M., & Schmader, T. (2008). Stereotype threat and executive resource depletion: Examining the influence of emotion regulation. *Journal of experimental psychology. General, 137*(4), 691–705. https://doi.org/10.1037/a0013834

Johns, M., Schmader, T., & Martens, A. (2005). Knowing is half the battle: Teaching stereotype threat as a means of improving women's math performance. *Psychological science, 16*(3), 175–179. https://doi.org/10.1111/j.0956-7976.2005.00799.x

Johnson, D. W., Johnson, R. T., & Smith, K. A. (2014). Cooperative learning: Improving university instruction by basing practice on validated theory. *Journal on excellence in college teaching, 25*(3/4), 85–118. https://doi.org/http://doi.org/10.1037/0003-066X.58.11.934

Johnston-Goodstar, K., & VeLure Roholt, R. (2017). "Our kids aren't dropping out; they're being pushed out": Native American students and racial microaggressions in schools. *Journal of ethnic & cultural diversity in social work, 26*(1/2), 30–47. https://doi.org/10.1080/15313204.2016.1263818

Jost, J. T. (2019). The IAT is dead, long live the IAT: Context-sensitive measures of implicit attitudes are indispensable to social and political psychology. *Current directions in psychological science, 28*(1), 10–19. https://doi.org/10.1177/0963721418797309

Jost, J. T., & Hunyady, O. (2005). Antecedents and consequences of system-justifying ideologies. *Current directions in psychological science, 14*(5), 260–265. https://doi.org/10.1111/j.0963-7214.2005.00377.x

Jury, M., Smeding, A., Stephens, N. M., Nelson, J. E., Aelenei, C., & Darnon, C. (2017). The experience of low-SES students in higher education: Psychological barriers to success and interventions to reduce social-class inequality. *The Journal of social issues, 73*(1), 23–41. https://doi.org/10.1111/josi.12202

Jusuf, C. C., Monteith, M. J., & Hildebrand, L. K. (2019, February). *Perceptions of ally confrontations* [Poster presentation]. 20th Annual Meeting of the Society for Personality and Social Psychology.

Karau, S. J., & Williams, K. D. (1993). Social loafing: A meta-analytic review and theoretical integration. *Journal of personality and social psychology, 65*(4), 681–706. https://doi.org/10.1037/0022-3514.65.4.681

Karau, S. J., & Williams, K. D. (1995). Social loafing: Research findings, implications, and future directions. *Current directions in psychological science, 4*(5), 134–139. https://doi.org/10.1111/1467-8721.ep10772570

Kattari, S. K., Olzman, M., & Hanna, M. D. (2018). "You look fine!": Ableist experiences by people with invisible disabilities. *Affilia, 33*(4), 477–492. https://doi.org/10.1177/0886109918778073

Katz, I., & Hass, R. G. (1988). Racial ambivalence and American value conflict: Correlation and prime studies of dual cognitive structures. *Journal of Personality and Social Psychology, 55*(6), 893–905.

Keels, M., Durkee, M., & Hope, E. (2017). The psychological and academic costs of school-based racial and ethnic microaggressions. *American educational research journal, 54*(6), 1316–1344. https://doi.org/10.3102/0002831217722120

Kendi, I. X. (2019). *How to be an antiracist.* New York: One World.

Kenney, M. (2001). *Mapping gay LA.: The intersection of place and politics.* Temple University Press.

Keum, B. T., Brady, J. L., Sharma, R., Lu, Y., Kim, Y. H., & Thai, C. J. (2018). Gendered racial microaggressions scale for Asian American women: Development and initial validation. *Journal of counseling psychology, 65*(5), 571–585. https://doi.org/10.1037/cou0000305

Kibler, J. (2011). Cognitive disequilibrium. In S. Goldstein & J. A. Naglieri (Eds.), *Encyclopedia of Child Behavior and Development* (p. 380). Springer.

King, P., & Kitchener, K. (1994). *Developing reflective judgment: Understanding and promoting intellectual growth and critical thinking in adolescents and adults.* Jossey-Bass.

King, R. S. (2013). They ask, should we tell? Thoughts on disclosure in the classroom. *Thought and Action, 29*, 101–111.

Kite, M. E., & Whitley, B. E., Jr. (2016). Introducing the concepts of stereotyping, prejudice, and discrimination. In *Psychology of prejudice and discrimination* (3rd ed.). Routledge.

Klein, O., & Snyder, M. (2003). Stereotypes and behavioral confirmation: From interpersonal to intergroup perspectives. In M. P. Zanna (Ed.), *Advances in experimental social psychology* (Vol. 35, pp. 153–234). Academic Press.

Knowles, E. D., Lowery, B. S., Chow, R. M., & Unzueta, M. M. (2014). Deny, distance, or dismantle? how white Americans manage a privileged identity. *Perspectives on Psychological Science, 9*(6), 594–609. https://doi.org/10.1177/1745691614554658

Knox, E. (Ed.). (2017). *Trigger warnings: History, theory, and context.* Rowman & Littlefield.

Kornell, N. (2009). Optimizing learning using flashcards: Spacing is more effective than cramming. *Applied cognitive psychology, 23*(9), 1297–1317. https://doi.org/10.1002/acp.1537

Kornell, N., & Bjork, R. A. (2008). Learning concepts and categories: Is spacing the "enemy of induction"? *Psychological science, 19*(6), 585–592. https://doi.org/10.1111/j.1467-9280.2008.02127.x

Kornell, N., & Son, L. K. (2009). Learners' choices and beliefs about self-testing. *Memory, 17*(5), 493–501. https://doi.org/10.1080/09658210902832915

Kuh, G. D. (2008). *High-impact educational practices: What they are, who has access to them, and why they matter.* Association of American Colleges & Universities.

Kumar, S., & Jagacinski, C. M. (2006). Imposters have goals, too: The imposter phenomenon and its relationship to achievement goal theory. *Personality and individual differences, 40*(1), 147–157. https://doi.org/10.1016/j.paid.2005.05.014

Kunda, Z., & Sherman-Williams, B. (1993). Stereotypes and the construal of individuating information. *Personality and Social Psychology Bulletin, 19*(1), 90–99. https://doi.org/10.1177/0146167293191010

LaBossiere, M. (2014, June 18). Trigger warnings and academic freedom I. *Talking Philosophy.* http://blog.talkingphilosophy.com/?p=7986

Ladson-Billings, G. (1995). But that's just good teaching! The case for culturally relevant pedagogy. *Theory Into Practice, 34*(3), 159–165.

Lai, C. K., Skinner, A. L., Cooley, E., Murrar, S., Brauer, M., Devos, T., Calanchini, J., Xiao, Y. J., Pedram, C., Marshburn, C. K., Simon, S., Blanchar, J. C., Joy-Gaba, J. A., Conway, J., Redford, L., Klein, R. A., Roussos, G., Schellhaas, F. M. H., Burns, M., & Nosek, B. A. (2016). Reducing implicit racial preferences: II. intervention effectiveness across time. *Journal of experimental psychology. General, 145*(8), 1001–1016. https://doi.org/10.1037/xge0000179

Landis, K. (Ed.). (2008). *Start talking: A handbook for engaging difficult dialogues in higher education.* University of Alaska and Alaska Pacific University.

Latu, I. M., Mast, M. S., Lammers, J., & Bombari, D. (2013). Successful female leaders empower women's behavior in leadership tasks. *Journal of experimental social psychology, 49*(3), 444–448. https://doi.org/10.1016/j.jesp.2013.01.003

Leary, M. R., Tambor, E. S., Terdal, S. K., & Downs, D. L. (1995). Self-Esteem as an interpersonal monitor: The sociometer hypothesis. *Journal of personality and social psychology, 68*(3), 518–530. https://doi.org/10.1037/0022-3514.68.3.518

Legge, M. M., Flanders, C. E., & Robinson, M. (2018). Young bisexual people's experiences of microaggression: Implications for social work. *Social Work in Mental Health, 16*(2), 125–144.

Lei, S. A. (2010). Classroom physical design influencing student learning and evaluations of college instructors: A review of literature. *Education, 131*(1), 128–133.

Leibowitz, B., Bozalek, V., Rohleder, P., Carolissen, R., & Swartz, L. (2010). "Ah, but the whiteys love to talk about themselves": Discomfort as a pedagogy for change. *Race Ethnicity and Education, 13*(1), 83–100. https://doi.org/10.1080/13613320903364523

Leonardo, Z., & Porter, R. K. (2010). Pedagogy of fear: Toward a Fanonian theory of "safety" in race dialogue. *Race Ethnicity and Education, 13*(2), 139–157. https://doi.org/10.1080/13613324.2010.482898

Lerner, M. J. (1980). *The belief in a just world*. Plenum.

Levesque, C., Zuehlke, A. N., Stanek, L. R., & Ryan, R. M. (2004). Autonomy and competence in German and American university students: A comparative study based on self-determination theory. *Journal of educational psychology, 96*(1), 68–84. https://doi.org/10.1037/0022-0663.96.1.68

Lewin, K. (1946). Behavior and development as a function of the total situation. In D. Cartwright (Eds.), *Field theory in social sciences: Selected theoretical papers by Kurt Lewin* (pp. 238–303). Harper & Row.

Lewis, J. A., Mendenhall, R., Harwood, S. A., & Huntt, B. M. (2016). "Ain't I a woman?": Perceived gendered racial microaggressions experienced by Black women. *The Counseling psychologist, 44*(5), 758–780. https://doi.org/10.1177/0011000016641193

Lewis, M. M. (2011). Body of knowledge: Black queer feminist pedagogy, praxis, and embodied text. *Journal of Lesbian Studies, 15*(1), 49–57. https://doi.org/10.1080/10894160.2010.508411

Lilienfeld, S. O. (2017). Microaggressions: Strong claims, inadequate evidence. *Association for Psychological Science, 12*(1), 138–169. https://doi.org/10.1177/1745691616659391

Lin, M. H., Kwan, V. S. Y., Cheung, A., & Fiske, S. T. (2005). Stereotype content model explains prejudice for an envied outgroup: Scale of anti-Asian American stereotypes. *Personality and Social Psychology Bulletin, 31*(1), 34–47. https://doi.org/10.1177/0146167204271320

Lippincott, J. (2009). Learning spaces: Involving faculty to improve pedagogy. *Educause, 44*(2), 17–25. https://doi.org/https://er.educause.edu/articles/2009/3/learning-spaces-involving-faculty-to-improve-pedagogy

Littleford, L. N., & Nolan, S. A. (2013). Your sphere of influence: How to infuse cultural diversity into your psychology class: Strategies for ensuring that diversity is an integral part of the psychology curriculum. *Psychology Teacher Network, 23*(1). https://doi.org/https://www.apa.org/ed/precollege/ptn/2013/05/cultural-diversity

Lopez, G. E. (2004). Interethnic contact, curriculum, and attitudes in the first year of college. *Journal of Social Issues, 60*(1), 75–94. https://doi.org/10.1111/j.0022-4537.2004.00100.x

Lowe, P. (2015). Lessening sensitivity: Student experiences of teaching and learning sensitive issues. *Teaching in Higher Education, 20*(1), 119–129. https://doi.org/10.1080/13562517.2014.957272

Lowe, P., & Jones, H. (2010). Teaching and learning sensitive topics. *Enhancing Learning in the Social Sciences, 2*(3), 1–7. https://doi.org/10.11120/elss.2010.02030001

Ludlow, J. (2004). From safe space to contested space in the feminist classroom. *Transformations: The Journal of Inclusive Scholarship and Pedagogy, 15*(1), 40–56.

Lui, P. P., & Quezada, L. (2019). Associations between microaggression and adjustment outcomes: A meta-analytic and narrative review. *Psychological Bulletin, 145*(1), 45–78. https://doi.org/10.1037/bul0000172

Luker, M., & Morris, B. (2016). Five things I learned from working with the student-consultant for teaching and learning program. *Teaching and Learning Together in Higher Education, 1*(17), 1–5. https://doi.org/https://repository.brynmawr.edu/tlthe/vol1/iss17/2

Luyckx, K., Vansteenkiste, M., Goossens, L., & Duriez, B. (2009). Basic need satisfaction and identity formation: Bridging self-determination theory and process-oriented identity research. *Journal of Counseling Psychology, 56*(2), 276–288. https://doi.org/10.1037/a0015349

Macdonald, H. M. (2013). Inviting discomfort: Foregrounding emotional labour in teaching anthropology in post-apartheid South Africa. *Teaching in Higher Education, 18*(6), 670–682. https://doi.org/10.1080/13562517.2013.795938

Mace, R. L., Hardie, G. J., & Place, J. P. (1991). Accessible environments: Toward universal design. In W. E. Preiser, J. C. Vischer, & E. T. White (Eds.), *Design intervention: Toward a more humane architecture* (pp. 155–176). Van Nostrand Reinhold.

Macrae, C. N., & Bodenhausen, G. V. (2000). Social cognition: Thinking categorically about others. *Annual Review of Psychology, 51*(1), 93–120. https://doi.org/10.1146/annurev.psych.51.1.93

Madera, J. M., Hebl, M. R., & Martin, R. C. (2009). Gender and letters of recommendation for academia: Agentic and communal differences. *Journal of Applied Psychology, 94*(6), 1591–1599. https://doi.org/10.1037/a0016539

Markus, H. R., & Conner, A. L. (2013). *Clash! 8 cultural conflicts that make us who we are.* Penguin Group.

Markus, H. R., & Kitayama, S. (1991). Culture and the self: Implications for cognition, emotion, and motivation. *Psychological Review, 98*(2), 224–253. https://doi.org/10.1037/0033-295X.98.2.224

Markus, H. R., & Kitayama, S. (1994). A collective fear of the collective: Implications for selves and theories of selves. *Personality and Social Psychology Bulletin, 20*(5), 568–579. https://doi.org/10.1177/0146167294205013

Markus, H. R., & Kitayama, S. (2003). Models of agency: Sociocultural diversity in the construction of action. In V. Murphy-Berman & J. J. Berman (Eds.), *Nebraska symposium on motivation: Vol. 49. Cross-cultural differences in perspectives on self* (pp. 1–57). University of Nebraska Press.

Martens, A., Johns, M., Greenberg, J., & Schimel, J. (2006). Combating stereotype threat: The effect of self-affirmation on women's intellectual performance. *Journal of Experimental Social Psychology, 42*(2), 236–243. https://doi.org/10.1016/j.jesp.2005.04.010

Maxwell, M. (2018, April 23). Diversifying the canon: Interview with Robert Sanchez [blog post]. American Philosophical Association. https://blog .apaonline.org/2018/04/23/diversifying-the-canon-interview-with-robert -sanchez/

McCarthy, T. (2018, May 16). Israel's violent rule increasingly driving liberal American Jews on to the streets. *The Guardian.* https://www.theguardian.com/ world/2018/may/16/israel-palestine-protests-american-jewish-groups

McClain, K. S., & Perry, A. (2017). Where did they go: Retention rates for students of color at predominantly white institutions. *College Student Affairs Leadership*, *4*(1).

McGregor, L. N., Gee, D. E., & Posey, K. E. (2008). I feel like a fraud and it depresses me: The relation between the imposter phenomenon and depression. *Social Behavior and Personality*, *36*(1), 43–48. https://doi.org/10.2224/sbp.2008 .36.1.43

McLean, K. C., Syed, M., & Shucard, H. (2016). Bringing identity content to the fore: Links to identity development processes. *Emerging adulthood*, *4*(5), 356–364. https://doi.org/10.1177/2167696815626820

Mekawi, Y., & Todd, N. R. (2018). Okay to say?: Initial validation of the acceptability of racial Microaggressions scale. *Cultural Diversity and Ethnic Minority Psychology*, *24*(3), 346–362. https://doi.org/10.1037/cdp0000201

Mendoza, S. A., Gollwitzer, P. M., & Amodio, D. M. (2010). Reducing the expression of implicit stereotypes: Reflexive control through implementation intentions. *Personality and Social Psychology Bulletin*, *36*(4), 512–523. https://doi .org/10.1177/0146167210362789

Mendoza-Denton, R., Downey, G., Purdie, V. J., Davis, A., & Pietrzak, J. (2002). Sensitivity to status-based rejection: Implications for African American students' college experience. *Journal of Personality and Social Psychology*, *83*(4), 896–918. https://doi.org/10.1037/0022-3514.83.4.896

Merculieff, I., & Roderick, L. (2013). *Stop talking: Indigenous ways of teaching and learning and difficult dialogues in higher education.* University of Alaska Anchorage.

Meyer, A., Rose, D. H., & Gordon, D. (2014). *Universal design for learning: Theory and practice.* CAST.

Meyers, S. A. (1997). Increasing student participation and productivity in small-group activities for psychology classes. *Teaching of Psychology*, *24*(2), 105–115. https://doi.org/10.1207/s15328023top2402_5

Micari, M., & Drane, D. (2011). Intimidation in small learning groups: The roles of social-comparison concern, comfort, and individual characteristics in student academic outcomes. *Active Learning in Higher Education*, *12*(3), 175–187. https://doi.org/10.1177/1469787411415078

Micari, M., & Pazos, P. (2014). Worrying about what others think: A social-comparison concern intervention in small learning groups. *Active Learning in Higher Education*, *15*(3), 249–262. https://doi.org/10.1177/1469787414544874

Michaelsen, L. K., & Sweet, M. (2008). The essential elements of team-based learning. In L. K. Michaelsen, M. Sweet, & D. X. Parmalee (Eds.), *Team-based learning: Small group learning's next big step* (New Directions for Teaching and Learning, No. 116, pp. 7–27). Jossey-Bass. https://doi.org/10.1002/tl.330

Miklikowska, M. (2016). Like parent, like child? development of prejudice and tolerance towards immigrants. *British Journal of Psychology, 107*(1), 95–116. https://doi.org/10.1111/bjop.12124

Milkman, K. L., Akinola, M., & Chugh, D. (2015). What happens before? A field experiment exploring how pay and representation differentially shape bias on the pathway into organizations. *Journal of Applied Psychology, 100*(6), 1678–1712. https://doi.org/10.1037/apl0000022

Miller, J., & Chamberlin, M. (2000). Women are teachers, men are professors: A study of student perceptions. *Teaching Sociology, 28*(4), 283–298. https://doi.org/10.2307/1318580

Minikel-Lacocque, J. (2013). Racism, college, and the power of words: Racial microaggressions reconsidered. *American Educational Research Journal, 50*(3), 432–465.

Miyake, A., Kost-Smith, L. E., Finkelstein, N. D., Pollock, S. J., Cohen, G. L., & Ito, T. A. (2010). Reducing the gender achievement gap in college science: A classroom study of values affirmation. *Science, 330*(6008), 1234–1237. https://doi.org/10.1126/science.1195996

Monteith, M. J. (1993). Self-regulation of prejudiced responses: Implications for progress in prejudice-reduction efforts. *Journal of Personality and Social Psychology, 65*(3), 469–485. https://doi.org/10.1037/0022-3514.65.3.469

Monteith, M. J., Ashburn-Nardo, L., Voils, C. I., & Czopp, A. M. (2002). Putting the brakes on prejudice: On the development and operation of cues for control. *Journal of Personality and Social Psychology, 83*(5), 1029–1050. https://doi.org/10.1037/0022-3514.83.5.1029

Monteith, M. J., Lybarger, J. E., & Woodcock, A. (2009). Schooling the cognitive monster: The role of motivation in the regulation and control of prejudice. *Social and Personality Psychology Compass, 3*(3), 211–226. https://doi.org/10.1111/j.1751-9004.2009.00177.x

Monteith, M. J., Parker, L. R., & Burns, M. D. (2016). The self-regulation of prejudice. In T. D. Nelson (Ed.), *Handbook of stereotyping, prejudice, and discrimination* (pp.409–432). Psychology Press.

Moroz, S. (2015). *Discrimination is in the eye of the beholder: Perception of discrimination and microaggressions* [Master's thesis, University of Western Ontario]. Electronic Thesis and Dissertation Repository, 3147. https://ir.lib.uwo.ca/etd/3147/

Mosely, M. M., & Obear, K. (2019). *Navigating triggering events: critical competencies for facilitating difficult dialogues.* [Workshop presentation]. 2019 National Conference on Race and Ethnicity in American Higher Education.

Murphy, M. C., Richeson, J. A., Shelton, J. N., Rheinschmidt, M. L., & Bergsieker, H. B. (2013). Cognitive and behavioral costs of subtle v. blatant racial prejudice during interracial interactions. *Group Processes and Intergroup Relations, 16*(5), 560–571.

Murphy, R. R., Hammerslough, S., Kaufman, S., MacCalman, M., Pearlman, S., Shrader, A., & Oleson, K. C. (2018, June). *Bias-aware critical self-reflection predicts university student and faculty prejudice-confrontation beliefs* [Poster presentation]. 14th Meeting of the Society for the Psychological Study of Social Issues.

Murphy, R. R., & Oleson, K. C. (2019, February). *When awareness isn't enough: Joint effect of bias awareness and perceived changeability on prejudice* [Poster presentation]. 20th Annual Meeting of the Society for Personality and Social Psychology.

Nadal, K. L., Davidoff, K. C., Davis, L. S., & Wong, Y. (2014). Emotional, behavioral, and cognitive reactions to microaggressions: Transgender perspectives. *Psychology of Sexual Orientation and Gender Diversity, 1*(1), 72–81. https://doi.org/10.1037/sgd0000011

Nadal, K. L., Griffin, K. E., Hamit, S., Leon, J., Tobio, M., & Rivera, D. P. (2012). Subtle and overt forms of Islamophobia: Microaggressions toward Muslim Americans. *Journal of Muslim Mental Health, 6*(2), 16–37. https://doi.org/10.3998/jmmh.10381607.0006.203

Nadal, K. L., Griffin, K. E., Wong, Y., Hamit, S., & Rasmus, M. (2014). The impact of racial microaggressions on mental health: Counseling implications for clients of color. *Journal of Counseling and Development, 92*(1), 57–66. https://doi.org/10.1002/j.1556-6676.2014.00130.x

Nadal, K. L., Hamit, S., Lyons, O., Weinberg, A., & Corman, L. (2013). Gender microaggressions: Perceptions, processes, and coping mechanisms of women. In M. A. Paludi (Ed.), *The psychology of business success, Vol. 1: Juggling, balancing, and integrating work and family role and responsibilities* (pp. 193–220). Praeger.

Nadan, Y., & Stark, M. (2017). The pedagogy of discomfort: Enhancing reflectivity on stereotypes and bias. *British journal of social work, 47*(3), 683–700. https://doi.org/10.1093/bjsw/bcw023

Nadga, B. A., & Gurin, P. (2013). The practice of intergroup dialogue. In P. Gurin, B. A. Nagda, & X. Zúñiga (Eds.), *Dialogue across difference: Practice, theory, and research on intergroup dialogue* (pp. 32–73). Russell Sage Foundation.

Nagda, B. A., Yeakley, A., Gurin, P., & Sorensen, N. (2012). Intergroup dialogue: A critical-dialogic model for conflict engagement. In L. R. Tropp (Ed.), *The Oxford handbook of intergroup conflict* (pp. 210–228). Oxford University Press.

Nagda, Biren (Ratnesh) A.. (2006). Breaking barriers, crossing borders, building bridges: Communication processes in intergroup dialogues. *Journal of Social Issues, 62*(3), 553–576. https://doi.org/10.1111/j.1540-4560.2006.00473.x

Nakamura, K. (2019, May). *Disability, race, class, and social justice in education.* [Workshop presentation]. 2019 National Conference on Race and Ethnicity in American Higher Education.

Nario-Redmond, M. R. (2010). Cultural stereotypes of disabled and non-disabled men and women: Consensus for global category representations and diagnostic domains. *British Journal of Social Psychology, 49*(3), 471–488. https://doi.org/10.1348/014466609X468411

Nario-Redmond, M. R. (2016, June). *Universal design: Principles and strategies for teaching all students.* [Paper presentation]. 12th Meeting of the Society for the Psychological Study of Social Issues.

Nario-Redmond, M. R. (2018, June). *Implementing universally-designed practices in a diverse first-year student writing course* [Paper presentation]. 14th Meeting of the Society for the Psychological Study of Social Issues.

Nario-Redmond, M. R., Gospodinov, D., & Cobb, A. (2017). Crip for a day: The unintended negative consequences of disability simulations. *Rehabilitation Psychology, 62*(3), 324–333. https://doi.org/10.1037/rep0000127

National Commission for the Protection of Human Subjects of Biomedical and Behavioral Research. (1979). *The Belmont report: Ethical principles and guidelines for the protection of human subjects of research.* U.S. Department of Health and Human Services. https://www.hhs.gov/ohrp/regulations-and-policy/belmont -report/read-the-belmont-report/index.html

National Survey of Student Engagement (NSSE). (2015). Engagement indicators and high-impact practices. http://nsse.indiana.edu/ pdf/ EIs_and_HIPs_2015 .pdf https://doi.org/10.1007/s11162-010-9210-3

Nelson, J. C., Adams, G., & Salter, P. S. (2013). The Marley hypothesis: Denial of racism reflects ignorance of history. *Psychological science, 24*(2), 213–218. https:// doi.org/10.1177/0956797612451466

Nelson Laird, T. F. (2011, 9). Measuring the diversity inclusivity of college courses. *Research in Higher Education, 52*(6), 572–588. https://doi.org/10.1007/s11162 -010-9210-3

Neville, H. A., Awad, G. H., Brooks, J. E., Flores, M. P., & Bluemel, J. (2013). Color-blind racial ideology: Theory, training, and measurement implications in psychology. *American Psychologist, 68*(6), 455–466. https://doi.org/10.1037/ a0033282

Neville, H. A., Poteat, V. P., Lewis, J. A., & Spanierman, L. B. (2014). Changes in White college students' color-blind racial ideology over four years: Do diversity experiences make a difference? *Journal of Counseling Psychology, 61*(2), 179–190. https://doi.org/10.1037/a0035168

Nickerson, R. S. (1998). Confirmation bias: A ubiquitous phenomenon in many guises. *Review of General Psychology, 2*(2), 175–220. https://doi.org/10.1037/ 1089-2680.2.2.175

Niemann, C. G. (2012). The making of a token: A case study of stereotype threat, stigma, racism, and tokenism in academe. In G. Gutierrez y Muhs, Y. F. Niemann, C. G. Gonzalez, & A. P. Harris (Eds.), *Presumed incompetent: The intersections of race and class for women in academia* (pp. 336–355). University Press of Colorado.

Niemiec, C. P., & Ryan, R. M. (2009). Autonomy, competence, and relatedness in the classroom: Applying self-determination theory to educational practice. *Theory and Research in Education, 7*(2), 133–144. https://doi.org/10.1177/ 1477878509104318

Nosek, B. A., Smyth, F. L., Hansen, J. J., Devos, T., Lindner, N. M., Ranganath, K. A., Smith, C. T., Olson, K. R., Chugh, D., Greenwald, A. G., & Banaji,

M. R. (2007). Pervasiveness and correlates of implicit attitudes and stereotypes. *European Review of Social Psychology*, *18*(1), 36–88. https://doi.org/10.1080/10463280701489053

O'Brien, L. T., Crandall, C. S., Horstman-Reser, A., Warner, R., Alsbrooks, A., & Blodorn, A. (2010). But I'm no bigot: How prejudiced White Americans maintain unprejudiced self-images. *Journal of Applied Social Psychology*, *40*(4), 917–946. https://doi.org/10.1111/j.1559-1816.2010.00604.x

Ohland, M. W., Loughry, M. L., Woehr, D. J., Bullard, L. G., Felder, R. M., Finelli, C. J., Layton, R. A., Pomeranz, H. R., & Schmucker, D. G. (2012). The comprehensive assessment of team member effectiveness: Development of a behaviorally anchored rating scale for self- and peer evaluation. *Journal of Management Learning and Education*, *11*(4), 609–630. https://doi.org/10.5465/amle.2010.0177

Oleson, K. C. (2015, September 1). The art of the conference: Is there a secret formula for great class discussion? *Reed Magazine*, *94*(3), 20.

Oleson, K. C. (2016). Introduction: Collaborating to develop and improve classroom teaching: Student-consultant for teaching and learning program at Reed College. *Teaching and Learning Together in Higher Education,*, *1*(17), 1–3.

Oleson, K. C. (2017). [Qualitative interviews on classroom dynamics] Unpublished raw data. For quotes: data have been transcribed verbatim except that fillers (e.g., umm, like, repeated phrases) have been deleted

Oleson, K. C. (2019). [Social psychology lab studies on discomfort and safety in the university classroom] Unpublished raw data.

Oleson, K. C., & Hovakimyan, K. (2017). Reflections on developing the student consultants for teaching and learning program at Reed College, USA. *International Journal for Students as Partners*, *1*(1), 1–8. https://doi.org/10.15173/ijsap.v1i1.3094

Oleson, K. C., Poehlmann, K. M., Yost, J. H., Lynch, M. E., & Arkin, R. M. (2000). Subjective overachievement: Individual differences in self-doubt and concern with performance. *Journal of Personality*, *68*(3), 491–524. https://doi.org/10.1111/1467-6494.00104

Oleson, K. C., & Steckler, M. T. (2010). The phenotypic expressions of self-doubt about ability in academic contexts: Strategies of self-handicapping and subjective overachievement. In R. M. Arkin, K. C. Oleson, & P. J. Carroll (Eds.), *Handbook of the uncertain self* (pp. 379–398). Psychology Press.

Oleson, K. C., Vinton, E., Buttrill, S., Murphy, R., & Harris, A. (2018, March). *Faculty and student misperceptions about safety, challenge, and discomfort in higher education classrooms.* [Poster presentation]. 19th Annual Meeting of the Society of Personality and Social Psychology.

Oleson, K. C., Vinton, E., Buttrill, S., Murphy, R., Harris, A., & Yang, T. (2018, June). *Faculty and student perceptions of discomfort in higher education classrooms.* [Paper presentation]. 14th Meeting of the Society for the Psychological Study of Social Issues.

Ollin, R. (2008). Silent pedagogy and rethinking classroom practice: Structuring teaching through silence rather than talk. *Cambridge Journal of Education, 38*(2), 265–280. https://doi.org/10.1080/03057640802063528

Oluo, I. (2019). *So you want to talk about race*. New York: Seal Press. https://doi.org/10.1080/03057640802063528

Ong, A. D., Burrow, A. L., Fuller-Rowell, T. E., Ja, N. M., & Sue, D. W. (2013). Racial microaggressions and daily well-being among Asian Americans. *Journal of Counseling Psychology, 60*(2), 188–199. https://doi.org/10.1037/a0031736

Oyserman, D., Elmore, K., Novin, S., Fisher, O., & Smith, G. C. (2018). Guiding people to interpret their experienced difficulty as importance highlights their academic possibilities and improves their academic performance. *Frontiers in Psychology, 9*, 781. https://doi.org/10.3389/fpsyg.2018.00781

Oyserman, D., & Lewis, N. A. (2017). Seeing the destination and the path: Using identity-based motivation to understand and reduce racial disparities in academic achievement. *Social Issues and Policy Review, 11*(1), 159–194. https://doi.org/10.1111/sipr.12030

Parsons, C. S. (2017). Reforming the environment: The influence of the roundtable classroom design on interactive learning. *Journal of Learning Spaces, 6*(3), 23–33.

Pasque, P. A., Chesler, M. A., Charbeneau, J., & Carlson, C. (2013). Pedagogical approaches to student racial conflict in the classroom. *Journal of Diversity in Higher Education, 6*(1), 1–16. https://doi.org/10.1037/a0031695

Patton, L. D. (2016). Disrupting postsecondary prose: Toward a critical race theory of higher education. *Urban Education, 51*(3), 315–342.

Patton, L. D., & Simmons, S. L. (2008). Exploring complexities of multiple identities of lesbians in a Black college environment. *Negro Educational Review, 59*(3/4), 197–237.

Pérez Huber, L., & Solórzano, D. G. (2018). Teaching racial microaggressions: Implications of critical race hypos for social work praxis. *Journal of Ethnic and Cultural Diversity in Social Work, 27*(1), 54–71. https://doi.org/10.1080/15313204.2017.1417944

Perry, G., Moore, H., Edwards, C., Acosta, K., & Frey, C. (2009). Maintaining credibility and authority as an instructor of color in diversity-education classrooms: A qualitative inquiry. *Journal of Higher Education, 80*(1), 80–105. https://doi.org/10.1080/00221546.2009.11772131

Perry, S. P., Murphy, M. C., & Dovidio, J. F. (2015). Modern prejudice: Subtle, but unconscious? The role of bias awareness in Whites' perceptions of personal and others' biases. *Journal of Experimental Social Psychology, 61*, 64–78. https://doi.org/10.1016/j.jesp.2015.06.007

Perry, W. G. (1970). *Forms of intellectual and ethical development in the college years: A scheme*. Holt.

Persellin, D. C., & Daniels, M. B. (2018). *A concise guide to teaching with desirable difficulties*. Stylus.

Peteet, B. J., Brown, C. M., Lige, Q. M., & Lanaway, D. A. (2015). Impostorism is associated with greater psychological distress and lower self-esteem for African

American students. *Current Psychology, 34*(1), 154–163. https://doi.org/10.1007/s12144-014-9248-z

Petrie, K. J., & Rief, W. (2019). Psychobiological mechanisms of placebo and nocebo effects: Pathways to improve treatments and reduce side effects. *Annual review of psychology, 70,* 599–625. https://doi.org/10.1146/annurev-psych-010418-102907

Petrone, M. C. (2004). Supporting diversity with faculty learning communities: Teaching and learning across boundaries. In M. D. Cox & L. Richlin (Eds.), *Building faculty learning communities* (New Directions for Teaching and Learning, No. 97, pp. 111–125). Jossey-Bass. https://doi.org/10.1002/tl.138

Pettigrew, T. F. (1998). Intergroup contact theory. *Annual review of psychology, 49,* 65–85. https://doi.org/10.1146/annurev.psych.49.1.65

Pettigrew, T. F., & Tropp, L. R. (2006). A meta-analytic test of intergroup contact theory. *Journal of personality and social psychology, 90*(5), 751–783. https://doi.org/10.1037/0022-3514.90.5.751

Piaget, J. (1983). Piaget's theory. In P. Mussen (Ed.), *Handbook of child psychology* (4th ed., Vol. 1). Wiley.

Piaget, J. (1985). *The equilibration of cognitive structures: The central problem of intellectual development.* University of Chicago Press.

Pierce, C., Carew, J., Pierce-Gonzalez, D., & Wills, D. (1978). An experiment in racism: TV commercials. In C. Pierce (Ed.), *Television and education* (pp.62–88). Sage.

Pierce, C. M. (1970). Offensive mechanisms. In F. B. Barbour (Ed.), *The Black seventies* (pp. 265–282). Porter Sargent.

Pittman, C. T. (2010). Race and gender oppression in the classroom: The experiences of women faculty of color with white male students. *Teaching Sociology, 38*(3), 183–196. https://doi.org/10.1177/0092055X10370120

Plaut, V. C., Garnett, F. G., Buffardi, L. E., & Sanchez-Burks, J. (2011, Aug). "What about me?" Perceptions of exclusion and Whites' reactions to multiculturalism. *Journal of Personality and Social Psychology, 101*(2), 337–353. https://doi.org/10.1037/a0022832

Project Implicit. (2011). Ethical considerations. https://implicit.harvard.edu/implicit/ethics.html

Purdie-Vaughns, V., Steele, C. M., Davies, P. G., Ditlmann, R., & Crosby, J. R. (2008, Apr). Social identity contingencies: How diversity cues signal threat or safety for African Americans in mainstream institutions. *Journal of Personality and Social Psychology, 94*(4), 615–630. https://doi.org/10.1037/0022-3514.94.4.615

Quaye, S. J. (2012). Think before you teach: Preparing for dialogues about racism realities. *Journal of college student development, 53*(4), 542–562. https://doi.org/http://doi.org/%2010.1353/csd.2012.0056

Rabinowitz, N. (2014). Introduction: Difficult and sensitive discussions. In N. Rabinowitz & F. McHardy (Eds.), *From abortion to pederasty: Addressing difficult topics in the classics classroom.* The Ohio State University Press.

Rabinowitz, N., & McHardy, F. (Eds.). (2014). *From abortion to pederasty: Addressing difficult topics in the classics classroom.* The Ohio State University Press.

Rands, M. L., & Gansemer-Topf, A. M. (2017). The room itself is active: How classroom design impacts student engagement. *Journal of Learning Spaces, 6*(1), 26–33.

Rasinski, H. M., Geers, A. L., & Czopp, A. M. (2013). "I guess what he said wasn't that bad": Dissonance in nonconforming targets of prejudice. *Personality and Social Psychology Bulletin, 39*(7), 856–860. https://doi.org/10.1177/0146167213484769

Rattan, A., & Ambady, N. (2011). Diversity ideologies and intergroup relations: An examination of colorblindness and multiculturalism. *European journal of social psychology, 43*(1), 12–21. https://doi.org/10.1002/ejsp.1892

Reardon, S. F., Kalogrides, D., & Shores, K. (2019). The geography of racial/ethnic test score gaps. *The American journal of sociology, 124*(4), 1164–1221. https://doi.org/10.1086/700678

Redmond, M. (2010). Safe space oddity: Revisiting critical pedagogy. *Journal of Teaching in Social Work, 30*(1), 1–14.

Reshamwala, S. (2016, December). Check our bias to wreck our bias [Video]. *New York Times.* https://www.nytimes.com/video/us/100000004818668/check-our-bias-to-wreck-our-bias.html

Richeson, J. A., & Nussbaum, R. J. (2004). The impact of multiculturalism versus color-blindness on racial bias. *Journal of experimental social psychology, 40*(3), 417–423. https://doi.org/10.1016/j.jesp.2003.09.002

Rios, D. (2018, June). *When the professor experiences stereotype threat.* [Paper presentation] 14th Meeting of the Society for the Psychological Study of Social Issues.

Ro, H. K., & Loya, K. I. (2015). The effect of gender and race intersectionality on student learning outcomes in engineering. *The review of higher education, 38*((3), 359–396. https://doi.org/http://doi.org/10.1353/rhe.2015.0014

Roberts, K. D., Park, H. J., Brown, S., & Cook, B. (2011). Universal design for instruction in postsecondary education: A systematic review of empirically based articles. *Journal of Postsecondary Education and Disability, 24*(1), 5–15.

Roff, S. (2014). May). treatment, not trigger warnings. *The Chronicle of higher education.* https://doi.org/https://www.chronicle.com/blogs/conversation/2014/05/23/treatment-not-trigger-warnings/

Rogler, L. H. (1989). The meaning of culturally sensitive research in mental health. *American Journal of Psychiatry, 146*(3), 296–303.

Rosenthal, L. (2016). Incorporating intersectionality into psychology: An opportunity to promote social justice and equity. *The American psychologist, 71*(6), 474–485. https://doi.org/10.1037/a0040323

Ruble, D. N. (1994). A phase model of transitions: Cognitive and motivational consequences. In M. P. Zanna (Ed.), *Advances in experimental social psychology* (Vol. 26, pp. 63–214). Academic Press.

Rudman, L. A., Ashmore, R. D., & Gary, M. L. (2001). "Unlearning" automatic biases: The malleability of implicit stereotypes and prejudice. *Journal of personality and social psychology, 81*(5), 856–868. https://doi.org/10.1037/0022-3514.81.5.856

Ruscher, J. B. (2001). The news media. In J. B. Ruscher (Ed.), *Prejudiced communication: A social psychological perspective* (pp. 137–165). Guilford Press.

Russ, T. L., Simonds, C. J., & Hunt, S. K. (2002). Coming out in the classroom . . . an occupational hazard? The influence of sexual orientation on teacher credibility and perceived student learning. *Communication Education, 51*(3), 311–324. https://doi.org/10.1080/03634520216516

Ryan, R. M., & Deci, E. L. (2000). Self-determination theory and the facilitation of intrinsic motivation, social development, and well-being. *The American psychologist, 55*(1), 68–78. https://doi.org/10.1037/0003-066X.55.1.68

Ryan, R. M., & Deci, E. L. (2017). *Self-determination theory: Basic psychological needs in motivation, development, and wellness.* Guilford Press.

Rydell, R. J., McConnell, A. R., & Beilock, S. L. (2009). Multiple social identities and stereotype threat: Imbalance, accessibility, and working memory. *Journal of personality and social psychology, 96*(5), 949–966. https://doi.org/10.1037/a0014846

Sakulku, J., & Alexander, J. (2011). The impostor phenomenon. *International Journal of Behavioral Science, 6*(1), 75–97. https://doi.org/10.14456/ijbs.2011.6

Salter, P., & Adams, G. (2013). Toward a critical race psychology. *Social and personality psychology compass, 7*(11), 781–793. https://doi.org/10.1111/spc3.12068

Sam, D. L., & Berry, J. W. (2010). Acculturation: When individuals and groups of different cultural backgrounds meet. *Perspectives on Psychological Science, 5*(4), 472–481. https://doi.org/10.1177/1745691610373075

Samuels, D. R. (2014). *The culturally inclusive educator: Preparing for a multicultural world.* Teachers College Press.

San Pedro, T. (2015). Silence as weapons: Transformative praxis among native American students in the urban Southwest. *Equality & Excellence, 48*(4), 511–528. https://doi.org/http://doi.org/10.1080/10665684.2015.1083915

Sanders, M. J. (2013). Classroom design and student engagement. *Proceedings of the Human Factors and Ergonomics Society ... Annual Meeting, 57*(1), 496–500. https://doi.org/10.1177/1541931213571107

Sanson, M., Strange, D., & Garry, M. (2019). Trigger warnings are trivially helpful at reducing negative affect, intrusive thoughts, and avoidance. *Clinical Psychological Science, 7*(4), 778–793. https://doi.org/10.1177/2167702619827018

Sassenrath, C., Hodges, S. D., & Pfattheicher, S. (2016). It's all about the self: When perspective taking backfires. *Current directions in psychological science, 25*(6), 405–410. https://doi.org/10.1177/0963721416659253

Saunders, S., & Kardia, D. (1997). *Creating inclusive college classrooms.* Center for Research on Learning and Teaching. http://www.crlt.umich.edu/gsis/p3_1

Sax, L. J. (1996). The dynamics of "tokenism": How college students are affected by the proportion of women in their major. *Research in higher education*, *37*(4), 389–425. https://doi.org/https://www.jstor.org/stable/40196217

Schmader, T., & Hall, W. M. (2014). Stereotype threat in school and at work: Putting science into practice. *Policy insights from the behavioral and brain sciences*, *1*(1), 30–37. https://doi.org/10.1177/2372732214548861

Schmader, T., & Sedikides, C. (2018). State authenticity as fit to environment: The implications of social identity fit, authenticity, and self-segregation. *Personality and Social Psychology Review*, *22*(3), 228–259. https://doi.org/10.1177/1088868317734080

Schmader, T., Whitehead, J., & Wysocki, V. H. (2007). A linguistic comparison of letters of recommendation for male and female chemistry and biochemistry job applicants. *Sex roles*, *57*(7/8), 509–514. https://doi.org/10.1007/s11199-007-9291-4

Schmitt, M. T., Davies, K., Hung, M., & Wright, S. C. (2010). Identity moderates the effects of Christmas displays on mood, self-esteem, and inclusion. *Journal of experimental social psychology*, *46*(6), 1017–1022. https://doi.org/10.1016/j.jesp.2010.05.026

Schrader, D. E. (2004). Intellectual safety, moral atmosphere, and epistemology in college classrooms. *Journal of Adult Development*, *11*(2), 87–102.

Scott, S., McGuire, J. M., & Shaw, S. (2003). Universal design for instruction: A new paradigm for adult instruction in postsecondary education. *Remedial and Special Education*, *24*(6), 369–379. https://doi.org/10.1177/07419325030240060801

Sensoy, Ö., & DiAngelo, R. (2014). Respect differences? challenging the common guidelines in social justice education. *Democracy and Education*, *22*(2), 1–10. https://doi.org/http://democracyeducationjournal.org/home/vol22/iss2/1

Shaffer, E. S., Marx, D. M., & Prislin, R. (2013). Mind the gap: Framing of women's success and representation in STEM affects women's math performance under threat. *Sex Roles*, *68*(7-8), 454–463.

Sharkey, P., Schwartz, A. E., Ellen, I. G., & Lacoe, J. (2014). High stakes in the classroom, high stakes on the street: The effects of community violence on students' standardized test performance. *Sociological science*, *1*, 199–220. https://doi.org/http://doi.org/10.15195/v1.a14

Sheldon, K. M., & Krieger, L. S. (2007). Understanding the negative effects of legal education on law students: A longitudinal test of self-determination theory. *Personality and Social Psychology Bulletin*, *33*(6), 883–897. https://doi.org/10.1177/0146167207301014

Sieber, J. E., & Sorensen, J. L. (1992). Ethical issues in community-based research and intervention. In F. B. Bryant, J. Edwards, R. S. Tindale, E. J. Posavac, L. Heath, E. Henderson, & Y. Suarez-Balcazar (Eds.), *Methodological issues in applied social psychology* (pp. 43–63). Plenum Press.

Silver, P., Bourke, A., & Strehorn, K. C. (1998). Universal instructional design in higher education: An approach for inclusion. *Equity & Excellence in Education*, *31*(2), 47–51. https://doi.org/10.1080/1066568980310206

Simpson, K. (2009). "Did I just share too much information?" Results of a national survey on faculty self-disclosure. *International Journal of Teaching and Learning in Higher Education, 20*(2), 91–97.

Singleton, G. E., & Linton, C. (2006). *Courageous conversations about race: A field guide for achieving equity in schools.* Corwin Press.

Sjöblom, K., Mälkkl, K., Sandström, N., & Lonka, K. (2016). Does physical environment contribute to basic psychological needs? A self-determination theory perspective on learning in the chemistry laboratory. *Frontline learning research, 4*(2), 12–39. https://doi.org/10.14786/flr.v4i1.217

Slavin, R. A., & Cooper, R. (1999). Improving intergroup relations: Lessons learned from cooperative learning programs. *The Journal of social issues, 55*(4), 647–663. https://doi.org/10.1111/0022-4537.00140

Smeding, A., Darnon, C., Souchal, C., Toczek-Capelle, M. -C., & Butera, F. (2013). Reducing the socio-economic status achievement gap at university by promoting mastery-oriented assessment. *PloS one, 8*(8), e71678. https://doi.org/10.1371/journal.pone.0071678

Smith, J. H., Lewis, K. L., Hawthorne, L., & Hodges, S. D. (2013). When trying hard isn't natural: Women's belonging with and motivation for male dominated STEM fields as a function of effort expenditure concerns. *Personality and Social Psychology Bulletin, 39*(2), 131–143. https://doi.org/http://doi.org/10.1177/0146167212468332

Solórzano, D., Ceja, M., & Yosso, T. (2000). Critical race theory, microaggressions, and campus racial climate: The experience of African American college students. *The Journal of Negro education, 69*(1/2), 60–73. https://doi.org/https://www.jstor.org/stable/2696265

Sorensen, G. (1989). The relationships among teachers' self-disclosive statements, students' perceptions, and affective learning. *Communication Education, 38*(3), 259–276.

Soria, K. M., & Johnson, M. (2017). High-impact educational practices and the development of college students' pluralistic outcomes. *College Student Affairs Journal, 35*(2), 100–116.

Souza, T. (2018). Responding to microaggressions in the classroom: taking action. *Faculty Focus.* https://www.facultyfocus.com/articles/effective-classroom-management/responding-to-microaggressions-in-the-classroom

Souza, T., Ganote, C., Roderick, L., & Cheung, F. (2018, Winter). *Resources for supporting our campuses in politically fraught times.* POD Network News. https://podnetwork.org/publications/networknews/

Souza, T., Vizenor, N., Sherlip, D., & Raser, L. (2016). Transforming conflict in the classroom: Best practices for facilitating difficult dialogues and creating an inclusive communication climate. In P. M. Kellett & T. G. Matyok (Eds.), *Transforming conflict through communication: Personal to working relationships* (pp. 373–395). Lexington Books.

Spencer, L. G., & Kulbaga, T. A. (2018). Trigger warnings as respect for student boundaries in university classrooms. *Journal of Curriculum and Pedagogy, 15*(1), 106–122.

Spencer, S. J., Logel, C., & Davies, P. G. (2016). Stereotype threat. *Annual review of psychology, 67*, 415–437. https://doi.org/10.1146/annurev-psych-073115-103235

Spencer, S. J., Steele, C. M., & Quinn, D. M. (1999). Stereotype threat and women's math performance. *Journal of Experimental Social Psychology, 35*(4), 4–28. https://doi.org/10.1080/15505170.2018.1438936

Spodek, J. (2018, September 4). Trigger warnings, microaggressions, safe spaces, and what to do about them. *Inc.* https://www.inc.com/joshua-spodek/handling-trigger-warnings-microaggressions-safe-spaces-other-outrages.html

Springer, L., Stanne, M. E., & Donovan, S. S. (1999). Effects of small-group learning on undergraduates in science, mathematics, engineering, and technology: A meta-analysis. *Review of educational research, 69*(1), 21–51. https://doi.org/10.3102/00346543069001021

Stebleton, M. J., Soria, K. M., & Cherney, B. (2013). The high impact of education abroad: College students' engagement in international experiences and the development of intercultural competencies. *Frontiers: The Interdisciplinary Journal of Study Abroad, 22*, 1–24.

Steele, C. M. (2010). *Whistling Vivaldi and other clues to how stereotypes affect us.* W. W. Norton.

Steele, C. M., & Aronson, J. (1995). Stereotype threat and the intellectual test performance of African Americans. *Journal of personality and social psychology, 69*(5), 797–811. https://doi.org/http://doi.org/10.1037//0022-3514.69.5.797

Steiger, K. (2011, January 19). 'Portlandia' Edges into 'stuff White people like' territory. *Generation Progress.* http://genprogress.org/voices/2011/01/19/16219/portlandia-edges-into-stuff-white-people-like-territory/

Stephan, W. G., & Stephan, C. W. (1985). Intergroup anxiety. *The Journal of social issues, 41*(3), 157–175. https://doi.org/10.1111/j.1540-4560.1985.tb01134.x

Stephens, N. M., Brannon, T. N., Markus, H. R., & Nelson, J. E. (2015). Feeling at home in college: Fortifying school-relevant selves to reduce social class disparities in higher education. *Social issues and policy review, 9*(1), 1–24. https://doi.org/10.1111/sipr.12008

Stephens, N. M., Fryberg, S. A., & Markus, H. R. (2012). It's your choice: How the middle class model of independence disadvantages working class Americans. In S. T. Fiske & H. R. Markus (Eds.), *Facing social class: How societal rank influences interaction* (pp. 87–106). Russell Sage Foundation.

Stephens, N. M., Fryberg, S. A., Markus, H. R., Johnson, C., & Covarrubias, R. (2012). Unseen disadvantage: How American universities' focus on independence undermines the academic performance of first-generation college students. *Journal of personality and social psychology, 102*(6), 1178–1197. https://doi.org/10.1037/a0027143

Stephens, N. M., Hamedani, M. G., & Destin, M. (2014). Closing the social-class achievement gap: A difference-education intervention improves first-generation students' academic performance and all students' college transition. *Psychological science, 25*(4), 943–953. https://doi.org/10.1177/0956797613518349

Stephens, N. M., Townsend, S. S. M., Hamedani, M. G., Destin, M., & Manzo, V. (2015). A difference-education intervention equips first-generation college students to thrive in the face of stressful College situations. *Psychological science, 26*(10), 1556–1566. https://doi.org/http://doi.org/10.1177/0956797615593501

Stephens, N. M., Townsend, S. S. M., Markus, H. R., & Phillips, L. T. (2012). A cultural mismatch: Independent cultural norms produce greater increases in cortisol and more negative emotions among first-generation college students. *Journal of experimental social psychology, 48*(6), 1389–1393. https://doi.org/10.1016/j.jesp.2012.07.008

Stone, D., Patton, B., & Heen, S. (2010). *Difficult conversations: How to discuss what matters most*(2nd ed.). Viking Press.

Stoudt, B. G., Fox, M., & Fine, M. (2012). Contesting privilege with critical participatory action research. *The Journal of social issues, 68*(1), 178–193. https://doi.org/10.1111/j.1540-4560.2011.01743.x

Strange, C. C., & Banning, J. H. (2015). *Designing for learning: Creating campus environments for student success* (2nd ed.). Jossey-Bass.

Strayhorn, T. L. (2012). *College students' sense of belonging: A key to educational success for all students*. Routledge.

Stringer, R. (2016). Trigger warnings in university teaching. *Women's Studies Journal, 30*(2), 62–66. https://doi.org/10.1080/15505170.2018.1438936

Suárez-Orozco, C., Casanova, S., Martin, M., Katsiaficas, D., Cuellar, V., Smith, N. A., & Dias, S. I. (2015). Toxic rain in class: Classroom interpersonal microaggressions. *Educational Researcher, 44*(3), 151–160. https://doi.org/10.3102/0013189X15580314

Sue, D. W. (2003). *Overcoming our racism: The journey to liberation*. Jossey-Bass.

Sue, D. W. (2013). Race talk: The psychology of racial dialogues. *The American psychologist, 68*(8), 663–672. https://doi.org/10.1037/a0033681

Sue, D. W. (2015). *Race talk and the conspiracy of silence: Understanding and facilitating difficult dialogues on race*. Wiley.

Sue, D. W., Alsaidi, S., Awad, M. N., Glaeser, E., Calle, C. Z., & Mendez, N. (2019). Disarming racial microaggressions: Microintervention strategies for targets, white allies, and bystanders. *The American psychologist, 79*(1), 128–142. https://doi.org/10.1037/amp0000296

Sue, D. W., Bucceri, J., Lin, A., Nadal, K., & Torino, G. (2007). Racial microaggressions and the Asian American experience. *Cultural Diversity and Ethnic Minority Psychology, 13*(1), 72–81. https://doi.org/http://doi.org/10.1037/1099-9809.13.1.72

Sue, D. W., Capodilupo, C. M., & Holder, A. M. B. (2008). Racial microaggressions in the life experience of black Americans. *Professional Psychology: Research and Practice, 39*(3), 329–336. https://doi.org/10.1037/0003-066X.62.4.271

Sue, D. W., Capodilupo, C. M., Torino, G. C., Bucceri, J. M., Holder, A. M. B., Nadal, K. L., & Esquilin, M. (2007). Racial microaggressions in everyday life: Implications for clinical practice. *The American psychologist, 62*(4), 271–286. https://doi.org/10.1037/0003-066X.62.4.271

Sue, D. W., & Constantine, M. G. (2007). Racial microaggressions as instigators of difficult dialogues on race: Implications for student Affairs educators and students. *College Student Affairs Journal, 62*(2), 136–143. https://doi.org/10 .1037/a0014191

Sue, D. W., Rivera, D. P., Watkins, N. L., Kim, R. H., Kim, S., & Williams, C. D. (2011). Racial dialogues: Challenges faculty of color face in the classroom. *Cultural Diversity and Ethnic Minority Psychology, 17*(3), 331–340. https://doi .org/http://doi.org/10.1037/a0024190

Sue, D. W., Torino, G. C., Capodilupo, C. M., Rivera, D. P., & Lin, A. I. (2009). How white faculty perceive and react to difficult dialogues on race: Implications for education and training. *Counseling Psychologist,, 37*(8), 1090–1115. https:// doi.org/10.1177/0011000009340443

Syed, M., & Azmitia, M. (2016). Narrative and ethnic identity exploration: A longitudinal account of emerging adults' ethnicity-related experiences. *Developmental Psychology, 46*(1), 208–219. https://doi.org/10.1037/a0017825

Tajfel, H., & Turner, J. C. (1986). The social identity theory of intergroup behavior. In S. Worchel & W. G. Austin (Eds.), *Psychology of intergroup relations* (pp. 7–24). Nelson-Hall.

Tatum, B. D. (2017). *Why are all the Black kids sitting together in the cafeteria? And other conversations about race.* Basic Books.

Taylor, H. (2017). Accessibility on campus: Posttraumatic stress disorder, duty to accommodate, and trigger warnings. In E. Knox (Ed.), *Trigger warnings: History, theory, and context* (pp. 22–36). Rowman & Littlefield.

Tervalon, M., & Murray-Garcia, J. (1998). Cultural humility versus cultural competence: A critical distinction in defining physician training outcomes in multicultural education. *Journal of Health Care to the Poor and Underserved, 9*(2), 117–125. https://doi.org/10.1353/hpu.2010.0233

Thakur, S. (2014). Challenges in teaching sexual violence and rape: A male perspective. In N. Rabinowitz & F. McHardy (Eds.), *From abortion to pederasty: Addressing difficult topics in the classics classroom.* The Ohio State University Press.

Theobald, E. J., Eddy, S. L., Grunspan, D. Z., Wiggins, B. L., & Crowe, A. J. (2017). Student perception of group dynamics predicts individual performance: Comfort and equity matter. *PLoS ONE, 12*(7), e0181336. https://doi.org/10 .1371/journal.pone.0181336

Thoman, D. B., Smith, J. L., Brown, E. R., Chase, J., & Lee, J. Y. K. (2013). Beyond performance: A motivational experiences model of stereotype threat. *Educational Psychology Review, 25*(2), 211–243. https://doi.org/10.1007/s10648-013-9219-1

Thompson, T., Davis, H., & Davison, J. (1998, 8). Attributional and affective responses of impostors to academic success and failure outcomes. *Personality and*

Individual Differences, 25(2), 381–396. https://doi.org/10.1016/S0191-8869(98)00065-8

Thorpe, M. E. (2016). Trigger warnings, the organic classroom, and civil discourse. *First Amendment Studies, 50*(2), 83–94. https://doi.org/10.1080/21689725.2016.1219270

Thurber, A., & DiAngelo, R. (2018). Microaggressions: Intervening in three acts. *Journal of Ethnic & Cultural Diversity in Social Work, 27*(1), 17–27. https://doi.org/10.1080/15313204.2017.1417941

Tobin, L. (2010). Self-disclosure as a strategic teaching tool: What I do—and I don't—tell my students. *College English, 73*(2), 196–206. https://doi.org/https://www.jstor.org/stable/25790469

Tobin, T. J., & Behling, K. T. (2018). *Reach everyone, teach everyone: Universal design for learning in higher education.* West Virginia University Press.

Tolman, A. O., & Kremling, J. (Eds.). (2016). *Why students resist learning: A practical model for understanding and helping students.* Stylus.

Topping, M. E., & Kimmel, E. B. (1985). The impostor phenomenon: Feeling phony. *Academic Psychology Bulletin, 7*(2), 213–226.

Trần, N. L. (2013). Calling in: A less disposable way to hold each other accountable. BGD. http://www.bgdblog.org/2013/12/calling-less-disposable-way-holding-accountable/

Trimble, J. E., Stevenson, M. R., & Worell, J. P. (2004). *Toward an inclusive psychology: Infusing the introductory psychology textbook with diversity content.* American Psychological Association.

Troxell Whitman, Z., & Oleson, K. C. (2016a, September). *Motivated disclosure patterns: disability identity management in the higher education environment* [Paper presentation]. 2016 International Disability Studies Conference

Troxell Whitman, Z., & Oleson, K. C. (2016b, October). *Disability disclosure: Strategy for academic and interpersonal success among American college students.* [Poster presentation]. 7th ICEEPSY International Conference on Education and Educational Psychology.

Turner, R. N., Hewstone, M., & Voci, A. (2007). Reducing explicit and implicit outgroup prejudice via direct and extended contact: The mediating role of self-disclosure and intergroup anxiety. *Journal of Personality and Social Psychology, 93*(3), 369–388. https://doi.org/10.1037/0022-3514.93.3.369

Uhlmann, E. L., & Cohen, G. L. (2005). Constructing criteria: Redefining merit to justify discrimination. *Psychological science, 16*(6), 474–480. https://doi.org/http://doi.org/10.1111/j.0956-7976.2005.01559.x

Ukpokodu, N. (2002). Breaking through preservice teachers' defensive dispositions in a multicultural education course: A reflective practice. *Multicultural Education, 9*(3), 25–32.

Vaccaro, A., & Koob, R. M. (2018). A critical and intersectional model of LGBTQ microaggressions: Toward a more comprehensive understanding. *Journal of Homosexuality, 66*(10), 1317–1344. https://doi.org/10.1080/00918369.2018.1539583

van Laar, C., Sidanius, J., & Levin, S. (2008). Ethnic-related curricula and intergroup attitudes in college: Movement toward and away from the in-group. *Journal of Applied Social Psychology*, *38*(6), 1601–1638. https://doi.org/10.1111/j.1559 -1816.2008.00361.x

Verduzco-Baker, L. (2018). Modified brave spaces: Calling in brave instructors. *Sociology of Race and Ethnicity*, *4*(4), 585–592. https://doi.org/10.1177/ 2332649218763696

Verschelden, C. (2017). *Bandwidth recovery: Helping students reclaim cognitive resources lost to poverty, racism, and social marginalization*. Stylus.

Vespa, J., Armstrong, D. M., & Medina, L. (2020, February). Demographic turning points for the United States: population projections for 2020 to 2060. Current population reports, P25-1144, U.S. Census Bureau. https://www.census.gov/ content/dam/Census/library/publications/2020/demo/p25-1144.pdf

Vick, B. (2016, June). *Capitalizing on teachable moments: Difficult dialogues in the inclusive classroom*. [Paper presentation] 12th Meeting of the Society for the Psychological Study of Social Issues.

Vinton, E. (2016). *Safety and discomfort in the classroom: Naïve realism and productive discomfort in higher education* [Unpublished senior thesis]. Reed College.

Vinton, E., & Oleson, K. C. (2017, January). *Safety and discomfort in the classroom: Naïve realism and productive discomfort in higher education.* [Poster presentation] 18th Annual Meeting of the Society of Personality and Social Psychology.

Volk, S. (2015, September). Revealing the secret handshakes: The rules of clear assignment design. Center for Teaching Innovation and Excellence. http:// languages.oberlin.edu/blogs/ctie/2015/09/27/revealing-the-secret-handshakes -the-rules-of-clear-assignment-design/

Vorauer, J. D., Hunter, A. J., Main, K. J., & Roy, S. A. (2000). Meta-stereotype activation: Evidence from indirect measures for specific evaluative concerns experienced by members of dominant groups in intergroup interaction. *Journal of Personality and Social Psychology*, *78*(4), 690–707. https://doi.org/10.1037/0022 -3514.78.4.690

Vorauer, J. D., Main, K. J., & O'Connell, G. B. (1998). How do individuals expect to be viewed by members of lower status groups? content and implications of meta-stereotypes. *Journal of Personality and Social Psychology*, *75*(4), 917–937. https://doi.org/10.1037/0022-3514.75.4.917

Vygotsky, L. S. (1978). *Mind in society: The development of higher psychological processes*. In M. Cole, V. John-Steiner, S. Scribner, & E. Souberman (Eds.), Harvard University Press.

Wagner-McCoy, S., & Schwartz, E. (2016). Gaining new perspectives on discussion-based classes in English and the humanities. *Teaching and Learning Together in Higher Education*, *1*(17), 1–9. https://doi.org/http://repository.brynmawr.edu/ tlthe/vol1/iss17/3

Walton, G. M., & Cohen, G. L. (2007). A question of belonging: Race, social fit, and achievement. *Journal of Personality and Social Psychology*, *92*(1), 82–96. https://doi.org/10.1037/0022-3514.92.1.82

Walton, G. M., & Cohen, G. L. (2011). A brief social-belonging intervention improves academic and health outcomes of minority students. *Science, 331*(6023), 1447–1451. https://doi.org/10.1126/science.1198364

Walton, G. M., Cohen, G. L., & Steele, C. M. (2012). 1-page guide on ways to reduce stereotype threat.. Gregory M. Walton website. http://gregorywalton -stanford.weebly.com/uploads/4/9/4/4/ 49448111/strategiestoreducestereotype threat.pdf

Walton, G. M., & Spencer, S. J. (2009). Latent ability: Grades and test scores systematically underestimate the intellectual ability of negatively stereotyped students. *Psychological science, 20*, 1132–1139. https://doi.org/http://doi.org/10 .1111/j.1467-9280.2009.02417.x

Warner, L. R. (2008). A best practices guide to intersectional approaches in psychological research. *Sex Roles, 59*(5–6), 454–463. https://doi.org/10.1007/ s11199-008-9504-5

Warren, L. (2005). Strategic action in hot moments. In M. L. Ouellett (Ed.), *Teaching inclusively: Resources for courses, departments, & institutional change in higher education* (pp. 620–630). New Forum Press.

Warren, L. (n. d). Managing hot moments in the classroom. Derek Bok Center for Teaching and Learning. https://www.elon.edu/u/academics/catl/wp-content/ uploads/sites/126/2017/04/Managing-Hot-Moments-in-the-Classroom-Harvard_ University.pdf

Watt, S. K. (2007). Difficult dialogues, privilege and social justice: Uses of the privileged identity exploration (PIE) model in student affairs practices. *College Student Affairs Journal, 26*(2), 114–126.

Weaver, S. (2013). A rhetorical discourse analysis of online anti-Muslim and anti-semitic jokes. *Ethnic and Racial Studies, 36*(3), 483–499. https://doi.org/10 .1080/01419870.2013.734386

Weinstein, R. S., Gregory, A., & Strambler, M. J. (2004). Intractable self-fulfilling prophecies fifty years after Brown v. Board of Education. *American Psychologist, 59*(6), 511–520. https://doi.org/10.1037/0003-066X.59.6.511

Weisz, C. (2016). *Inclusive teaching of research methods: Making science relevant and revolutionary.* [Paper presentation] 12th Meeting of the Society for the Psychological Study of Social Issues.

West, E. J. (2004). Perry's legacy: Models of epistemological development. *Journal of adult development, 11*(2), 61–70. https://doi.org/10.1023/B:JADE.0000024540 .12150.69

West, K. (2019). Testing hypersensitive responses: Ethnic minorities are not more sensitive to microaggressions, they just experience them more frequently. *Personality and Social Psychology Bulletin, 45*(11), 1619–1632. https://doi.org/10 .1177/0146167219838790

White, R. W. (1959). Motivation reconsidered: The concept of competence. *Psychological Review, 66*(5), 297–333. https://doi.org/10.1037/h0040934

Wiggins, G., & McTighe, J. (2006). *Understanding by design* (expanded 2nd ed.). Association for Supervision and Curriculum Development.

Wilkins, C. L., Hirsch, A. A., Kaiser, C. R., & Inkles, M. P. (2017). The threat of racial progress and the self-protective nature of perceiving anti-White bias. *Group Processes and Intergroup Relations, 20*(6), 801–812. https://doi.org/10.1177/1368430216631030

Wilkins-Yel, K. G., Hyman, J., & Zounlome, N. O. O. (2018). Linking intersectional invisibility and hypervisibility to experiences of microaggressions among graduate women of color in STEM. *Journal of Vocational Behavior, 113*, 51–61. https://doi.org/10.1016/j.jvb.2018.10.018

Williams, G. C., & Deci, E. L. (1996). Internalization of biopsychosocial values by medical students: A test of self-determination theory. *Journal of Personality and Social Psychology, 70*(4), 767–779. https://doi.org/10.1037/0022-3514.70.4.767

Williams, M. T. (2020). Psychology cannot afford to ignore the many harms caused by microaggressions. *Perspectives on Psychological Science, 15*(1), 38–43. https://doi.org/10.1177/1745691619893362

Wilson, R. (2015). Students' requests for trigger warnings grow more varied. *The Chronicle of higher education*. https://doi.org/http://chronicle.com.proxy.library.reed.edu/article/Students-Requests-for/233043

Winkelmes, M., Boye, A., & Tapp, S. (Eds.). (2019). *A guide to implementing the transparency framework institution-wide to improve learning and retention*. Stylus.

Winkelmes, M.-A., Bernacki, M., Butler, J., Zochowski, M., Golanics, J., & Weavil, K. H. (2016). A teaching intervention that increases underserved college students' success. *Peer Review, 18*(1/2).

Wise Interventions. (n.d). *Wise Interventions: A searchable database of psychologically "wise" interventions to help people flourish*. www.wiseinterventions.org

Wong-Padoongpatt, G., Zane, N., Okazaki, S., & Saw, A. (2017). Decreases in implicit self-esteem explain the racial impact of microaggressions among Asian Americans. *Journal of Counseling Psychology, 64*(5), 574–583. https://doi.org/10.1037/cou0000217

Wyatt, W., & Society for Ethics Across the Curriculum. (2016). The ethics of trigger warnings. *Teaching Ethics, 16*(1), 17–35. https://doi.org/10.5840/tej201632427

Yeager, D. S., & Dweck, C. S. (2012). Mindsets that promote resilience: When students believe that personal characteristics can be developed. *Educational Psychologist, 47*(4), 302–314. https://doi.org/10.1080/00461520.2012.722805

Yeager, D. S., Purdie-Vaughns, V., Garcia, J., Apfel, N., Brzustoski, P., Master, A., Hessert, W. T., Williams, M. E., & Cohen, G. L. (2014). Breaking the cycle of mistrust: Wise interventions to provide critical feedback across the racial divide. *Journal of Experimental Psychology: General, 143*(2), 804–824. https://doi.org/10.1037/a0033906

Yerkes, R. M., & Dodson, J. D. (1908). The relation of strength of stimulus to rapidity of habit-formation. *Journal of Comparative Neurology and Psychology, 18*(5), 459–482. https://doi.org/10.1002/cne.920180503

Yosso, T., Smith, W., Ceja, M., & Solórzano, D. (2009). Critical race theory, racial microaggressions, and campus racial climate for Latina/o undergraduates.

Harvard Educational Review, *79*(4), 659–691. https://doi.org/10.17763/haer.79.4.m6867014157m707l

Young, G. (2003). Dealing with difficult classroom dialogue. In P. Bronstein & K. Quina (Eds.), *Teaching gender and multicultural awareness: Resources for the psychology classroom* (pp. 347–360). American Psychological Association.

Zembylas, M. (2012). Pedagogies of strategic empathy: Navigating through the emotional complexities of anti-racism in higher education. *Teaching in Higher Education*, *17*(2), 113–125. https://doi.org/10.1080/13562517.2011.611869

Zembylas, M. (2015). 'Pedagogy of discomfort' and its ethical implications: the tensions of ethical violence in social justice education. *Ethics and Education*, *10*(2), 163–174. https://doi.org/10.1080/17449642.2015.1039274

Zembylas, M., & McGlynn, C. (2012). Discomforting pedagogies: Emotional tensions, ethical dilemmas and transformative possibilities. *British Educational Research Journal*, *38*(1), 41–59. https://doi.org/10.1080/01411926.2010.523779

Zembylas, M., & Papmichael, E. (2017). Pedagogies of discomfort and empathy in multicultural teacher education. *Intercultural Education*, *28*(1), 1–19. https://doi.org/10.1080/14675986.2017.1288448

Zheng, L. (2016, May 15). Why your brave space sucks. *Stanford Daily*. http://www.stanforddaily.com/2016/05/15/why-your-brave-space-sucks/

Zumbrunn, S., McKim, C., Buhs, E., & Hawley, L. R. (2014). Support, belonging, motivation, and engagement in the college classroom: A mixed method study. *Instructional Science*, *42*(5), 661–684. https://doi.org/10.1007/s11251-014-9310-0

Zúñiga, X., Nagda, B. A., Chesler, M., & Cytron-Walker, A. (2007). *Intergroup dialogues in higher education: Meaningful learning about social justice* (ASHE Higher Education Report, Vol. 32, No. 4). Jossey-Bass.

ABOUT THE AUTHORS

Kathryn (Kathy) C. Oleson is dean of the faculty at Reed College. Before becoming dean in July 2020, she was professor of psychology and inaugural director of the Center for Teaching and Learning (2014–2016) at Reed. Prior to coming to Reed in 1995, she was a National Institute of Mental Health postdoctoral fellow at The Ohio State University after finishing her PhD in social psychology at Princeton University. With Robert Arkin and Patrick Carroll, she coedited the *Handbook of the Uncertain Self* (Psychology Press, 2009). She is a teacher-scholar who conducts collaborative research with undergraduates. Much of her research has examined students' reactions in challenging academic contexts, concentrating on self-doubt, achievement goals, academic procrastination, and behavioral strategies. Currently, her research primarily explores ways to create inclusive classroom dynamics in higher education, with a particular focus on productive discomfort.

Robert (Robby) R. Murphy currently conducts nonprofit evaluation research in New York City public schools as a junior research associate with Glass Frog Solutions. He grew up in New Jersey before moving to Portland, Oregon, to attend Reed College. He graduated in 2018 with a BA in psychology. Murphy has worked closely with Kathryn Oleson as a research assistant, conducting research on the psychology of prejudice in higher education as well as bias reduction more broadly. He has also held research positions at Florida International University, University of Wisconsin–Madison, and Purdue University. He plans to pursue a PhD and is particularly interested in the systemic and interpersonal roots of and solutions to inequality and prejudice.

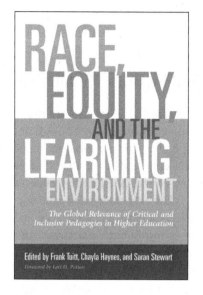

Straddling Class in the Academy

Sonja Ardoin and becky martinez

Foreword by Jamie Washington

"*Straddling Class in the Academy* is a must-read for students and educators. Ardoin, martinez, and their contributors masterfully challenge the myth that class is invisible by sharing their lived experiences navigating class and classism in and outside of the academy. The intersectional nature of contributors' narratives and Ardoin and martinez's analysis highlights the powerful effects of classism and calls for action if we are to create more inclusive and socially just institutions."—*Rosemary J. Perez, Assistant Professor, School of Education, Iowa State University*

Creating the Path to Success in the Classroom

Teaching to Close the Graduation Gap for Minority, First-Generation, and Academically Unprepared Students

Kathleen F. Gabriel

Foreword by Stephen Carroll

"*Creating the Path to Success in the Classroom* totally delivers. As noted in this book, graduation rates for students in both 4-year and 2-year educational institutions are depressing. Something has to change, and this book is an important component in bringing about that change by noting how best to help our most vulnerable students. Chapter by chapter, Gabriel dissects and describes fundamental components that impact student success and provides specific strategies for bringing about successful learning outcomes. *Creating a Path to Success in the Classroom* will have a prominent place on my bookcase of essential resources for helping students to succeed in college."—*Todd Zakrajsek, Associate Professor, School of Medicine, University of North Carolina at Chapel Hill*

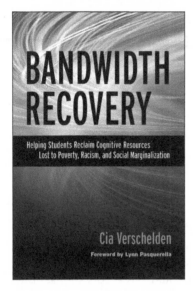

Bandwidth Recovery

Helping Students Reclaim Cognitive Resources Lost to Poverty, Racism, and Social Marginalization

Cia Verschelden

Foreword by Lynn Pasquerella

"Verschelden makes the convincing case that many lower income and minority students struggle in college not because of lower ability or poor preparation, but because they deal with life situations that deplete cognitive resources that are needed for learning. Offering us a distinctly different lens through which to view these students, she describes concrete strategies we can implement to replenish their cognitive resources so that they don't just survive, but thrive in the college environment with recovered 'bandwidth.'"—***Saundra McGuire***, *(Ret.) Assistant Vice Chancellor & Professor of Chemistry; Director Emerita, Center for Academic Success, Louisiana State University; author of* Teach Students How to Learn

22883 Quicksilver Drive
Sterling, VA 20166-2019   Subscribe to our e-mail alerts: www.Styluspub.com